Other People's Pain

CULTURAL HISTORY AND LITERARY IMAGINATION

EDITED BY CHRISTIAN J. EMDEN & DAVID MIDGLEY

VOL. 18

PETER LANG

Oxford · Bern · Berlin · Bruxelles · Frankfurt am Main · New York · Wien

Other People's Pain

Narratives of Trauma and the Question of Ethics

Martin Modlinger and Philipp Sonntag (eds)

PETER LANG

Oxford · Bern · Berlin · Bruxelles · Frankfurt am Main · New York · Wien

Bibliographic information published by Die Deutsche Nationalbibliothek
Die Deutsche Nationalbibliothek lists this publication in the Deutsche Nationalbiblio-
grafie; detailed bibliographic data is available on the Internet at http://dnb.d-nb.de.

A catalogue record for this book is available from the British Library.

Library of Congress Cataloging-in-Publication Data:

Other people's pain : narratives of trauma and the question of ethics /
Martin Modlinger and Philipp Sonntag (eds).
    p. cm. -- (Cultural history and literary imagination ; 18)
 Includes bibliographical references and index.
 ISBN 978-3-0343-0260-9 (alk. paper)
 1. Violence in literature. 2. Violence--Psychological aspects. 3.
Psychic trauma in literature. 4. Ethics in literature. I. Modlinger,
Martin, 1981- II. Sonntag, Philipp.
 PN56.V53075 2011
 809'.933552--dc22
                        2011009000

ISSN 1660-6205
ISBN 978-3-0343-0260-9

© Peter Lang AG, International Academic Publishers, Bern 2011
Hochfeldstrasse 32, CH-3012 Bern, Switzerland
info@peterlang.com, www.peterlang.com, www.peterlang.net

Printed in Germany

Contents

vi

Acknowledgements

We would like to thank all those who participated in the international and interdisciplinary conference 'Other People's Pain: Narratives of Trauma and the Question of Ethics', which was held at the Centre for Research in the Arts, Social Sciences and Humanities (CRASSH) in Cambridge in March 2010, on which this volume is based, especially our co-organizer Christopher M. Geissler, the Department of German and Dutch at the University of Cambridge, particularly Chris Young and David Midgley, Acting Director of CRASSH Andrew Webber, and our conference administrator Anna Malinowska, who made this event possible.

The conference was generously supported by CRASSH at the University of Cambridge, the Ethics of Textual Cultures honours graduate programme at the Universities of Erlangen-Nuremberg and Augsburg, the Tiarks Fund of the Department of German and Dutch at the University of Cambridge, and the Gates Cambridge Trust.

We are very grateful to the Ethics of Textual Cultures honours graduate programme at the Universities of Erlangen-Nuremberg and Augsburg for its generous support of the publication of this volume. Furthermore, we would like to thank Edinburgh University Press (<http://www.eup-publishing.com>) for their kind permission to reprint a revised version of Susannah Radstone's article 'Trauma Theory: Contexts, Politics, Ethics', which was previously published in a special issue of *Paragraph* 30/1 (2007), entitled 'Trauma, Therapy and Representation', edited by Nerea Arruti with Bob Plant.

— MARTIN MODLINGER AND PHILIPP SONNTAG
Cambridge/Erlangen, December 2010

MARTIN MODLINGER AND PHILIPP SONNTAG

Introduction: Other People's Pain – Narratives of Trauma and the Question of Ethics

In *Regarding the Pain of Others*, Susan Sontag opens a discussion of the photography of suffering with a reference to Virginia Woolf's *Three Guineas*, described by Sontag as Woolf's 'brave, unwelcomed reflections on the roots of war.'[1] Woolf claims therein that the shock of horrific pictures cannot fail to unite 'people of good will'; that photographs of war will invariably create a 'we' that is opposed to the atrocities before 'our' eyes. Susan Sontag begs to differ. 'No "we" should be taken for granted when the subject is looking at other people's pain.'[2]

In the last twenty years, a new 'we' seems to have emerged with respect to horrific histories and their deeply disturbing forms of representation: the unifying field of trauma studies. Other people's pain has become one of the core interests of literary and cultural studies. While narratives of loss, oppression, marginalization, and physical and psychological trauma are by no means new to readers and viewers, the particular dedication of the humanities to these issues has reached a new quality. '[W]e inhabit an academic world that is busy consuming trauma [...]. We are obsessed with stories that must be passed on, that must not be passed over', writes Patricia Yaeger, and asks, 'What happens when we "textualize" bodies, when we write about other people's deaths [...] as something one reads?'[3]

This new interest in pain and death, in the suppressed histories of persecuted and annihilated peoples – not only a trend but also a method

---

1   Susan Sontag, *Regarding the Pain of Others* (London: Penguin, 2004), 3.
2   *Ibid.*, 6.
3   Patricia Yaeger, 'Consuming Trauma; or, The Pleasures of Merely Circulating', in Nancy K. Miller and Jason Tougaw, eds, *Extremities. Trauma, Testimony and the Community* (Chicago: University of Illinois Press, 2002), 25–51, 29.

that Peter Middleton has called 'New Memoryism'[4] – draws especially on insights from psychoanalysis and psychotherapy, fields that are still very much influenced by Sigmund Freud and his followers. Sigmund Freud, who himself often resorted to literature to explicate his concepts of psychosexual development and their possible connection to neurosis, formulated the first steps towards a theory of trauma together with Josef Breuer in *Studies on Hysteria* in 1895. As Craig Piers summarizes nearly one hundred years after Freud's and Breuer's study, the idea that 'hysterics "suffer from reminiscences" or the return to consciousness of an anxiety-provoking idea/ memory or "exciting event" in symbolic and symptomatic form' is now at the core of recent debates on the nature, transmission, treatment – and telling – of trauma. Piers found it necessary to return to these first attempts at classifying and explaining the traumatized condition in order to systematize contemporary trauma theory within the framework of psychoanalysis and psychotherapy, where Freud's theorizing, 'in many respects is as much the source of debate now, as it was during his own times.'[5]

At that point in time, trauma studies had already been taken up by literary scholars who quickly appropriated the findings of memory studies and psychoanalysis for their discussions and analysis of what became known as 'trauma texts', in particular survivor testimonies from the Holocaust and the Vietnam War, but also from the Rwandan Genocide, South African apartheid, and, more recently, the attacks on the World Trade Center of 9/11. Shoshana Felman and Dori Laub first addressed the earlier cases in their 1992 study on the crises of witnessing, in which they explored the role of testimony in literature, psychoanalysis and history and where they addressed the possibility – and necessity – of participatory re-creation of trauma. Teaching traumatic texts and histories, 'teaching as such, takes place precisely only through a crisis: if teaching does not hit upon some sort of crisis, if it does not encounter either vulnerability or the explosiveness of a (explicit or implicit) critical and unpredictable

---

4   Peter Middleton, 'The New Memoryism: How Computers Changed the Way We Read', *New Formations* 50 (2003), 57–74, 58.

5   Craig Piers, 'A return to the source: Rereading Freud in the midst of contemporary trauma theory', *Psychotherapy*, 33/4 (1996), 539–48, 539.

dimension, it has perhaps *not truly taught*,[6] writes Shoshana Felman. In this view, a permutation of Virginia Woolf's thoughts on war photography, only the re-creation of trauma ('creating in the class the highest state of crisis that it could withstand')[7] can form the 'we' that has truly understood the nature of trauma and can adequately address the crisis of witnessing. This rather bold idea is still very prominent in the academic discourse on trauma within the humanities; it found its way into the highly influential volume *Trauma: Explorations in Memory*, edited by Cathy Caruth in 1995, as well as Caruth's later monograph that expanded the scope of the project into narrative.[8]

The re-creation of trauma as proposed by Shoshana Felman raises an ethical question. As Anne Whitehead has stated in an article on Geoffrey Hartman's place in trauma theory, the reader's/viewer's position and perspective on traumatic events unavoidably leads to ethical considerations. Questions regarding '*how we see* and *from where we see*'[9] determine all 'efforts to confront and remember the past'.[10] 'Prior to all efforts at commemoration, explanation or understanding,' Ulrich Baer writes, 'we must find a place and a position from which we may then gain access to the event.'[11] An ethical vantage point has to be found from which those not directly affected by the traumatic event itself can access the stories and histories of pain. Again, there is no 'we' to be taken for granted when looking for access to these narratives of trauma.

6   Shoshana Felman, 'Education and Crisis, or the Vicissitudes of Teaching', in Shoshana Felman and Dori Laub, *Testimony: Crises of Witnessing in Literature, Psychoanalysis, and History* (New York and London: Routledge, 1992), 1–56, 53 (emphasis in the original).
7   *Ibid.*
8   Cathy Caruth, ed., *Trauma: Explorations in Memory* (Baltimore and London: Johns Hopkins University Press, 1995), Cathy Caruth, *Unclaimed Experience: Trauma, Narrative and History* (Baltimore and London: Johns Hopkins University Press, 1996).
9   Anne Whitehead, 'Geoffrey Hartman and the Ethics of Place: Landscape, Memory, Trauma', *European Journal of English Studies* 7/3 (2003), 275–92, 276.
10 *Ibid.* (emphasis in the original).
11 Ulrich Baer, 'To Give Memory a Place: Holocaust Photography and the Landscape Tradition', *Representations* 69 (2000), 38–62, 43.

When neuroscientists Bessel A. van der Kolk, Alexander C. McFarlane and Onno van der Hart wrote on the nature of traumatic memories, they did so with the clear aim of treating a psychological disorder: 'Traumatic memories need to become like memories of everyday experience, that is, they need to be modified and transformed by being placed in their proper content and restructured into a meaningful narrative. [...]. Thus, in therapy, memory paradoxically becomes an act of creation rather than the static (fixation) recording of events that is characteristic of trauma-based memories.'[12] In her brilliant *Trauma: A Genealogy*, Ruth Leys criticizes this approach to trauma, particularly the notion of 'a literal imprint of an external trauma that, lodged in the brain in a special traumatic memory system, defies all possibility of representation.'[13] Nevertheless, following the works of van der Kolk, Felman, Laub and Caruth, the integration of literally imprinted traumatic memories into narratives of trauma has become the focal point of trauma literature and art.

Where cultural work engages with other people's trauma, it does so with a double emphasis on contradictory terms: the impossibility of fully grasping the traumatic moment and of translating it into language (especially in regard to the Holocaust), and the necessity to transmit knowledge of these traumas and to translate them for new audiences. Roger Luckhurst has called these two sides to the study of other people's pain the 'trauma paradigm': 'Given the narrative/anti-narrative tension at the core of trauma, aesthetics might step into this area because its task is (like that of the cultural critic) to "play with contradictions".'[14] Cultural forms, he argues, have provided 'the genres and narrative forms in which traumatic disruption is temporalized and rendered transmissible. Trauma has become a paradigm because it has been turned into a repertoire of compelling stories about

---

12   Bessel A. van der Kolk, Alexander C. McFarlane and Onno van der Hart, 'A General Approach to Treatment of Posttraumatic Stress Disorder', in Bessel A. van der Kolk, Alexander C. McFarlane and Lars Weisaeth, eds, *Traumatic Stress: The Effects of Overwhelming Experience on Mind, Body, and Society* (New York: Guilford, 1996), 417–40, 420.

13   Ruth Leys, *Trauma. A Genealogy* (Chicago: University of Chicago Press, 2000), 16.

14   Roger Luckhurst, *The Trauma Question* (London: Routledge, 2008), 80.

the enigmas of identity, memory and selfhood that have saturated Western cultural life.'[15] In light of Judith Herman's highly significant findings, this breadth of issues is not surprising.[16] When Herman introduced the concept of complex post-traumatic stress disorder, she emphasized that the manifestations of trauma are much more varied than commonly thought and underlines her argument with the findings of eminent psychiatrists who first worked with Holocaust survivors. William Niederland found that '"the concept of traumatic neurosis does not appear sufficient to cover the multitude and severity of clinical manifestations" of the survivor syndrome'. Further, Emmanuel Tanay observed that the 'psychopathology may be hidden in characterological changes that are manifest only in disturbed object relationships and attitudes towards work, the world, man and God.'[17]

Such disturbed relationships to the world, man, and God are very much at the core of modern and especially postmodern literature and art, with postmodernism particularly suited to address the fragmentation and breakdown of ordering principles in a post-Holocaust world. The enormous 'repertoire of compelling stories' about trauma, however, is, as Luckhurst himself admits, 'at odds with some of the most influential cultural theories of trauma, where the term trauma can be defined *in opposition* to narrative.'[18] Most prominent of these positions on trauma as a point of narrative impossibility is Jean-Francois Lyotard's definition of the traumatic experience. 'What art can do, is bear witness not to the sublime, but to this aporia of art and to its pain. It does not say the unsayable, but says that it cannot say it.'[19] This leads Luckhurst to conclude that '[t]rauma can therefore only be an

15 *Ibid.*
16 Judith Herman, *Trauma and Recovery: The Aftermath of Violence from Domestic Abuse to Political Terror* (New York: Basic Books, 1997).
17 Quoted in Judith Herman, 'Complex PTSD: A Syndrome in Survivors of Prolonged and Repeated Trauma', *Journal of Traumatic Stress* 5/3 (1992), 377–91, 378.
18 Luckhurst, *Trauma Question*, 80 (emphasis in the original).
19 Jean-François Lyotard, *Heidegger and 'the jews'*, trans. Andreas Michel and Mark S. Roberts (Minneapolis: University of Minnesota Press, 1990), 47.

aporia in narrative, and any narrative temporalization is an unethical act.'[20] Severe trauma, he writes, 'can only be conveyed by the catastrophic rupture of narrative possibility'.[21] Thus, if not only the participatory re-creation of trauma compromises ethical boundaries, but also any representation of other people's pain that goes beyond stating narrative impossibility, what is left for literature, art and their critics to do?

Roger Luckhurst soon changed his mind about the 'unethical act' of narrating trauma: Looking back on *The Trauma Question* in a journal article in 2010 (notably a journal on English literature),[22] he realizes that his earlier study was heavily influenced by the images of Abu Ghraib, images that defined 'an era saturated with the question of torture.'[23] Whereas Jean Améry described his torture by the Germans in 1943 as incomparable and therefore indescribable, marking 'the limit of the capacity of language to communicate',[24] the infliction of bodily pain in Abu Ghraib (the place that imprinted itself as the *image* of the 'war on terror') was not met with speechlessness but with immediate reappropriation. 'The images were not diluted or disrespected; that their meanings were continually de- and re-contextualized was part of their explosive power. In this phase, at least, an aesthetic of unspeakability or unrepresentability would fail to register how cultural forms have actually responded to our torturous times',[25] writes Luckhurst. Art is no longer only to bear witness to the aporia of pain. Luckhurst concludes: 'I would rather move beyond that, and follow the extraordinary flowering of cultural work that is using every register to assess these torturous times.'[26]

20   Luckhurst, *Trauma Question*, 81.
21   *Ibid.*
22   Roger Luckhurst, 'Beyond Trauma: Torturous times', *European Journal of English Studies* 14/1 (2010), 11–21.
23   *Ibid.*, 13.
24   Jean Améry, *At the Mind's Limits: Contemplations by a Survivor on Auschwitz and its Realities* (London: Granta, 1999 [1966]), 33.
25   Luckhurst, 'Beyond Trauma', 15.
26   *Ibid.*, 19.

This would lead back to Cathy Caruth's idea of trauma as a means of connecting with the other, of 'a speaking and a listening *from the site of trauma*'[27]: 'In a catastrophic age, that is, trauma itself may provide the very link between cultures: not as a simple understanding of the pasts of others but rather, within the traumas of contemporary history, as our ability to listen through the departures we have all taken from ourselves.'[28] Just as the translation of concepts from psychology and the transfer of the psychologist–patient relationship to that of art and its readership and audience pose ethical questions, so too does this configuration of trauma as a link between cultures. As Nancy Miller and Jason Tougaw observe, 'in a culture of trauma, accounts of extreme situations sell books. Narratives of illness, sexual abuse, torture or the death of loved ones have come to rival the classic, heroic adventure as a test of limits that offers the reader the suspicious thrill of borrowed emotion.'[29]

A 'culture of trauma' is in danger of losing contact with history, fears Dominick LaCapra: 'the significance or force of particular historical losses (for example, those of apartheid or the Shoah) may be obfuscated or rashly generalized. As a consequence one encounters the dubious ideas that everyone (including perpetrators or collaborators) is a victim, that all history is trauma, or that we all share a pathological public sphere or a "wound culture".'[30] Necessary distinctions are blurred in the all-encompassing 'wound-culture' approach to the trauma paradigm. Jean Améry wrote as the traumatized victim of torture; the reactions to the images of Abu Ghraib on the part of journalists, film-makers, and the public are, in contrast to this, at best a case of secondary witnessing. Notwithstanding the fact that 'torturous times' might in themselves be able to wound the national psyche or harm the personal and private sets of beliefs and convictions of readers and viewers, a clearer distinction on the one hand between primary victims

27 Cathy Caruth, 'Introduction', in Caruth, *Trauma: Explorations in Memory*, 3–11, 11 (emphasis in the original).

28 *Ibid.*

29 Nancy K. Miller and Jason Tougaw, 'Introduction: Extremities' in *Extremities*, 1–24, 2.

30 Dominick LaCapra, *Writing History, Writing Trauma* (Baltimore and London: Johns Hopkins University Press, 2001), 64.

who, in Freud's terms, 'suffer from reminiscences', and people influenced by this pain, on the other, has to be upheld. For LaCapra, the necessary boundary is that of 'empathic unsettlement': 'At the very least, empathic unsettlement poses a barrier to closure in discourse and places in jeopardy harmonizing or spiritually uplifting accounts of extreme events from which we attempt to derive reassurance or a benefit (for example, unearned confidence about the ability of the human spirit to endure any adversity with dignity and nobility).'[31]

Otherwise, if all engagement with horrific events is subsumed under the equalizing term of trauma, there will be no 'we' left at all to talk about other people's pain. The tendency to welcome empathic understanding (as opposed to unsettlement) as a way to experience the pain of the other, thereby assuming at least in part the position of the traumatized victim, might in fact disavow the victim of his or her most personal experience and history. Psychiatrist Dori Laub, for example, claims that 'the listener to trauma comes to be a participant and a co-owner of the traumatic event: through his very listening, he comes to partially experience trauma in himself'.[32] While this may be true in the case of the psychiatrist listening to his patient's trauma in a psychological sense,[33] it becomes ethically problematic when transferred imprudently and without distinction to literature and literary and cultural criticism.

Literature can indeed engage with trauma. It has always done so. Yet the narratives of trauma that 'we' are being offered about other people's pain in literature, film, photography and art are, in the overwhelming number of cases, not the same ones that psychologists and psychotherapists are dealing with in their treatment of real victims and witnesses. Distinguishing

---

31   *Ibid.*, 41–2. As an example for this 'unearned and incongruous spiritual uplift', LaCapra mentions Melissa Mueller, *Anne Frank: The Biography* (New York: Henry Holt, 1998).

32   Dori Laub, 'Bearing Witness, or the Vicissitudes of Listening', in Shoshana Felman and Dori Laub, *Testimony: Crises of Witnessing*, 57–74, 57.

33   As, for instance, Heather M. Moulden and Philip Firestone have pointed out in their review of descriptive and empirical literature examining vicarious traumatization: 'Vicarious Traumatization. The Impact on Therapists who Work With Sexual Offenders', *Trauma, Violence & Abuse* 8/1 (2007), 67–83.

between the two would seem, therefore, to be not only a question of proper procedure, but of ethics. Art can mirror the nature of traumatic memories and their 'need to be modified and transformed by being placed in their proper content and restructured into a meaningful narrative', but this 'act of creation'[34] should not be a claim to co-ownership of real trauma. Art, in particular postmodern art, can navigate brilliantly the territories of trauma, but it should be careful not to succumb to voyeuristic and arrogant spectatorship.

At the end of *Regarding the Pain of Others*, Susan Sontag takes up this idea of the unified spectatorship, of the 'we', again in a passage describing Jeff Wall's photograph *Dead Troops Talk (A Vision After an Ambush of a Red Army Patrol near Moquor, Afghanistan, Winter 1986)*, a digital montage of a 'made-up event in a savage war that had been much in the news.'[35] In the style of a nineteenth-century history painting, Wall arranges the 'antithesis of a document',[36] a disturbingly 'real' picture of the face of war where the dead talk to each other. Yet these dead 'are supremely uninterested in the living: in those who took their lives; in witnesses – and in us. [...] "We" – this "we" is everyone who has never experienced anything like what they went through – don't understand. We don't get it. [...] Can't understand, can't imagine.'[37] If this is true, all engagement with trauma literature and art is pointless. There must be something left that literature and art can do in the face of trauma; if not offer understanding, then at least a perspective on that which 'we' have not experienced. It is this question of the possibilities and limitations of narratives of trauma in regard to other people's pain and the question of ethics that this volume sets out to address.

The following contributions approach the vast – though not unlimited – field of trauma studies and its complexity by examining a variety of literary trauma narratives and the ethical implications involved in the production, reception and analysis of other people's pain from a multidisciplinary

34   van der Kolk, McFarlane and van der Hart, 'A General Approach to Treatment of PTSD', 420.
35   Sontag, *Regarding the Pain of Others*, 111.
36   *Ibid.*
37   *Ibid.*, 113.

perspective. Examining the theoretical framework of trauma studies, its place within academic discourse and society, the following articles explore the representation of other people's pain from the viewpoint of cultural studies and provide critical readings of literary texts from the disciplines of French, German, American and English studies, which link the theory of trauma studies to individual in-depth analyses. These case studies engage with a variety of distinct forms of collective/historical and individual traumatic experience, such as persecution and mass genocide in the Holocaust, the atrocities of forced labour concentration camps, the Second World War, the Vietnam War, the 9/11 terrorist attacks, slavery, European imperialism and colonialism in Africa, apartheid in South Africa, sexual abuse, racism and racial segregation, and anti-Semitism.

In his expository article 'Trauma and Ethics: Telling the Other's Story', COLIN DAVIS explores the dangers of secondary witnessing and the temptations of participating in the story and trauma of others. 'Who should speak for those who do not speak for themselves, the dead, the mute, the traumatized, those who cannot or will not tell their own stories, or those who have no story to tell?' Davis's question draws attention to the fundamental dilemma of speaking about other people's pain. If to speak for the other inevitably involves participation in the other's pain, and if to remain silent perpetuates the initial violence and neglects the memory of the other, speaking about other people's pain turns into 'an ethical minefield'. Davis's analysis of Giorgio Agamben's *Remnants of Auschwitz* and of Shoshana Felman's account of a class in crisis shows that these two seminal texts of trauma theory seem to lack an adequate understanding of this ethical dilemma. Pointing out that Agamben's identification of the Muselmann, the 'living dead', as the 'principal figure for the understanding of Auschwitz' is based on a misreading of Primo Levi, Davis shows how Agamben elevates his own position and 'asserts his authority as interpreter over subjects who can no longer speak for themselves'. In Levi's account the survivor can speak for the Muselmann 'by proxy' and 'in ignorance and incomprehension' of his experience. There is nothing to learn from the figure of the Muselmann. In contrast, in Agamben's account 'the witness speaks for the Muselmann, and Agamben speaks for the witness', thus emphasizing his general 'view of the human subject as lacking intention and agency'. The ethically problematic nature of Agamben's appropriation of the other's trauma is reflected in Felman's approach to teaching narratives of trauma in the form of 'participatory re-creation of trauma'. Davis criticises Felman's ideal of teaching trauma by forcing her students to identify with the victims of traumatic experience, turning them into secondary victims, and to 'work through' the pain that has become their own. Instead of creating a state of 'trauma envy' and participating in the pain of others, Davis argues 'that witnessing the other's trauma is precisely *not* to share it'. In the third section of his essay, Davis provides a literary example that avoids these dangers of 'secondary trauma'. Here, Davis gives an analysis of Charlotte Delbo's *Measure of our Days*, which tells the stories of other people's pain from a first-person perspective, but refuses 'to exert authority over the stories of the survivors by imposing a coherent meaning on them'.

ALEIDA ASSMANN in her essay 'From Collective Violence to a Common Future: Four Models for Dealing with a Traumatic Past' draws attention to the ethics and politics involved in the processes of remembering and forgetting a traumatic history of violence both at the individual and at the collective level. In contrast to the recent development of a 'Culture of Remembrance', the first model, which Assmann presents as 'dialogic forgetting', considers the ability to forget as a 'cultural achievement' that has been used since antiquity to achieve the 'closure of a violent past in a symmetric situation of power'. It is a way of 'shared forgetting' that can provide a basis for a common future. The atrocities of the Holocaust and the radically asymmetric experience of traumatic violence, in contrast, demand a radically different way of dealing with the past. The closure provided by the first model is here 'exactly what had to be prevented by all means'. Instead, only a pact of 'remembering in order never to forget' that achieved 'ethical recognition' of the victims could provide for an appropriate answer to the 'historically unprecedented crime of the Holocaust'. Yet in contrast to this 'semi-religious memorialization' of the past, the third model Assmann presents, 'remembering in order to overcome', also aims at the ethical recognition of the victims of a traumatic past, but intends to achieve reconciliation 'in order to be able to imagine a common future'. The fourth model, which Assmann terms 'dialogic remembering', applies to nations which share a history of traumatic violence and mutually acknowledge their own responsibility for the suffering that each has inflicted on the other. From Assmann's perspective this last model especially, although it is not a practised reality yet, could provide future possibilities for overcoming international conflicts about the ethics and politics of remembering and acknowledging other people's pain.

In her article 'Trauma Studies: Contexts, Politics, Ethics', SUSANNAH RADSTONE provides a critical analysis of the development and the place of trauma theory within the humanities today. Radstone approaches trauma studies from the perspective of its ethical and political implications, its mechanisms of exclusion and inclusion, and its inherent danger of inferiorizing the victims of trauma from an outside perspective of secondary witnessing, as described by Dominick LaCapra. Defining the notion of a fundamental 'lack of agency' on the part of the primary witness and victim as a central characteristic of traumatic experience, Radstone draws attention to the normative element involved in the construction of the victim of traumatic experience as 'helpless' that might easily turn secondary witnessing into pitying spectatorship and voyeurism of other people's pain. By identifying trauma studies within the humanities as a 'kind of tertiary witnessing' Radstone raises awareness of the 'necessity of interrogating' the ethics and politics involved in the practice of trauma studies itself. Rather than perpetuating an, at least ethically, questionable notion of witnessing, Radstone's approach demands 'an active, engaged and agentic practice that intervenes in and practices a politics and an ethics open to critique, negotiation and transformation'. Taking its cues from Laplanchian psychoanalytic theory and object relations theory, Radstone's article furthermore critically examines the concept of the subject underlying canonical texts of trauma studies by Cathy Caruth and Dori Laub and Shoshana Felman. In Ruth Leys's criticism, Radstone identifies the model of a mimetic variation of trauma theory that focuses on the dissociation of the self and an anti-mimetic variation that focuses on the traumatic event. Examining the connections between trauma studies and history, memory and testimony, as well as theories of referentiality and representation, Radstone offers a critique of the tendency in trauma studies toward emphasizing the anti-mimetic event, thus contributing to the construction of a strict dichotomy between the autonomy of the subject and the externality of the traumatic event. Instead of perpetuating these binary oppositions, thus advocating 'cultural and political Manicheanism', Radstone concludes that trauma studies should not extend its boundaries but should rather self-reflexively engage with its own mechanism of inclusion and exclusion and the 'inevitability of ethical impurity'.

MARÍA JESÚS MARTÍNEZ-ALFARO in her essay 'Narrating the Holocaust and its Legacy: The Complexities of Identity, Trauma and Representation in Art Spiegelman's *Maus*' explores the limits of representing the Holocaust in the form of a radically different and seemingly disconcerting literary genre, the comic book, which subverts the traditional idea of decorum. Taking its cues from Marianna Hirsch's concept of 'postmemory', which describes the transgenerational transmission of traumatic memory from the victims of trauma to their descendants, Martínez discusses Spiegelman's struggle in his *Maus: A Survivor's Tale* to recover the 'absent memories' of his own family's traumatic past. Spiegelman's textual and graphic narrative tells the story of the protagonist Artie, who serves as the author's persona, and who tries to cope with his father's traumatic past as a survivor of Auschwitz. The after-effects of traumatization and the traumatic memories of persecution and the Holocaust not only invade the present life of Artie's father himself, but also result in Artie's struggle with his identity as a survivor's descendant and the moral responsibilities of the second generation of survivors in general. Spiegelman's narrative manages to negotiate the representation of the Holocaust, Martínez shows, by explicitly and self-consciously reflecting on the act of textual and graphic narration, on the representation of the unspeakable events, on the ethical dilemma of using other people's pain as a source of artistic expression and the risk of commodification involved in this. It is precisely this awareness of the limits of representation, Martínez concludes, that enables *Maus* to represent the unspeakable events of the Holocaust. Spiegelman achieves this by laying bare the silence and absence of those who did not survive, by showing the unbridgeable gaps and paradoxes of traumatic memories, and by avoiding the imposition of closure on the textual and graphic narrative of this *Survivor's Tale*.

In her essay 'Zero – A Gaping Mouth: The Discourse of the Camps in Herta Müller's *Atemschaukel* between Literary Theory and Political Philosophy', BETTINA BANNASCH analyses Müller's account of the deportation of a young Romanian German to a labour camp by the Soviet Union and his struggle to survive the camp, an account based on the life stories of survivors, in particular that of the writer Oskar Pastior. Drawing on Roland Barthes's writing about 'the ideal case of narration' Bannasch explores the significance of the 'ineffable' zero point in *Atemschaukel* that marks Müller's 'critical engagement with the discourse about the literary depiction of the camps' surrounding Theodor W. Adorno's pronouncement about literature after Auschwitz and Paul Celan's remarks on the zero point of history. Yet, as Bannasch points out, Müller's novel makes a 'different kind of claim to universal validity' that is not concerned with the question of the legitimacy of storytelling after Auschwitz but which 'pursues a fundamentally different question, namely that of a *politically relevant ethic*'. The narrative composition of *Atemschaukel*, Bannasch argues, manages to avoid such comparisons as continue to dominate the literary discourse of the Shoah, using instead the mathematical precision of equations, in what Barthes terms the 'honest' stance of the writer, to express the 'gaping mouth of the zero', and thus emphasizing the 'existential quality of the narration'. The 'zero' is the hunger of the camp inmates that challenges their sense of personal identity and, Bannasch emphasizes, represents the 'ethical centre of the novel'. It creates a 'state of emergency' that, in contrast to the notions of Giorgio Agamben and Carl Schmitt, is not depicted from the external perspective of the sovereign power that determines the 'state of emergency', but rather from the first-person perspective of the narrator who experiences this situation. By its 'precision in dealing with language', also reflected in Müller's use of metaphors, the text manages to resist 'the construction of a beautiful world of art that promises refuge from an ugly reality', depicting the 'state of emergency' and the ethical dilemma of camp life, whilst maintaining, Bannasch concludes, a distinction between 'right and wrong', between the 'state of emergency and normality'.

HUBERT ZAPF in his contribution 'Trauma, Narrative and Ethics in Recent American Fiction' explores the significance of trauma as a narrative topic and ethical challenge in selected works of recent American fiction, with a particular emphasis on Leslie Marmon Silko's *Ceremony* and Toni Morrison's *Beloved*. Taking Torquato Tasso's epic *Jerusalem Liberated* as a starting-point for his analysis, Zapf emphasizes the importance of trauma and traumatization as a literary topic. The special function and status of imaginative literature, its 'metaphorical and mythopoetic mode of textualizing experience', calls for a supplementation of 'psychoanalytic or

psychocultural' trauma theory by a 'poetics of trauma'. American literary
history, Zapf argues, from Nathanial Hawthorne's *The Scarlet Letter* to William Faulkner's *The Sound and the Fury*, and twentieth-century literature in
particular, offers a variety of trauma narratives. Although Silko's *Ceremony*,
which connects the protagonist's traumatic experience of the Second World
War with the traumatizing loss of his cultural identity as a Native American,
and Morrison's *Beloved*, which is set against the background of the historical experience of the enslavement of African Americans, draw on diverg-
ing forms of historical trauma, Zapf shows that both narratives refer to
traditional story-telling and ecocultural counter-discourses as regenerative
means for the individuals, who act as representatives of traumatic historical experiences. The connection of various forms of traumatic experience,
as Zapf points out in his survey of trauma narratives in recent American
literature, also marks one characteristic feature of twenty-first century fiction. The novels of Philip Roth, Richard Powers, Siri Hustvedt, Jonathan
Safran Foer and Don DeLillo link 'public and private, extreme and everyday,
physical and psychological traumas' in their fictionalized accounts of other
people's pain and experience of the Holocaust, the Second World War, the
Vietnam War, racism and anti-Semitism, or the 9/11 terrorist attacks. It is
precisely the 'fictional status' of all these narratives of trauma, Zapf argues
in conclusion, their setting in 'a depragmatized and metadiscursive space'
that makes these narratives ethically relevant for the reader, thus contributing 'towards a collectively experienced historical reality'.

RUDOLF FREIBURG in his essay 'Trauma as Normalcy: Pain in Philip
Roth's *The Human Stain*' explores the negotiation of personal and national
identity in its relation to pain and trauma in Roth's 'American tragedy'
from a perspective informed by the literary history of catastrophe and
traumatic experiences and dominant positions in contemporary trauma
studies. Drawing particularly on the literary tradition of Greek tragedy,
Freiburg shows how the multifarious forms of individual traumatization,
represented in the novel by the traumatic life stories of Nathan Zuckerman,
Coleman Silk, and Faunia and Les Farley, not only affect significantly the
continuous construction and revision – the 'performance' – of personal
identity, but are also reflected on the collective national level of American
history which then comes to be seen as a sequence of atrocious events.
The Human Stain, the third part of Roth's 'American Trilogy', examines

American society against the backdrop of its recent history, in particular
the Clinton–Lewinsky affair, which, as Freiburg points out, mirrors the
human stain – the 'inevitable result of typically human weakness of character and nature' – on the level of the individual characters in the novel.
Roth's narrative uses his traumatized characters who suffer from post-
traumatic stress disorder as a consequence of the Vietnam War, sexual abuse
and racial discrimination to portray the 'genetically predetermined habit
of all human beings to create evil, to torment each other'. Identifying this
omnipresence of pain and trauma as the central characteristic of the text,
Freiburg argues that *The Human Stain* challenges the exceptionality usually
ascribed to traumatization, thus inverting the standard definition of trauma.
In Roth's disillusioning depiction of the American 'wound culture', Freiburg
concludes, other people's pain is likely to turn into one's own suffering and
the condition of traumatization then becomes normalcy.

   In the concluding essay 'Trauma, Shame and Ethical Responsibility
for the Death of the Other in J. M. Coetzee's *Waiting for the Barbarians*',
SUSANA ONEGA draws attention to the limitations of trauma studies,
which are revealed by its primary dedication to the analysis of historical
catastrophes from a Western perspective, thus often neglecting other cultures and literary fields. Onega enlarges the scope of other people's pain
by analysing *Waiting for the Barbarians* as an example of contemporary
postcolonial African literatures and the challenge of 'providing healing
narratives' for the atrocities of colonialism and the after-effects of a traumatic history of genocide, civil war and oppressive dictatorship. Coetzee's
third novel, which engages with the dominant individual and collective
trauma of contemporary South Africa, the institutionalization of racial
hatred and violence by the apartheid regime, Onega argues, serves as a
paradigmatic example of the 'ethical demand and of the extraordinary
difficulty' of creating narratives of trauma that manage to incorporate
the pain of the victims and the shame of the perpetrators. Drawing on
the 'cathartic effect of abreaction', described by Freud and Breuer, Onega
stresses the 'crucial role of narrative in the healing of trauma' and the rejection with which postmodern and experimental writers, such as Coetzee, are
confronted when they engage with the historical 'truth'. Contrary to these
'realism-biased' expectations, Coetzee's narrative manages to give voice to
'the barbarians', 'the white minority's absolute other' and their experience of

'structural' and 'manifest' violence through the perspective of an unnamed country magistrate, whose quiet life and harmonious coexistence with the local community and with nature in a remote fort on the border of the Empire comes to an abrupt end with the arrival of the cruel and pitiless Colonel of Police, Joll. Traumatized by the extreme physical torture and the death of 'barbarian' prisoners, ordered and executed by Joll himself, the protagonist gradually comes to realize his shame and responsibility as an active participant in the apartheid system and as a complicit witness of extreme violence. Identifying the mutual gaze of colonizer and colonized as 'the definitive humanizing event', Onega argues, informed by Emmanuel Levinas's ethics of alterity, that the protagonist assumes responsibility for the unjust death of the other, thus overcoming his shame and trauma. Yet, as consoling as it might be, Onega finally warns against an interpretation of the text which ignores 'the troubling fact' that the protagonist tries to speak for the 'barbarian' other, the victims of his own crimes. Although he is tortured himself as a result of his 'ethical awakening' – some form of penance and reparation – the narrative fails to establish hope for a lasting affective relationship between colonizer and colonized except for 'the reader's participation in the minimal existential freedom' achieved by the protagonist's assumption of responsibility for other people's pain.

Bibliography

Améry, Jean, *At the Mind's Limits: Contemplations by a Survivor on Auschwitz and its Realities* (London: Granta, 1999 [1966]).

Baer, Ulrich, 'To Give Memory a Place: Holocaust Photography and the Landscape Tradition', *Representations* 69 (2000), 38–62.

Caruth, Cathy, ed., *Trauma: Explorations in Memory* (Baltimore and London: Johns Hopkins University Press, 1995).

——, *Unclaimed Experience: Trauma, Narrative and History* (Baltimore and London: Johns Hopkins University Press, 1996).

Felman, Shoshana, 'Education and Crisis, or the Vicissitudes of Teaching', in Shoshana Felman and Dori Laub, *Testimony: Crises of Witnessing in Literature, Psychoanalysis, and History* (New York and London: Routledge, 1992), 1–56.

Herman, Judith, 'Complex PTSD: A Syndrome in Survivors of Prolonged and Repeated Trauma', *Journal of Traumatic Stress* 5/3 (1992), 377–91.

——, *Trauma and Recovery: The Aftermath of Violence from Domestic Abuse to Political Terror* (New York: Basic Books, 1997).

LaCapra, Dominick, *Writing History, Writing Trauma* (Baltimore and London: Johns Hopkins University Press, 2001).

Laub, Dori, 'Bearing Witness, or the Vicissitudes of Listening', in Shoshana Felman and Dori Laub, *Testimony: Crises of Witnessing in Literature, Psychoanalysis, and History* (New York and London: Routledge, 1992), 57–74.

Leys, Ruth, *Trauma. A Genealogy* (Chicago: University of Chicago Press, 2000).

Luckhurst, Roger, *The Trauma Question* (London: Routledge, 2008).

——, 'Beyond Trauma: Torturous times', *European Journal of English Studies* 14/1 (2010), 11–21.

Lyotard, Jean-François, *Heidegger and 'the jews'*, trans. Andreas Michel and Mark S. Roberts (Minneapolis: University of Minnesota Press, 1990).

Middleton, Peter. 'The New Memoryism: How Computers Changed the Way We Read', *New Formations* 50 (2003), 57–74.

Miller, Nancy K., and Jason Tougaw, 'Introduction: Extremities', in Nancy K. Miller and Jason Tougaw, eds, *Extremities. Trauma, Testimony and the Community* (Chicago: University of Illinois Press, 2002), 1–24.

Moulden, Heather M., and Philip Firestone, 'Vicarious Traumatization. The Impact on Therapists who Work With Sexual Offenders', *Trauma, Violence & Abuse* 8/1 (2007), 67–83.

Piers, Craig, 'A return to the source: Rereading Freud in the midst of contemporary trauma theory', *Psychotherapy* 33/4 (1996), 539–48.

Sontag, Susan, *Regarding the Pain of Others* (London: Penguin, 2004).

Yaeger, Patricia, 'Consuming Trauma; or, The Pleasures of Merely Circulating', in Nancy K. Miller and Jason Tougaw, eds, *Extremities. Trauma, Testimony and the Community* (Chicago: University of Illinois Press, 2002), 25–51.

van der Kolk, Bessel A., Alexander C. McFarlane and Onno van der Hart, 'A General Approach to Treatment of Posttraumatic Stress Disorder', in Bessel A. van der Kolk, Alexander C. McFarlane and Lars Weisaeth, eds, *Traumatic Stress: The Effects of Overwhelming Experience on Mind, Body, and Society* (New York: Guilford, 1996), 417–40.

Whitehead, Anne, 'Geoffrey Hartman and the Ethics of Place: Landscape, Memory, Trauma', *European Journal of English Studies* 7/3 (2003), 275–92.

COLIN DAVIS

Trauma and Ethics: Telling the Other's Story

Who should speak for those who do not speak for themselves, the dead, the mute, the traumatized, those who cannot or will not tell their own stories, or those who have no story to tell? In his 'Plea for the Dead', Auschwitz survivor Elie Wiesel is adamant that no one has the right to speak in the place of the victims of atrocity: 'To want to speak in the name of those who died [...] is precisely to humiliate them. [...] Leave them in peace.'[1] We cannot speak on their behalf, nor should we even try to understand them: 'You want to understand? There is nothing more to understand. You want to know? There is nothing more to know. It is not by playing with words and with the dead that you will understand and know. On the contrary. The Ancients used to say: "Those who know do not speak; those who speak do not know".'[2] We should not have the arrogance to assume that we can share some part of what happened to the victims. And yet not to speak for those who have been silenced, not to recall or to study what happened to them in the hope of learning something from their stories, would be an act of barbarity in itself, hideously complicit with the forces which sought to eliminate them. As Wiesel puts it elsewhere, 'To forget the dead would be to betray them. To forget the victims would be to take the side of their executioners'.[3]

Talking of the other's trauma is, then, an ethical minefield. The duty to preserve the memory of pain has been asserted so frequently that it has become difficult to contest; this chapter focuses rather on the less evi-

1   Elie Wiesel, 'Plaidoyer pour les morts', in *Le Chant des morts* (Paris: Seuil, 1966), 191–220, 197. Translations from Wiesel and other French texts are my own.
2   *Ibid.*, 219.
3   Elie Wiesel, *Discours d'Oslo* (Paris: Grasset, 1987), 27.

dent but insidious dangers inherent in secondary witnessing and vicarious
trauma. In one of the key texts for the development of modern trauma
studies, the psychiatrist Dori Laub says that 'the listener to trauma comes
to be a participant and a co-owner of the traumatic event: through his very
listening, he comes to partially experience trauma in himself'.[4] This may be
psychologically correct, but I find Laub's formulation ethically problematic.
My argument here is that we do not participate in or co-own the other's
trauma; and the sense or desire that we do should be resisted because it
gives us the potentially self-serving illusion of empathic understanding.
Rather than the 'unsettlement' described by Dominick LaCapra,[5] it might
be used to confirm the authority of the analyst and produce premature,
unwarranted closure. This chapter examines briefly two authors, Giorgio
Agamben and Shoshana Felman, who represent different but equally wor-
rying ways of encroaching on traumas which are not their own; and then at
slightly greater length it considers Charlotte Delbo, whose book *Measure
of our Days* seems to do precisely what I am arguing against by purport-
ing to speak in the place of traumatized others. The chapter asks how it is
that Delbo avoids the charge of over-hastily appropriating the other's pain
which I shall level against Agamben and Felman.

Is it theoretically possible to settle the meaning of another's story
without delusion or falsification? In her book *Giving an Account of Oneself,* Judith Butler suggests that we cannot even give final form to our own
stories, let alone those of others. There are a number of what she calls
'vexations' which prevent me from giving a narrative account of myself: I

4   Dori Laub, 'Bearing Witness, or the Vicissitudes of Listening', in Shoshana Felman
     and Dori Laub, *Testimony: Crises of Witnessing in Literature, Psychoanalysis, and
     History* (New York and London: Routledge, 1992), 57–74, 57.
5   On 'empathic unsettlement', see for example Dominick LaCapra, *Writing History,
     Writing Trauma* (Baltimore and London: Johns Hopkins University Press, 2001),
     41–2: 'At the very least, empathic unsettlement poses a barrier to closure in discourse
     and places in jeopardy harmonizing or spiritually uplifting accounts of extreme events
     from which we attempt to derive reassurance or a benefit (for example, unearned
     confidence about the ability of the human spirit to endure any adversity with dignity
     and nobility).'

cannot narrate the exposure to the other which establishes my singularity in the first place; the primary relations which form lasting impressions on the course of my life are irrecoverable; there is a history which I do not own and which makes me partially opaque to myself; the norms that enable my narrative are not authored by me, so they rob me of my singularity at the very moment I seek to assert it; and because every account is an account given to someone else, it is superseded by the structure of address in which it takes place.[6] As Butler puts it succinctly, 'There is that in me and of me for which I can give no account'.[7] We cannot offer narrative closure for our lives because we are, Butler argues, 'interrupted by alterity'.[8]

An important point here is that what Butler calls 'my own foreignness to myself'[9] also entails our foreignness to others and their foreignness to us. The Italian philosopher Adriana Cavarero, who is an important interlocutor for Butler in *Giving an Account of Oneself*, argues against the empathy, identification or confusion through which one person's story may be appropriated by another; as she insists, 'your story is never my story'.[10] This view goes together with distrust of the first person plural 'we', which implies the existence of a community where there is none: 'No matter how much the larger traits of our life-stories are similar, I still do not recognize myself *in* you and, even less, in the collective *we*.'[11] Butler is less hostile to the first person plural than Cavarero,[12] but we can use it, she suggests, only on the understanding that our fundamental sociality is constituted on the basis of our foreignness to one another. There is no final account of our own lives and no secure bridge between our experience and that of other people.

6   Judith Butler, *Giving an Account of Oneself* (New York: Fordham University Press, 2005), 39.
7   *Ibid.*, 40.
8   *Ibid.*, 64.
9   *Ibid.*, 84.
10   Adriana Cavarero, *Relating Narratives: Storytelling and Selfhood*, trans. Paul A. Kottman (London and New York: Routledge, 2000), 92.
11   *Ibid.* (emphasis in original).
12   Butler, *Account of Oneself*, 33.

Butler gives good reasons why we cannot provide a definitive narrative of our own lives. It follows that it will be all the more impossible to account without distortion for the lives and deaths of others. We cannot possess our own stories, and *a fortiori* we cannot claim to possess the stories of others. And yet, as critics, historians, analysts, teachers, students and readers, we are bound to attempt to do so. As inevitable and indeed important as this may be, the current chapter suggests that it is fraught with intellectual and ethical dangers.

Agamben and the Other's Truth

Giorgio Agamben's *Remnants of Auschwitz: The Witness and the Archive* has rapidly become an important and widely-cited text in Holocaust and trauma studies.[13] It has not been, though, exempt from criticism, particularly for its central move of making the so-called Muselmann the principal figure for the understanding of Auschwitz.[14] The word *Muselmann*

13   Giorgio Agamben, *Remnants of Auschwitz: The Witness and the Archive*, trans. Daniel Heller-Roazen (New York: Zone Books, 1999).
14   For criticisms of Agamben's book, see Philippe Mesnard and Claudine Cahan, *Giorgio Agamben à l'épreuve d'Auschwitz* (Paris: Kimé, 2001); Robert Eaglestone, 'On Giorgio Agamben's Holocaust', in *Paragraph* 25/2 (2002), 51–67; Fethi Benslama, 'La Représentation et l'impossible', in Jean-Luc Nancy, ed., *L'Art et la mémoire des camps: Représenter exterminer* (Paris: Seuil, 2001), 59–80; Ruth Leys, 'The Shame of Auschwitz', in *From Guilt to Shame: Auschwitz and After* (Princeton and Oxford: Princeton University Press, 2007), 157–79; and Colin Davis, 'Speaking with the Dead: De Man, Levinas, Agamben', in *Haunted Subjects: Deconstruction, Psychoanalysis and the Return of the Dead* (London: Palgrave Macmillan, 2007), 111–27. Whilst Agamben's account of the Muselmann has attracted a great deal of criticism, it has been readily accepted by some readers. Notably, Slavoj Žižek repeatedly returns to the figure of the Muselmann, basically agreeing with and building on Agamben's analysis; see for example Slavoj Žižek, *The Puppet and the Dwarf: The Perverse Core of Christianity* (Cambridge, MA, and London: The MIT Press, 2003), 155–9;

(Muslim) was used at Auschwitz and some other camps to designate a type of prisoner who seemed to have given up on life, surviving precariously as a set of biological functions. They are a kind of living dead. Agamben elevates the Muselmann to being the key which will unlock the significance of Auschwitz. He describes the Muselmann's status between life and death as 'the perfect cipher of the camp'; and he insists that 'we will not understand what Auschwitz is if we do not first understand who or what the *Muselmann* is'.[15] He then goes on to reveal to us the true meaning of the Muselmann, which is also the true meaning of Auschwitz and the whole concentrationary universe. Auschwitz appears as a kind of terrible experiment which lays bare 'the hidden structure of all subjectivity and consciousness'.[16] The Muselmann is what this experiment reveals to be the limit point of human existence: 'he marks the threshold between the human and the inhuman'; he is 'the final biopolitical substance to be isolated in the biological continuum'.[17]

In his account of the Muselmann, Agamben draws on the testimony of a number of camp survivors, in particular that of Primo Levi. Indeed, *Remnants of Auschwitz* can be viewed as an extended commentary on a few passages from Levi's work. In a quotation to which Agamben repeatedly refers, Levi describes the Muselmänner as 'the true witnesses [...] the complete witnesses, the ones whose deposition would have a general significance'; but, 'just as no one ever returned to recount his own death', they can not tell of their experiences.[18] In consequence, according to Levi, the survivors 'speak in their stead, by proxy'.[19] This statement might appear to

---

The Parallax View (Cambridge, MA, and London: The MIT Press, 2006), 112–13; 'Neighbors and Other Monsters: A Plea for Ethical Violence', in Slavoj Žižek, Eric L. Santner and Kenneth Reinhard, *The Neighbor: Three Inquiries in Political Theology* (Chicago and London: The University of Chicago Press, 2005), 134–90, 160–2.

15   Agamben, *Remnants*, 48, 52

16   *Ibid.*, 128.

17   *Ibid.*, 55, 85.

18   Primo Levi, *The Drowned and the Saved*, trans. Raymond Rosenthal (London: Abacus, 1989), 63–4.

19   *Ibid.*, 64.

contradict Wiesel's view, quoted above, that no one could or should speak in the name of the dead. In fact, though, the difference between Wiesel and Levi on this point is not so great as it might appear. Levi's formulation is characteristically exact. To speak in someone's stead or by proxy is not to assume their voice or to imply that their experience can be understood or narrated by another. The survivor speaks because someone has to, not because he has access to some otherwise barred knowledge. When Levi tells us that only the Muselmann's testimony would have 'general significance', he insists on the point that such testimony cannot be given and therefore the general significance of the camps will never be available. The Muselmänner, Levi insists, have no story to tell and no lesson to teach us.[20]

For all his close reliance on Levi, Agamben misses precisely this point. He endeavours to describe the significance of the Muselmann and his centrality to the experience of the camps despite Levi's implicit warning that this would be to find meaning – and comfort – where there is none. And Agamben's failure to understand Levi's point that the general significance of the Muselmann's testimony is not available leads him to misunderstand Levi's related point that survivors speak 'in their stead, by proxy'. Agamben takes this to mean that, despite the fact that no one returns to recount their death, 'it is in some way the *Muselmann* who bears witness'.[21] Provoked into speech by those who are speechless, the survivor nevertheless *in some way* testifies on behalf of the Muselmann. It is essential to Agamben's argument that, although the Muselmann does not bear witness for himself, there is still a lesson to be learned from his existence. So, even if centred subject positions are relinquished in Agamben's account of testimony, the speechless one nevertheless speaks. It is hard to avoid the suspicion, though, that the position of Agamben himself comes out of this all the stronger, as he asserts his authority as interpreter over subjects who can no longer speak for themselves. Levi's point is that speaking by

20   See Primo Levi, *If This is a Man / The Truce*, trans. Stuart Woolf (London: Abacus, 1987), 96: 'All the musselmans who finished in the gas chambers have the same story, or more exactly, have no story; they followed the slope down to the bottom, like streams that run down to the sea.'

21   Agamben, *Remnants*, 120.

proxy can never yield an understanding of the Muselmann. The survivor speaks 'in his stead' because he cannot speak for himself; but the survivor speaks in ignorance and incomprehension of the Muselmann's experience. Agamben turns this into something rather different. In this account, the witness speaks for the Muselmann, and Agamben speaks for the witness. In the absence of the Muselmann's testimony, he takes it upon himself to explain the meaning of the camps. This is confirmed by the final pages of *Remnants of Auschwitz*. Agamben's book ends with texts by a number of Muselmänner who survived the camps. Agamben wants, he says, to leave 'the last word' to the Muselmänner.[22] On the face of it, the words of the Muselmänner appear to contradict the claim that, by definition, they are unable to bear witness. Agamben is nevertheless unshaken, and concludes by insisting that the testimony of the Muselmänner 'fully verifies'[23] the paradox according to which they are the witnesses who cannot bear witness. By this point he has stopped listening; he has already decided what meaning the lives and deaths of the Muselmänner should have.

Agamben tells us that 'all witnesses speak of [the Muselmann] as a central experience'.[24] This is simply untrue, but it perfectly encapsulates Agamben's rush to generalize from fragmentary material and it decisively inflects his understanding of the camps. Moreover, it grossly neglects the variety of experiences of the camps by privileging one over all others. Making the Muselmann the key figure discounts all those whose experience was quite different: those who were killed on arrival at Auschwitz, or those who struggled and resisted and died, those who found comradeship and those who lost faith, those who improbably survived and those who were used in hideous experiments or gassed or shot or hanged. All these must take second place, in Agamben's account, to the unutterable yet somehow uttered experience of the Muselmann.

Agamben's understanding of the Muselmann entails, and is enabled by, a misreading of Levi's comments. Showing how Agamben may not

22   *Ibid.*, 165.
23   *Ibid.*
24   *Ibid.*, 52.

accurately represent the texts to which he refers (particularly works by
Levi and Robert Antelme), Ruth Leys states her disapproval of 'the partial
and misleading way he has of reading certain crucial passages, expound-
ing them in terms that are alien to the meaning of the texts in which they
appear'.[25] This misreading is not merely a matter of literary interpretation,
since it has far-reaching consequences for Agamben's thought. According
to Leys, it underpins his view of the human subject as lacking intention
and agency. Moreover, it is important because Agamben regards the concentration camps not simply as an anomalous occurrence but as, on the
contrary, the means to explain the modern world as a whole. The camps
are, he tells us in *Homo Sacer* and elsewhere, 'the hidden matrix and *nomos*
of the political space in which we are still living';[26] they appear 'as an event
that decisively signals the political space of modernity itself'.[27] Through
the suspension of the normal rule of law in the camps, the state creates
for itself a place where it can fulfil what is now one of its main functions,
according to Agamben: to manage 'bare life', which otherwise cannot
be inscribed in the order of the nation.[28] The Muselmann manifests this
bare life in its rawest form. So the Muselmann is presented as the key to
understanding the camps, and the camps are the key to understanding the
modern world. Agamben's rushed appropriation of the other's trauma in
his account of the Muselmann underlies and risks discrediting his conception of modernity in general.

---

25   Leys, *From Guilt to Shame: Auschwitz and After*, 180.
26   Giorgio Agamben, *Homo Sacer: Sovereign Power and Bare Life*, trans. Daniel Heller-
      Roazen (Stanford: Stanford University Press, 1998), 166. See also Giorgio Agamben,
      Means Without End: Notes on Politics, trans. Vincenzo Binette and Cesare Casarino
      (Minneapolis and London: University of Minnesota Press, 2000), 36.
27   Agamben, *Homo Sacer*, 174.
28   See *ibid.*, 174–6; Agamben, *Means Without End*, 41–4.

Felman and the Pedagogy of Trauma

If Agamben's study turns into a questionable appropriation of the other's suffering, in Felman's case it is the participatory re-creation of trauma which raises problems. The first chapter of the hugely influential book she wrote with Dori Laub, *Testimony: Crises of Witnessing in Literature, Psychoanalysis, and History*, includes her account of a graduate class she gave at Yale University in 1984.[29] The class and what happened to it played a significant role in the development of modern trauma studies since the crisis it underwent contained, as Felman writes, 'the germ – and the germination' of the book which describes it.[30] Entitled 'Literature and Testimony', the class covered works by Camus, Dostoyevsky, Freud, Mallarmé and Celan, and culminated with the screening of two testimonial videotapes borrowed from the Video Archive for Holocaust Testimony at Yale. Towards the conclusion of the class, something happened; as Felman puts it, 'The class itself broke out into a crisis'.[31] In Felman's account, she began getting phone calls from students at odd hours to discuss the class; colleagues reported that Felman's students could not focus on other work, and talked only about the class. The students were, Felman says, 'obsessed': 'They felt apart, and yet not quite together. They sought out each other and yet felt they could not reach each other. They kept turning to each other and to me. They felt alone, suddenly deprived of their bonding to the world and to one another. As I listened to their outpour, I realized the class was entirely at a loss, disoriented and uprooted'.[32]

After consulting with her colleague and future co-author Dori Laub, Felman concluded that in the final session of the class, when the second videotape was due to be screened, it was necessary for her – in her words

---

29 Felman, 'Education and Crisis, or the Vicissitudes of Teaching', in Felman and Laub, *Testimony: Crises of Witnessing*, 1–56.

30 *Ibid.*, 47.

31 *Ibid.*

32 *Ibid.*, 48.

– 'to reassume authority as the teacher of the class, and bring the students back into significance'.[33] She prepared a lecture which summarized and interpreted the students' reactions to the first videotape in the context of the rest of the course. In effect, she returned to them their own words and responses, but this time overlaid with significance which her position as teacher allowed her to supply. On reading the students' final term papers a few weeks later, Felman 'realized that the crisis, in effect, had been worked through and that a resolution had been reached, both on an intellectual and on a vital level'.[34]

Rather than breathing a sigh of relief that this difficult situation was resolved, Felman now goes on to theorize that a crisis such as the one undergone by her students is in fact essential to genuine teaching:

> I would venture to propose, today, that teaching in itself, teaching as such, takes place precisely only through a crisis: if teaching does not hit upon some sort of crisis, if it does not encounter either vulnerability or the explosiveness of a (explicit or implicit) critical and unpredictable dimension, it has perhaps *not truly taught* [...]. Looking back at the experience of that class, I therefore think that my job as teacher, paradoxical as it may sound, was that of creating in the class the highest state of crisis that it could withstand, without 'driving the students crazy' – without compromising the students' bounds.[35]

This is certainly a heady vision of teaching. Rather than enslaving ourselves and our students to the demands of the syllabus and examinations, we should be provoking crises and opening up ourselves and our students to traumatic encounters. It is striking that this exposure to trauma does not lead Felman to question her authority as a teacher. On the contrary, her account of what teaching should be involves maintaining her dominance over the classroom. She seems confident that she has the ability, the right and the wisdom to decide (to a degree that I, for example, could not) what does or does not compromise the students' bounds, and what does or does not drive other people crazy; and she appears to be comfortable with her

33   *Ibid.*
34   *Ibid.*, 52.
35   *Ibid.*, 53 (emphasis in original).

prerogative to put an end to the crisis by '[bringing] the students back into significance'.[36] She provokes the crisis and then resolves it, comparing her role to that of a psychoanalyst who helps her patients work through their trauma.[37]

Dominick LaCapra expresses what I believe are legitimate concerns about this approach, which entails the traumatization of students through encouraging them to identify with the victims of atrocity. It would be preferable, he suggests, 'to avoid or at least counteract such traumatization – or its histrionic simulacrum – rather than to seek means of assuaging it once it had been set in motion'.[38] The teacher's placing of herself in the role of therapist and the identification of her class with trauma victims and survivors are at best questionable and at worst positively dangerous. Once the complex dynamics of transference and countertransference have been unleashed, it may not be a straightforward matter to bring them back under control. The working-through which Felman believes has been achieved by the end of the course ('I realized that the crisis, in effect, had been worked through')[39] may be illusory. Freud concluded his classic paper on working-through by warning that the process may turn out to be 'an arduous task for the subject of the analysis and a trial of patience for the analyst'.[40] Even if trauma is vicarious rather than primary, it may not be quickly resolved by a final course assignment. For LaCapra, the teacher should endeavour to avoid or at least to minimize crisis; Felman, by contrast, insists that real teaching *depends upon* instigating the highest level of crisis that can be borne, to a degree and in a manner which might be thought to be reckless.

There is, moreover, a normative, even coercive, element in this transformation of the classroom into a site of vicarious trauma. After the outbreak of the crisis Felman reports how she called the students 'who had *failed* to

36 *Ibid.*, 48.
37 *Ibid.*, 53–4
38 LaCapra, *Writing History, Writing Trauma*, 102.
39 Felman, 'Education and Crisis', 52.
40 Sigmund Freud, 'Remembering, Repeating and Working-Through', in *The Standard Edition of the Complete Psychological Works of Sigmund Freud*, vol. 12, ed. James Strachey (London: Hogarth Press, 1958), 145–56, 155.

contact [her]' to discuss their reactions to what was occurring.[41] It turns out, then, that not all students were affected by events to the extent that they felt obliged to contact their teacher themselves; and this response or absence of response is designated as a *failure*. They are at fault for not participating in the crisis to an adequate degree or in the right way. Failing to be traumatized might lead to failing the class. Felman's narrative seems to recommend *forcing* students into crisis, sharing it with them and then imposing one's authority as teacher to resolve it:

> I lived the crisis with them, testified to it and made them testify to it. My own testimony to the class, which echoed their reactions, returning to them the expressions of their shock, their trauma and their disarray, bore witness nonetheless to the important fact that their experience, incoherent though it seemed, *made sense*, and that *it mattered*. My testimony was thus both an echo and a *return of significance*, both a repetition and an affirmation of the double fact that their response was *meaningful*, and that it *counted*.[42]

Describing her students' experience, Felman refers here to 'their shock, their trauma and their disarray'. The students of trauma have now become the victims of trauma, and their teacher wants her part of it too. I would argue, however, that witnessing the other's trauma is precisely *not* to share it. The responsibility of the witness is not to *become* the victim, to partake of the victim's pain; rather, I want to suggest, it is to regard the other's pain as something alien, unfathomable, and as an outrage which should be stopped. There is nothing enviable about suffering, and for most of us there is nothing to be gained by sharing in it unnecessarily. My objection to Agamben is that he wants to speak on behalf of the victims of trauma in order to tell us the meaning of their experience; Felman goes further, endeavouring to create and participate in a crisis that will turn her students into secondary victims. Both maintain their authority to understand, to bestow significance, and to theorize. Their magisterial positions remain strangely unaffected by the traumas they oversee.

---

41   Felman, 'Education and Crisis', 48 (my emphasis).
42   *Ibid.*, 54–5 (emphasis in original).

Delbo and the Other's Story

The work of Charlotte Delbo, and in particular her book *Measure of our Days*, speaks on behalf of the victims of trauma;[43] however, I shall suggest, it manages to avoid the appropriative assumption of authority which problematizes the work of Agamben and Felman. Delbo was twenty-eight in March 1942 when she was arrested in occupied France along with her husband Georges Dudach for resistance activities. She was allowed to visit her husband for the final time in May of that year on the day he was executed. She was subsequently deported to Auschwitz and later to Ravensbrück. She was one of the forty-nine survivors from the 230 women on the convoy in which she was transported to Auschwitz.[44] After the war she published, amongst other things, three remarkable works grouped together as a trilogy under the title *Auschwitz and After* which describe and comment on experiences in Auschwitz, Ravensbrück and in post-war France. In the current context it is the third part of the trilogy, *Measure of our Days* which is of most interest. The book presents a series of accounts of the lives of

43 Charlotte Delbo, *Mesure de nos jours* (Paris: Minuit, 1971). From the growing body of work devoted to Delbo, my understanding of her writing has benefited in particular from the following: Nicole Thatcher, *A Literary Analysis of Charlotte Delbo's Concentration Camp Re-Presentation* (Lewiston, Queenston, Lampeter: The Edwin Mellen Press, 2000), and *Charlotte Delbo: Une voix singulière. Mémoire, témoignage et littérature* (Paris: L'Harmattan, 2003); Margaret-Anne Hutton, 'Conclusion: The Case of Charlotte Delbo', in *Testimony from the Nazi Camps: French Women's Voices* (London and New York: Routledge, 2005), 210–19; and Kathryn Jones, '"A New Mode of Travel": Representations of Deportation in Charlotte Delbo's *Auschwitz et après* and Jorge Semprún's *Le Grand Voyage*', in *Journeys of Remembrance: Memories of the Second World War in French and German Literature, 1960–1980* (Oxford: Legenda, 2007), 34–53. Some of the issues discussed in this chapter, such as the question of community and the use of the first person, are brilliantly analysed in Thomas Trezise, 'The Question of Community in Charlotte Delbo's *Auschwitz and After*', *Modern Language Notes* 117/4 (2002), 858–86.

44 Delbo attempts to piece together the lives and deaths of the women on her convoy in *Le Convoi du 24 janvier* (Paris: Minuit, 1965).

camp survivors after their return to France. Most – though not all – of the survivors are women, and most are named in the title of the section which presents their story: Gilberte, Mado, Poupette, Marie-Louise, Ida, Loulou, Germaine, Jacques, Denise, Gaby, Louise, Marceline, Françoise. Most of these accounts are in the first person singular. No explanation is offered of how the narratives were gathered or composed, and no generic marker on the book indicates whether the reader should take them as biographical or fictional. It would seem that Delbo is doing exactly what I have been objecting to: speaking in the place of others, presenting their stories as first-person narratives when the words they use may not be their own.

One way in which Delbo avoids the dangers of asserting authority over the other's story is through the absence of any attempt to unify the disparate experiences of her narrators into a coherent aesthetic whole. Agamben's Muselmänner all betoken the same meaning; Felman speaks of her students as an undifferentiated block. By contrast, Delbo's approach preserves the specific difference of each narrative. There is no consistent theory or diagnosis of survival in *Measure of our Days*, only a series of diverse, contradictory stories: one woman recounts how she does not marry after her return to France, another marries but does not tell her husband about her experiences, another divorces; one shares everything with her husband and carefully preserves every memory of the camps; one thinks it would have been easier to marry a fellow survivor, another does marry a fellow survivor but finds that it is in fact no easier; some endeavour to forget the past, others insist on the importance of remembering. In a passage quoted above, Cavarero asserts that 'your story is never my story'; Delbo does not ask us to recognize ourselves in the stories of others. There is no thematic consistency to the lives of survivors which would allow us to interpret *Measure of our Days* monolithically as a work of, say, despair or hope. The text implies that there is no Story of the return from Auschwitz, rather we are offered a multiplicity of stories without overarching sense.

According to a key topos of survivor literature, there is a stark tension between the need or duty to narrate and the impossibility of narrating. Even as they endeavour to tell their stories, survivors are acutely aware of the limitations of their own narrative capabilities and the likely incredulity of their audience.[45] The impossibility which Butler ascribes to any attempt to give an account of oneself is felt with particular keenness by the survivors of trauma. Delbo certainly shares the intuition that a story cannot succeed in explaining a life to a listener or reader. This awareness can be seen in *Measure of our Days*, for example, in the strange incongruence between the determined attempt to tell the other's story as if it were one's own and the recurrent theme that it is impossible or pointless to talk of the camps. We are told that it is not worth trying to explain to those who cannot understand.[46] Referring to the title of the book, one speaker says that time that can be measured is not the measure of the survivors' time.[47] Their temporality is not ours, and we cannot share it. One survivor tells of her grief to her goats, as if only they can understand: 'Have you noticed how goats have those melancholic eyes? It's really as if they understand when you talk to them'.[48] The goats may understand, or they may not; what is repeatedly suggested, though, is that no human who is not a survivor of the camps can share the survivors' experience. We can be instructed of the facts, but we cannot partake of the meaning or the pain, as one of Delbo's narrators explains: 'As for others, I don't expect them

---

45   This is evident in the earliest accounts by survivors of the concentration camps, such as Robert Antelme's *L'Espèce humaine*, first published in 1947. The opening words of the book's introduction describe the survivors' dilemma: 'Two years ago, during the first days which followed our return, we were all, I think, prey to a real delirium. We wanted to speak, finally to be heard. We were told that our physical appearance was eloquent enough on its own. But we were just back, we were bringing with us our memory, our still vivid experience, and we felt a frenetic desire to tell it as it was. And yet from the very first days, it seemed to us to be impossible to bridge the distance which we discovered between the language at our disposal and that experience which, in the main, was still continuing in our bodies. How could we resign ourselves to not attempting to explain how we had got to that point? We were still there. And yet it was impossible. Hardly did we begin to recount than we began to suffocate. To ourselves, what we had to say began then to appear to us to be *unimaginable*.' Robert Antelme, *L'Espèce humaine* (Paris: Gallimard, 1957), 9 (emphasis in original).

46   Delbo, *Mesure de nos jours*, 44.

47   *Ibid.*, 48, see also 197.

48   *Ibid.*, 112.

to understand. I want them to know, even if they don't feel what I feel. That's what I mean when I say that they don't understand, that no one can understand. At least they have to know'.[49]

This sense of the necessary unintelligibility of one's own story is given further poignancy when the speaker insists that she is dead. In Edgar Allan Poe's story 'The Facts in the Case of M. Valdemar', the titular M. Valdemar says of himself '*I am dead*'.[50] Poe's text repeatedly marks its awareness that this claim will appear nonsensical, defying his narrator's and reader's frame of understanding. Delbo's *Measure of our Days* issues the same challenge. The section attributed to Mado begins with the words 'It seems to me that I am not alive'.[51] Listing the dead – 'Mounette, Viva, Sylviane, Rosie, all the others, all the others'[52] – Mado believes that no one could return from the camps alive. This recalls the title of the first volume of *Auschwitz and After, None of Us Will Return*.[53] The fact that *None of Us Will Return* exists suggests that, contrary to the title, some will return and that they will tell of their survival in Auschwitz; but they return with a sense that in fact they have not survived.[54] Their temporality is incommensurable with ours because they died in Auschwitz and return to tell of their deaths. Mado concludes: 'I am not alive. People believe that memories become vague, that they fade with time, that nothing can resist the effects of time. That's the difference; on me, on us, time does not pass. Nothing becomes hazy, nothing gets worn away. I am not alive. I died in Auschwitz and no one can see it.'[55]

---

49   *Ibid.*, 54–5.
50   Edgar Allan Poe, 'The Facts in the Case of M. Valdemar', in *The Portable Poe*, ed. Philip Van Doren Stern (Harmondsworth: Penguin, 1977), 268–80, 277 (emphasis in original).
51   Delbo, *Mesure de nos jours*, 47.
52   *Ibid.*
53   Charlotte Delbo, *Aucun de nous ne reviendra* (Paris: Minuit, 1970).
54   This is suggested by the play on the word *revenir* and the description of the female survivors as *revenantes*, which also means *ghosts*, implying that in some sense they have died. For discussion, see Davis, 'The Ghosts of Auschwitz: Charlotte Delbo', in *Haunted Subjects*, 93–110.
55   Delbo, *Mesure de nos jours*, 66.

The story of a woman who declares herself to be dead epitomizes the narrative deadlock of *Measure of our Days* and survivor literature more broadly. The death of the self is unnarratable, and the death of the other is irretrievable. At the same time survivor literature disturbs the boundaries between the living and the dead, and shows their eerie cohabitation. Robert Jay Lifton describes the survivors of massive traumas as fearing that they have become 'carriers of death'.[56] The dead and the living are no longer comfortably separate. The opening section of *Measure of our Days* describes how, on the return from captivity, the narrator finds herself still accompanied by her dead comrades, and she asks herself: 'If I confuse the dead and the living, which am I?'[57] None of us shall return, Delbo and others suggest, even if it might look to you, the non-survivors, as if we are back amongst you. The dead cannot tell their own story. The living would not, could not and – it is implied – *should* not understand it. The title of the second volume of *Auschwitz and After, Useless Knowledge*,[58] implies that what the dead know would be of no use to us; it can teach us nothing that will help us live more fully. We are better off not knowing.

Yet *Measure of our Days* does purport to tell the stories of the dead or the living dead who returned from the camps. What saves Delbo's work from what I regard as the failings of Agamben and Felman is not simply that she is a survivor herself. It is partly, as already suggested, her refusal to exert authority over the stories of the survivors by imposing a coherent meaning on them. It also lies, I want now to suggest, in the simultaneous merging of voices and loss of voice that constitute the intimate texture of her writing. We should note the first person plural which occurs in the title of both *None of Us Will Return* and *Measure of our Days*. Cavarero's distrust of the plural 'we' is a reluctance to allow a singular story to be subsumed in a generalizing narrative. Delbo, by contrast, frequently uses the first person plural. In her writing the terror of a loss of self is countered or

---

56   Robert Jay Lifton, *Death in Life: The Survivors of Hiroshima* (London: Weidenfeld and Nicolson, 1968), 517.
57   Delbo, *Mesure de nos jours*, 11.
58   Charlotte Delbo, *Une connaissance inutile* (Paris: Minuit, 1970).

at least palliated by the comfort of belonging to a community of sufferers.
Just as the lines between the living and the dead are blurred, so is the division between self and other; and in the process the subject's possession of
a unique voice is thrown into disarray. As Mado, ventriloquized by Delbo,
puts it: 'I am other. I speak and my voice sounds like another voice. My
words come from outside me. I speak and I am not the one who says what
I say'.[59] In this passage Mado reflects on the question of who is speaking
here. Her words are literally not her own because they are Delbo's; someone else speaks through her. But this ventriloquism is not simply Delbo
speaking on Mado's behalf or in her place, because every voice in this text
is inhabited by others. One of the narrators of *Measure of our Days* is identified as Charlotte, and of course we are likely to assume that this refers
to the author, Charlotte Delbo. But the textual Charlotte is no more wise
and all-knowing than any other character. The fact that she may be the
one who puts pen to paper does not make of her an authority figure who
bestows significance on everything around her.

The merging of voices becomes most evident in the section entitled
'The Burial' ('L'Enterrement'). A group of camp survivors, including the
narrator of this section who is addressed as Charlotte, meet at a railway
station on their way to attend the burial of one of their former comrades.
Some of the women have not seen each other for years, yet they fall easily
into a familiar conversation, exchanging and sharing memories and news.
Much of the section is set out as dialogue, sometimes with no indication
of who the speaker is at any given moment. It barely matters. The narrator explains the ease with which the group converses: 'Amongst ourselves,
there is no effort to be made, there is no constraint, not even that of normal
politeness. Amongst ourselves, we are ourselves'.[60] In the original French,
this final sentence is even more emphatic: 'Entre nous, nous sommes nous'.
The first person plural contains and exceeds the first person singular. Each
can tell the story of the other because, in this haunted community of survivors, each story belongs to all of them.

59   Delbo, *Mesure de nos jours*, 60.
60   *Ibid.*, 193–4.

And each death belongs to all of them also. The burial the women are attending is that of their comrade Germaine. In an earlier section, when Charlotte visits Germaine's death bed with two others, for a moment she is taken back in her mind to Auschwitz and a visit to another dying comrade, Sylviane, together with two different companions, Carmen and Lulu.[61] The scenes of death, their witnesses and the identity of the deceased become interchangeable. Delbo writes: 'I know that the two others who were with me on that day, the day when Germaine died, were neither Carmen nor Lulu. It is only because we were together, Lulu, Carmen and I, to say farewell to Sylviane, that I confuse them with the ones who were really with me when Germaine died'.[62] Scenes and identities are overlaid, as later events become confused with and substitutable for earlier ones. What happens outside Auschwitz merely repeats what happened inside it. The living and the dead merge across time. The funeral which the women attend is Germaine's, but also Sylviane's, and that of so many others, and their own. Each one survives with every other, and each dies with every death, along with and in place of the other. So to witness and to recount the death of the other is also to tell of one's own demise and one's own survival in the living death of those who can say, along with Mado, 'I died in Auschwitz and no one can see it'.

Delbo's use of the first person plural – 'we' – forges a community across the boundaries of death, trauma and survival. But we should not be misled into thinking that the reader – the non-survivor – can be admitted to this community. In *Regarding the Pain of Others* Susan Sontag writes that 'No "we" should be taken for granted when the subject is looking at other people's pain'.[63] Delbo freely uses the first person plural, but it is as exclusive as it is inclusive. The non-survivor is addressed as 'You', and thereby permanently distanced from the community of survivors. 'You' and 'we' can never understand one another. One of the passages which closes *Useless Knowledge* describes the barrier between the survivor and the non-survivor:

61   On Sylviane, see Delbo, *Le Convoi du 24 janvier*, 273–5.
62   Delbo, *Mesure de nos jours*, 149–50.
63   Susan Sontag, *Regarding the Pain of Others* (London: Penguin, 2003), 6.

> I returned from amongst the dead
> and I believed
> that that gave me the right
> to speak to others
> and when I found myself again in front of them
> I had nothing to say to them
> because
> I had learned
> back there
> that one cannot speak to others.[64]

The reader – the non-survivor – is not and cannot be part of the community which Delbo forms together with her living and dead comrades. In his study of the problematic sense of community in Delbo's *Auschwitz and After*, Thomas Trezise describes 'attentiveness to the irreducible difference between a survivor of Auschwitz and those not directly affected by the Holocaust' as 'an ethical prerequisite'.[65] Those of us who were not in the camps are excluded. The text repeatedly informs us that we can observe but not comprehend; our knowledge is not the survivors' knowledge. What Anne-Lise Stern calls *le savoir-déporté* is incommensurable with what we can know.[66] Charlotte and her comrades are both the source of the text and the only audience capable of receiving it fully. Indeed, we are warned that we are better off not comprehending, since only the dead can understand the dead, so that to take a share in their narratives would be to forego life.

64   Delbo, *Une connaissance inutile*, 188.
65   Trezise, 'Community in Delbo's *Auschwitz and After*', 886. Trezise's focus is slightly different from mine in that he is interested in the possibility of community between survivors and the 'you' to whom Delbo sometimes refers, whereas I use the word *community* in the current discussion to refer to the group formed by the survivors. In his nuanced and subtle reading of parts of *None of Us Will Return*, Trezise suggests that the irreducible difference between survivors and non-survivors does not preclude the possibility of a form of community which includes both groups: 'the tension between identification and estrangement is not a misfortune to be surmounted but a condition of community to be maintained'. *Ibid.*
66   Anne-Lise Stern, *Le Savoir-déporté: Camps, histoire, psychanalyse* (Paris: Seuil, 2004).

Delbo, the author, may speak in the voice of dead others; but that does not entitle the excluded reader to appropriate their stories and to respond to their pain as if it were our own. Agamben wants to tell us the meaning of the Muselmann's experience and its relevance for the post-Holocaust world; Felman wants to participate in the suffering of others and then to re-assert her authority by conferring significance on it. Delbo, by contrast, issues no invitation to explain or to share.

Conclusion

To conclude, I want to warn against the allure of trauma envy, that is, the temptation that those of us who witness the testimony of others appropriate to ourselves an unmerited, unearned part in the story of suffering. It has been argued that vicarious trauma may have socially and ethically useful effects;[67] but it may also be self-indulgent and ethically delusional. Those of us who study and teach emotionally gruelling material run the risk of succumbing to the dark glamour of vicarious trauma, regarding ourselves as traumatized subjects by proxy. When Felman refers to the modern world as 'post-traumatic',[68] she invites us to extend the scope of trauma by making of us all survivors and victims. Agamben also, according to Ruth Leys, offers a view of the human subject which has the result that 'a kind of traumatic abjection is held to characterize not only all the victims of the camps with-out differentiation but all human life after Auschwitz – including those

67 For discussion and references, see E. Ann Kaplan, *Trauma Culture: The Politics of Terror and Loss in Media and Literature* (New Brunswick and London: Rutgers University Press, 2005), for example 39–41, 87–93, 122–5. Kaplan states that '[a]rgu-ably, being vicariously traumatized invites members of a society to confront, rather than conceal, catastrophes, and in that way might be useful'; but she goes on to say that 'On the other hand, it might arouse anxiety and trigger defense against further exposure'. *Ibid.*, 87.

68 Felman, 'Education and Crisis', 1, 54.

of us who were never there'.[69] The danger of this is that it collapses the necessary distinction between, for example, those who were in Auschwitz and those who were not. Delbo reminds us uncompromisingly that those who survived the camps are unintelligible in the terms of those who did not know it at first hand. We are not the victims; we do not share or feel their pain. Dominick LaCapra insists that 'a historian or other academic, however empathetic a listener he or she may be, may not assume the voice of the victim'.[70] I would add that he or she may not assume the victim's trauma either. It should be possible to speak of these difficult topics with moral urgency, but also analytically and with respectful distance. Following Butler, we may not be able to give a final account of our life, and even less an account of others' lives; and we have no mandate to assume the pain or decide the meaning of the lives and deaths of others. As readers, the best we can do may be to try to attend as honourably as possible to the traces of that which remains foreign to us.

Bibliography

Agamben, Giorgio, *Homo Sacer: Sovereign Power and Bare Life*, trans. Daniel Heller-Roazen (Stanford: Stanford University Press, 1998).
——, *Remnants of Auschwitz: The Witness and the Archive*, trans. Daniel Heller-Roazen (New York: Zone Books, 1999).
——, *Means Without End: Notes on Politics*, trans. Vincenzo Binette and Cesare Casarino (Minneapolis and London: University of Minnesota Press, 2000).
Antelme, Robert, *L'Espèce humaine* (Paris: Gallimard, 1957).
Benslama, Fethi, 'La Représentation et l'impossible', in Jean-Luc Nancy, ed., *L'Art et la mémoire des camps: Représenter exterminer* (Paris: Seuil, 2001), 59–80.
Butler, Judith, *Giving an Account of Oneself* (New York: Fordham University Press, 2005).

69   Leys, *From Guilt to Shame*, 180.
70   LaCapra, *Writing History, Writing Trauma*, 98.

Cavarero, Adriana, *Relating Narratives: Storytelling and Selfhood*, trans. Paul A. Kottman (London and New York: Routledge, 2000).

Davis, Colin, *Haunted Subjects: Deconstruction, Psychoanalysis and the Return of the Dead* (London: Palgrave Macmillan, 2007).

Delbo, Charlotte, *Le Convoi du 24 janvier* (Paris: Minuit, 1965).

——, *Aucun de nous ne reviendra* (Paris: Minuit, 1970).

——, *Une connaissance inutile* (Paris: Minuit, 1970).

——, *Mesure de nos jours* (Paris: Minuit, 1971).

Eaglestone, Robert, 'On Giorgio Agamben's Holocaust', in *Paragraph* 25/2 (2002), 51–67.

Felman, Shoshana, and Dori Laub, *Testimony: Crises of Witnessing in Literature, Psychoanalysis, and History* (New York and London: Routledge, 1992).

Freud, Sigmund, 'Remembering, Repeating and Working-Through', in *The Standard Edition of the Complete Psychological Works of Sigmund Freud*, vol. 12, ed. James Strachey (London: Hogarth Press, 1958), 145–56.

Hutton, Margaret-Anne, *Testimony from the Nazi Camps: French Women's Voices* (London and New York: Routledge, 2005).

Jones, Kathryn, *Journeys of Remembrance: Memories of the Second World War in French and German Literature, 1960–1980* (Oxford: Legenda, 2007).

Kaplan, E. Ann, *Trauma Culture: The Politics of Terror and Loss in Media and Literature* (New Brunswick and London: Rutgers University Press, 2005).

LaCapra, Dominick, *Writing History, Writing Trauma* (Baltimore and London: Johns Hopkins University Press, 2001).

Levi, Primo, *If This is a Man / The Truce*, trans. Stuart Woolf (London: Abacus, 1987).

——, *The Drowned and the Saved*, trans. Raymond Rosenthal (London: Abacus, 1989).

Leys, Ruth, *From Guilt to Shame: Auschwitz and After* (Princeton and Oxford: Princeton University Press, 2007).

Lifton, Robert Jay, *Death in Life: The Survivors of Hiroshima* (London: Weidenfeld and Nicolson, 1968).

Mesnard, Philippe, and Claudine Cahan, *Giorgio Agamben à l'épreuve d'Auschwitz* (Paris: Kimé, 2001).

Poe, Edgar Allan, 'The Facts in the Case of M. Valdemar', in *The Portable Poe*, ed. Philip Van Doren Stern (Harmondsworth: Penguin, 1977), 268–80.

Sontag, Susan, *Regarding the Pain of Others* (London: Penguin, 2003).

Stern, Anne-Lise, *Le Savoir-déporté: Camps, histoire, psychanalyse* (Paris: Seuil, 2004).

Thatcher, Nicole, *A Literary Analysis of Charlotte Delbo's Concentration Camp Re-Presentation* (Lewiston, Queenston, Lampeter: The Edwin Mellen Press, 2000).

——, *Charlotte Delbo: Une voix singulière. Mémoire, témoignage et littérature* (Paris: L'Harmattan, 2003).

Trezise, Thomas, 'The Question of Community in Charlotte Delbo's *Auschwitz and After*', *Modern Language Notes* 117/4 (2002), 858–86.

Wiesel, Elie, *Le Chant des morts* (Paris: Seuil, 1966).

——, *Discours d'Oslo* (Paris: Grasset, 1987).

Žižek, Slavoj, *The Puppet and the Dwarf: The Perverse Core of Christianity* (Cambridge, MA, and London: The MIT Press, 2003).

——, 'Neighbors and Other Monsters: A Plea for Ethical Violence', in Slavoj Žižek, Eric L. Santner and Kenneth Reinhard, *The Neighbor: Three Inquiries in Political Theology* (Chicago and London, The University of Chicago Press, 2005), 134–90.

——, *The Parallax View* (Cambridge, MA, and London: The MIT Press, 2006).

ALEIDA ASSMANN

From Collective Violence to a Common Future: Four Models for Dealing with a Traumatic Past

The Israeli philosopher Avishai Margalit dedicated his book *The Ethics of Memory* to his parents, whom he introduces to the reader on the second page of his preface. 'From early childhood,' he writes, 'I witnessed an ongoing discussion between my parents about memory.' Margalit then reconstructs this parental dialogue, which started after the Second World War when it became obvious that both of their huge families in Europe had been destroyed. This is what the mother used to say:

> The Jews were irretrievably destroyed. What is left is just a pitiful remnant of the great Jewish people (by which she meant European Jewry). The only honorable role for the Jews that remains is to form communities of memory – to serve as 'soul candles' like the candles that are ritually kindled in memory of the dead.

This is what the father used to say:

> We, the remaining Jews, are people, not candles. It is a horrible prospect for anyone to live just for the sake of retaining the memory of the dead. That is what the Armenians opted to do. And they made a terrible mistake. We should avoid it at all costs. Better to create a community that thinks predominantly about the future and reacts to the present, not a community that is governed from mass graves.[1]

After 1945, it was first the father's position that prevailed – and not only in Israel. What mattered then in Israel was the collective project of founding a new state, of forging a new beginning for survivors and opening up the

1   Avishai Margalit, *The Ethics of Memory* (Cambridge, MA: Harvard University Press, 2003), vii–ix.

future for successive generations. Four decades later, during the 1980s, the mother's position became more and more dominant. The survivors turned to the past that they had held at a distance for so long. After the foundation of the state had been politically accomplished and confirmed by two wars, Yad Vashem became the symbolic cultural centre of the nation and Israeli society transformed itself more and more into a ritualistic community of memory.

Margalit has presented two paradigmatic solutions for the problem of dealing with a traumatic past: remembering or forgetting, either preservation of the past or orientation towards the future. I want to argue that today we are no longer dealing with only these two mutually exclusive models but are experimenting with three or perhaps with four. I will refer to them as

1. dialogic forgetting
2. remembering in order to never forget
3. remembering in order to overcome
4. dialogic remembering.

All four models are attempts at overcoming a traumatic history of violence; they all aim at diffusing the pernicious fuel of violence, be it through an oppressive regime of silence on the part of the victors, be it through the fuel of resentment and hatred on the part of the losers. One of the lessons of the First World War was that asymmetric memories and silences prepare the ground for further violence. All of the following models respond to traumatic violence by negotiating mutual strategies of memory and visions of the past. They were implemented after the Second World War and developed in response to new outbreaks of autocratic and genocidal violence (the Holocaust, Latin American dictatorships, South African apartheid, the Balkan War, Rwanda) as well as in response to the lasting impact of older genocides and crimes against humanity (such as European colonialism and slavery).

1. Dialogic Forgetting

During the 1990s, we saw the coining of the innovative term 'Culture of Remembrance', a term which provides a cultural framework within which we automatically assume that remembering is a beneficial obligation which we must fulfil. Remembering thus appears as a significant social and cultural resource. This picture has been thoroughly upset recently by Christian Meier, whose latest book *Das Gebot zu vergessen und die Unabweisbarkeit des Erinnerns* [The Imperative to Forget and the Inescapability of Remembering] posits the theory that it is the ability to forget which must be considered the cultural achievement; remembering is only to be recommended under one absolutely exceptional circumstance, which is Auschwitz.[2]

Meier argues as a historian, drawing attention to forgetting as an age-old strategy of containing the explosive force of conflictual memories. Forgetting was introduced, for instance, in ancient Greece after civil wars in order to achieve closure after a period of internal violence and to mark a new era in which a divided society could grow together again.[3] Of course the state could not directly influence the memories of its citizens, but it could prohibit the public articulation of resentments, that were liable to reactivate old hatred and new violence. After the Peloponnesian War, an Athenian law ordered such a form of stipulated forgetting.[4] The injunction to forget was legally enforced by restricting public communication through specific taboos. A new word was even coined to describe what was henceforth forbidden: 'mnesikakein' which means literally: 'to remember what is bad'. The same model was implemented after other civil wars, for instance

2   Christian Meier, *Das Gebot zu vergessen und die Unabweisbarkeit des Erinnerns. Vom öffentlichen Umgang mit schlimmer Vergangenheit* (Munich: Beck, 2010).
3   Hinderk Emrich and Gary Smith, eds, *Vom Nutzen des Vergessens* (Berlin: Akademie, 1996); Gary Smith and Avishai Margalit, eds, *Amnestie, oder Die Politik der Erinnerung* (Frankfurt am Main: Suhrkamp, 1997).
4   Nicole Loraux, *La Cité divisée. L'Oubli dans la Mémoire d'Athènes* (Paris: Payot, 1997).

the Thirty-Years-War. The 1648 peace treaty of Münster-Osnabrück contains the formula: 'perpetua oblivio et amnestia'.[5] This policy of forgetting often goes hand in hand with a blanket amnesty in order to end mutual hatred and achieve a new social integration of formerly opposed parties.

It is interesting to note that even after 1945 the model of dialogic forgetting was still widely used as a political resource. The international court of the Nuremberg trials had of course dispensed transitional justice by indicting major Nazi functionaries for the newly defined 'crime against humanity'. This, however, was an act of purging rather than remembering the past. In postwar Germany, the public sphere and that of official diplomacy remained largely shaped by what was called 'a pact of silence'. The term was used in 1983 in a retrospective description by Hermann Lübbe ('kollektives Beschweigen').[6] He made the controversial point that maintaining silence was a necessary pragmatic strategy adopted in postwar Germany (and supported by the Allies) to facilitate the economic and political reconstruction of the state and the integration of society. These goals were swiftly achieved in West Germany at the price of putting the former NS elites back into power. Dialogic forgetting or the pact of silence became also a strategy of European politics. It was widely adopted during the period of the Cold War in which much had to be forgotten in order to consolidate the new Western military alliance against that of the communist block.[7] As an example, we may refer to a speech that Winston Churchill gave in Zürich in 1946. From the vantage point of the newly constituted House of Europe, he was looking back on the Second World War as a civil war,

5   The peace treaty (Instrumentum Pacis Osnabrugensis of 24 October 1648) contains
     the following article: 'Both sides grant each other a perpetual forgetting and amnesty
     concerning every aggressive act committed in any place in any way by both parties
     here and there since the beginning of the war.' Arno Buschmann, *Kaiser und Reich.
     Verfassungsgeschichte des Heiligen Römischen Reiches Deutscher Nation vom Beginn des
     12. Jahrhunderts bis zum Jahre 1806 in Dokumenten* (Baden-Baden: Nomos, 1994),
     17.

6   See Aleida Assmann and Ute Frevert, *Geschichtsvergessenheit, Geschichtsversessenheit.
     Vom Umgang mit deutschen Vergangenheiten nach 1945* (Stuttgart: DVA, 1999),
     76–8.

7   See Tony Judt, *Postwar. A History of Europe Since 1945* (Harmondsworth: Penguin,
     2005).

which he hoped could be overcome by the tried and tested means of forgetting. After those most responsible had been condemned in Nuremberg, Churchill demanded an end to 'the process of reckoning', declaring:

> We must all turn our backs upon the horrors of the past. We must look to the future. We cannot afford to drag forward across the years that are to come the hatreds and revenges which have sprung from the injuries of the past. If Europe is to be saved from infinite misery, and indeed from final doom, there must be an act of faith in the European family and an act of oblivion against all the crimes and follies of the past.[8]

It is important to note that forgetting at that time was not equivalent to suppressing memory; a moralistic and therapeutic discourse was only developed in Germany in the 1960s.[9] In the 1940s and 1950s, forgetting was associated with a spirit of renewal and of opening up to the future. The general hope in the regenerative power of the future was a central value of modernism shared by European countries in both East and West.

2. Remembering in Order to Never Forget

Especially after civil wars, forgetting was prescribed as a potent remedy against socially dangerous and explosive forms of remembering to foster a speedy integration. Dialogic silence was a remedy but it was clearly no general cure for other situations to dispose of a traumatic past. The pact

8   Randolph S. Churchill, ed., *The Sinews of Peace. Post-War Speeches by Winston S. Churchill* (London: Cassell 1948), 200. (Thanks to Marco Duranti for drawing my attention to this speech.)

9   The school of critical theory in Frankfurt, represented by Theodor W. Adorno and Max Horkheimer had an important impact on the intellectual climate of West-German youth, as well as the reestablishment of psychoanalysis (Alexander and Margarete Mitscherlich). It eventually effected a change of paradigm in West-German public discourse, shifting the perspective from the point of view of the perpetrators to that of the victims who had suffered under the Nazis.

of forgetting works only after mutual forms of violence between combatants or under the pressure of a new military alliance like the NATO. It cannot work after situations of asymmetric relations in which all-powerful perpetrators attacked defenseless victims. The paradigmatic case of such an asymmetric situation of extreme violence is the Nazi genocide of the European Jews.

The paradigmatic shift from the model of *forgetting* to an orientation towards *remembering* occurred with the return of Holocaust memory after a period of latency. This memory returned in various steps. In the 1960s it reemerged together with the images of the Eichmann trial in Jerusalem, which were projected into a transnational public arena. The televised event transformed the silenced memories of Israeli and diasporic Jewish families into a new ethnic community of memory. After the broadcasting of the American television series *Holocaust* in 1978, the impact of this event spilled over to those who had no share in the historical experience, but joined the memory community on the basis of empathy. In the 1980s, a number of events happened in Germany that transformed the social consensus and made the nation of the former perpetrators ready to formally join the transnational Holocaust community of memory, beginning with the fortieth anniversary speech in 1985 by President Richard von Weizsäcker who taught the Germans to no longer think of 8 May 1945 in terms of defeat but of liberation, the scandal caused by Chancellor Kohl three days before when together with Ronald Reagan he visited the cemetery of Bitburg that included soldiers of the Waffen-SS, and the controversy among historians in 1986 in the course of which the singularity, normative status and ongoing impact of the Holocaust as 'unmasterable past' was established and enforced on a discursive level. Further commemorative events, exhibitions, monuments and media debates continued this trend throughout the 1990s. After 2000, the Holocaust memory community was further extended when it was officially taken up by other European states and the United Nations. This general turn from amnesia to anamnesis could be witnessed in Germany and the respective countries on all levels of personal and collective remembering; it was supported by books and films, public debates and exhibitions, museums, monuments and acts of commemoration on a social, national and transnational level. Holocaust memory today is supported by an extended community with a long-term commitment. This memory is sealed with a special pledge for an indefinite future: 'to remember in order to never forget'. Through its widening in space as well as time it has acquired the quality of a civil religion.

In the case of the Holocaust, the model of dialogic forgetting as a strategy of sealing a traumatic past and opening up a new future was no longer considered a viable solution for the problem. On the contrary, this form of closure was exactly what had to be prevented by all means. Remembering was the only adequate response to such collectively destructive and devastating experiences. It was rediscovered not only as a therapeutic remedy for the survivors but also as a spiritual and ethical obligation for the millions of dead victims. Thus slowly but inevitably, the pact of forgetting was transformed into a 'pact of remembering'. The aim of such a pact is to transform the *asymmetric* experience of violence into *shared* forms of remembering. To leave the memory of suffering to the affected victim group was now recognized as prolonging the original murderous constellation. The fatal polarity between perpetrator and victim could never be reconciled but it could be overcome by a shared memory based on an empathetic and ethical recognition of the victim's memories. The establishing of such a 'pact of remembering' between the Germans as the successors of the perpetrators and the Jews as the successors of the victims was a historically new and unique answer to the historically unprecedented crime of the Holocaust.

3. Remembering in Order to Overcome

The cumulative process of the returning Holocaust memory was a decisive event in the 1980s that brought about a profound change in sensibility also in other places of the world in dealing with historic traumas. Against this background of a new awareness of the suffering of victims, forgetting was no longer acceptable as a general policy in overcoming atrocities of the past.

Remembering became a universal ethical and political claim when dealing with other historic traumas, such as the dictatorships in South America, the South African regime of apartheid, colonial history or the crime of slavery. In most of these discourses about other atrocities, references and metaphorical allusions were made to the newly established memory icon of the Holocaust.

I want to argue, however, that although the Holocaust quickly became the prototype of traumatic memories and was and is regularly invoked in the rhetoric of memory activists all over the world, it was not chosen as a model. The transformation of traumatic suffering into a semi-religious transnational and perpetual memory of a 'normative past' is not what was and is aimed at in other contexts. Remembering in the context of the third model took on another quality, one that did not anxiously exclude but also included certain forms of forgetting. Since the 1980s and 1990s, we have witnessed a new policy of memory that is no longer in strict opposition to forgetting but somehow also in alliance with it. In this model, the aim is also in some sense 'forgetting', but the way to achieve this aim paradoxically leads through remembering. In this case, remembering is not implemented to memorialize an event of the past into an indefinite future but is introduced as a therapeutic tool to cleanse, to purge, to heal, to reconcile. It is not pursued as an end in itself but as a means to an end, which is the forging of a new beginning.

Whenever the term 'reconciliation' comes up in the Holocaust discourse, it is immediately refuted as a highly problematic term. In clear opposition to this, the contested term has become the central keyword in the context of the third model. Reconciliation is often proverbially connected to the two verbs 'forgive and forget'. The third model, however, clearly deviates from this common sense model of reconciliation. It decouples the two actions of forgiving and forgetting and connects in a new way forgiving to remembering. Remembering here means recognition of the victims' memories. Without a clear facing and working through the atrocities of the past from the point of view of those who suffered, the process of social, national or transnational reconciliation cannot begin. In this context, remembering is the beginning of a process, not its end.

Cultures in history have produced ample evidence for such forms of transitory and transitional remembering. In the ritual framework of Christian confession remembering is the introduction to forgetting: the sins have to be publicly articulated and listed before they can be blotted out through the absolution of the priest. A similar logic is at work in the artistic concept of *catharsis*: through the re-presentation of a painful event on stage a traumatic past can be once more collectively re-lived and over-come in the very process of doing so. According to the theory of Aristotle, the group that undergoes such a process is purged in this shared experience. Forgetting through remembering is at bottom also the goal of Freudian psychotherapy: a painful past has to be raised onto the level of language and consciousness in order to be able to move forward and leave it behind. 'To remember in order to forget' holds also true for the witness at court whose sole function is to support with his testimony the legal procedure of finding the truth and reaching a verdict. As the goal of every trial is the verdict and conclusion of the procedure, its aim is closure and therewith the final erasure of the event from social memory.[10] There is a world of a difference between the legal witness testifying to a crime within the insti-tution of the court and the 'moral witness' (Avishai Margalit) testifying to a crime against humanity publicly outside the courtroom before a moral community. While the former's narrative is subordinated to the legal pro-cess, the testimony of the latter is part of a civic culture of remembrance. A merging of the legal and therapeutic function was aimed at in the staging of remembering in South Africa. The Truth and Reconciliation Commis-sion as designed by Bishop Tutu und Alex Boraine created a new form of public ritual, which combined features of the tribunal, the cathartic drama, and the Christian confession. In these public rituals a traumatic event had to be publicly narrated and shared; the victim had to tell his or her experiences and they had to be witnessed and acknowledged by the accused before they could be relegated to the shared past.

10   See Thomas Henne, 'Zeugenschaft vor Gericht', in Michael Elm and Gottfried Kößler, eds, *Zeugenschaft des Holocaust. Zwischen Trauma, Tradierung und Ermittlung* (Frankfurt am Main and New York: Campus, 2007), 79–91.

The model of the Truth and Reconciliation Commission (TRC) was invented in South America when countries such as Chile, Uruguay, Argentina and Brazil transitioned from military dictatorships to democracies in the 1980s and 90s. By enforcing the moral human rights paradigm, new political and extremely influential concepts were coined such as 'human rights violations' and 'state terrorism'. This led to the establishment of investigative commissions, which became the antecedent of later truth commissions. They emphasized the transformative value of truth and stressed the importance of acts of remembrance. "'Remember, so as not to repeat" began to emerge as a message and as a cultural imperative."[11] Within the human rights framework, a new and highly influential concept of victimhood was constructed. It replaced the older frameworks within which power struggles used to be debated in terms of class struggles, national revolutions or political antagonisms. By resorting to the universal value of bodily integrity and human rights, the new terminology depoliticized the conflict and led to the elaboration of memory policies.[12] In the new framework of a human rights agenda and a new memory culture, also other forms of state violence could be addressed such as racial and gender discrimination, repression and the rights of indigenous people. When decades and sometimes centuries after a traumatic past justice in the full sense is no longer possible, memory was discovered as an important symbolic resource to retrospectively acknowledge these crimes against humanity. What the transnational movement of abolition was for the nineteenth century, the new transnational concept of victimhood is for the late twentieth and early twenty-first century. The important change is, however, that now the victims speak for themselves and claim their memories in a globalized public arena. The dissemination of their voices and their public visibility and audibility has created a new 'world ethos' that is not automatically enforced but makes it increasingly difficult for state authorities to continue a repressive policy of forgetting and silence.

11   Elizabeth Jelin, 'Memories of State Violence: The Past in the Present', Ms. 2007, 5; see also Elizabeth Jelin, *State Repression and the Labors of Memory* (Minneapolis: University of Minnesota Press, 2003).
12   Elizabeth Jelin, 'Memories of State Violence', 6.

A new response to the disenfranchised discourse of human rights and mutual global media observation is the memory policy of public apology. We are without doubt, writes Christopher Daase, 'living in an age of political apologies: The Pope apologizes for the inquisition, the United Nations apologize for their inactiveness during the genocide in Rwanda, the Queen apologizes for the repression of the Maori in New Zealand, President Jacques Chirac for the Dreyfus affair and President Bill Clinton for the slave trade.'[13] The list can go on and it does go on. Whatever we may think of these acts, they are evidence of new departures in the construction of nations as moral communities in the contemporary world of media observation. Democratic states and their societies distinguish themselves from others in taking the principles of care and public accountability seriously.[14] This involves a new memory policy and culture of remembrance that addresses unresolved issues of the past and listens with empathy to the voices of victims.

The TRC in South Africa placed 'truth' (rather than justice) in the first position. It was inspired by the idea of reconciliation and hence by negotiation, compromise and an orientation towards integration and a new beginning. Today there are almost thirty TRCs working all over the world, where the rules of the procedure have to be reinvented each time according to the specific circumstances. Their aim is first and foremost a pragmatic one: they are designed as instruments for 'mastering the past'.[15] The fact that the equivalent German term 'Vergangenheitsbewältigung'

---

13   Christopher Daase, 'Apologies and Reconciliation in International Relations', <http://www.bundesstiftung-friedensforschung.net/projektfoerderung/forschung/daase.html> accessed 9 December 2010. See his essay 'Addressing Painful Memories: Apologies as a New Practice in International Relations', in Aleida Assmann and Sebastian Conrad, eds, *Memory in a Global Age. Discourses, Practices, Trajectories* (London: Palgrave Macmillan, 2010), 19–31.

14   John Bornemann, 'Reconciliation after Ethnic Cleansing: Listening, Retribution, Affiliation', *Public Culture* 14/2 (2002), 281–304; Christopher Bennett, *The Apology Ritual. A Philosophical Theory of Punishment* (Cambridge: Cambridge University Press, 2008).

15   See Pierre Hazan, 'Das neue Mantra der Gerechtigkeit', *Überblick. Deutsche Zeitschrift für Entwicklungspolitik* 43/1+2 (2007), 10–22. The edition of May 2007 is dedicated to the problem of reestablishing justice after armed conflicts.

(mastering the past) has a negative ring is another indicator of the difference between the second and the third model that I am here proposing. 'Vergangenheitsbewältigung' in the sense of mastering the past is the explicit aim of the third model, while 'Vergangenheitsbewahrung' or perpetual preservation of a normative past is the aim of the second model. We have learned in the meantime that a new beginning cannot be forged on a *tabula rasa*, nor is there such a thing as a zero hour. To begin anew requires not forgetting but remembering. The road from authoritarian to civil societies leads through the needle's ear of facing, remembering and coming to terms with a burdened past. The transformation process of memory that starts with TRCs on the political level has to be deepened on the social level, which takes much more time. But however long it may take and how deep it may go, remembering is not the aim of the process but only its medium. The aim is to facilitate recognition, reconciliation and, eventually, 'forgetting' in the sense of putting a traumatic past behind in order to be able to imagine a common future.

4. Dialogic Remembering

With the third model, we have looked at cases in which a state transitions from dictatorship to democracy or confronts a traumatic history in order to create a shared moral consensus within its nation and society. My fourth model applies to situations that transcend such internal reconstructions of nations and societies. It concerns the memory policy of two or more states that share a common legacy of traumatic violence. Two countries engage in a dialogic memory if they face a shared history of mutual violence by mutually acknowledging their own guilt and empathy with the suffering they have inflicted on others.

As a rule, national memories are not dialogic but monologic. They are constructed in such a way that they are identity-enhancing and self-celebrating; their main function is generally to 'enhance and celebrate' a positive collective self-image. National memories are self-serving and therein closely aligned to national myths, which Peter Sloterdijk has appropriately termed modes of 'auto-hypnosis'.[16] With respect to traumatic events, these myths provide effective protection shields against events that a nation prefers to forget. When facing negative events in the past, there are only three dignified roles for the national collective to assume: that of the victor who has overcome the evil, that of the resistor who has heroically fought the evil and that of the victim who has passively suffered the evil. Everything else lies outside the scope of these memory perspectives and is conveniently forgotten.

After the Second World War, for instance, with the Germans in the evident role of the perpetrators, all the other national memories chose one of these dignified positions: the narrative of the victor was that of the Allies, the narrative of the resistor was assumed by the GDR and by France, the narrative of the victim was chosen by Poland and Austria. After 1989 and the demise of the Soviet Union, the opening of eastern European archives brought to light a number of documents that challenged some of these clear-cut memory constructions. The Holocaust that had been a peripheral site in the Second World War gradually began to move into its centre and to become its defining event. In the light of this shift in historical perspective, new evidence of active collaboration, passive support, and indifference to the crime of the Holocaust brought about a crisis in national memories. In Western Europe, the national constructions of memory have become more complex through the acknowledgement of collaboration. In many Eastern states, however, the memory of the Holocaust has to compete with the memory of one's own victimhood and suffering under communist oppression, which is a hot memory that emerged only after the end of the cold war.[17] Because there is a notorious shortage in memory capacity the atrocities that one has suffered claim more space than the atrocities that one has committed.

16   Sloterdijk defines nations as communities created by synchronized media effects, that wrap millions of people up in an effective hypnosis. Peter Sloterdijk, *Der starke Grund zusammen zu sein* (Frankfurt am Main: Suhrkamp, 1998), 23.

17   See Charles S. Maier, 'Heißes und kaltes Gedächtnis: Über die politische Halbwertszeit von Nazismus und Kommunismus', *Transit* 22 (2001/2002), 153–65.

Another lack of dialogic memory has become manifest in the relations between Russia and Eastern European nations. While Russian memory is centred around the great patriotic war and Stalin is celebrated today as the national hero, the nations that broke away from Soviet power maintain a strikingly different memory of Stalin that has to do with deportations, forced labor and mass killings. The triumphalist memory of Russia and the traumatic memory of Eastern European nations clash at the internal borders of Europe and fuel continuous irritations and conflicts.

There are dark incidents that are well-known to historians and emphatically commemorated by the traumatized country but totally forgotten by the nation that was immediately responsible for the suffering. While in the meantime they have learned a lot about the Holocaust, younger Germans today know next to nothing about the legacy of the Second World War and the atrocities committed by Germans against, for instance, their French, Polish and Russian neighbors. The name 'Oradour-sur-Glane'[18] is never mentioned in history classes; former German president Roman Herzog mistook the Warsaw Uprising (July 1944) for the Warsaw Ghetto Uprising (January 1943). Germans have rightly reclaimed the area bombing of Dresden for their national memory, but they have totally forgotten a key event of Russian memory, namely the Leningrad Blockade (1941–4) by the German Wehrmacht, during which 700,000 Russians were starved to death.[19] This event has never entered German national memory due to a lack of interest, empathy, and external pressure.

18   Editors' note: On 10 June 1944, soldiers of the 2nd SS-Panzer Division 'Das Reich' attacked and totally destroyed the town of Oradour-sur-Glane near Limoges in France. Having locked the whole town population into barns and the church, the SS set fire to the buildings and shot everyone trying to escape, killing 642 men, women, and children.

19   To quote from a recent historical account: The siege of Leningrad was 'an integral part of the unprecedented German war of extermination against the civilian population of the Soviet Union. [...] Considering the number of victims and the permanence of the terror, it was the greatest catastrophy that hit a city during the Second World War. The city was cut off from the outside world for almost 900 days from September 7th 1941 to 27th January 1944.' Jörg Ganzenmüller, *Das belagerte Leningrad 1941–1944*.

There are promising beginnings between teachers and historians of neighboring countries working on shared textbooks and mutual perceptions. On the whole, however, dialogic memory is still more of a project than a reality and is best exemplified by its absence. It must be emphasized, however, that the European Union creates a challenge to the solipsistic constructions of national memory and provides an ideal framework for dialogic remembering. As we all know, the European Union is itself the consequence of a traumatic legacy of an entangled history of unprecedented violence. If it is to develop further from an economic and political network to a community of shared values, the entangled histories will have to be transformed into mutually shared memories. Janusz Reiter, Polish ambassador in Germany between 1990 and 1995, commented on this situation: 'With respect to its memories, the European Union remains a split continent. After its extension, the line that separated the EU from other countries now runs right through it.' On the occasion of the sixtieth anniversary of the liberation of Buchenwald, the former prisoner of the concentration camp Jorge Semprún said: One of the most effective possibilities to forge a common future for the EU is 'to share our past, our remembrance, our hitherto divided memories'. And he added that the Eastern extension of the EU can only work 'once we will be able to share our memories, including those of the countries of the other Europe, the Europe that was caught up in Soviet totalitarianism'.[20]

Already in the 1920s, the historian Marc Bloch criticized the monologic character of national memory constructions, describing their solipsistic nature as a 'dialogue between the deaf'. Eighty years after Bloch the European Union is offering a framework which makes possible and demands the restructuring of monologic into dialogic memories. Dialogic remembering which is, of course, applicable in any region of the world has a special relevance for Europe; it could produce a new type of nation-state

---

Die Stadt in den Strategien von Angreifern und Verteidigern (Paderborn: Schoeningh, 2005), 20. See also Peter Jahn, '27 Millionen', *Die ZEIT* (14 June 2007).

20 Jorge Semprún, 'Niemand wird mehr sagen können: "Ja, so war es"', *Die ZEIT* (14 April 2005). (Transl. A. A.).

that is not exclusively grounded in pride but also accepts its quantum of guilt, thus ending a destructive history of violence by including the victims of this violence into one's own memory. Such an inclusive memory, which is based on the moral standard of accountability and human rights, can in turn help to back up the protection of human rights and support the values of a civil society.

Dialogic remembering links two nations through their common knowledge of a shared legacy of a traumatic past. This, however, does by no means entail a unified master narrative for Europe. Richard Sennet once remarked that it needs a plurality of contesting memories in order to acknowledge uncomfortable facts. That is exactly the potential that the frame of the EU has to offer: the transforming of solipsistic into dialogic memories, even though it may take another shift of sensibility before this potential will eventually be embraced by its member states.

Conclusion

The Israeli writer Amos Oz once remarked: 'If I had a say in the peace talks – no matter where, in Wye, Oslo or wherever – I would instruct the sound technicians to turn off the microphones as soon as one of the negotiating parties starts talking about the past. They are paid for finding solutions for the present and the future.'[21] Unfortunately, issues concerning the confronting of the past and the solving of urgent problem for the future are not always so easy to sever. On the contrary, all over the world acts of remembering are today part and parcel of the project of establishing the foundations of a more just society and a better future.

---

21   Amos Oz, 'Israelis und Araber: Der Heilungsprozeß', in Herbert Quandt-Stiftung, ed., *Trialog der Kulturen im Zeitalter der Globalisierung. Sinclair-Haus Gespräche (11. Gespräch 5.–8. Dezember 1998)* (Bad Homburg v.d. Höhe, Herbert Quandt-Stiftung, 1998), 82–9, 83.

It must be conceded, however, that memories are double-edged and can promote integration as well as disintegration: they are both part of the problem (as Amos Oz suggests) and of its solution. Whether memories are part of the problem by prolonging inequality and violence, as Meier insisted, or whether they are a means to transform historical antagonisms and overcome a divisive violent past depends purely on the way they are framed in a given political and social configuration. When we look back on the history of the twentieth century from the vantage of the present, we discover that our manners and methods of dealing with traumatic pasts have changed a number of times, elaborating different models.

The first model, dialogic forgetting, was imposed to achieve the closure of a violent past in a symmetric situation of power. This form of forgetting or silence can only work to create the basis for a new future where the aggression was not one-sided but mutual. While *repressive* silence is the 'automatic' form that perpetuates the structure of violence by prolonging oppressive power relations which protect the perpetrators and harm the victims, *dialogic* silence is built on a mutual agreement.

The second model, remembering in order to never forget, was developed as the unique answer to the singular historic trauma of the Holocaust. The shift from forgetting to remembering, which evolved over the last four decades, has irreversibly changed our moral sensibility on a global scale. While the memory of the Holocaust was conducive to the emergence of other memories, it did not, I would claim, become their prototype. The Holocaust is unique given the methods of its execution and the number of irredeemable and irreconcilable victims. The answer to it is a monumental memory that is semi-religious and an end in itself.

The third model, in contrast, is not unique at all but has been replicated in variations all over the world. It can be paraphrased as 'remembering in order to overcome' in the sense of mastering the past and putting it behind. I wanted to show that there is a clear difference between the semi-religious memorialization of the past (my second model) and the mastering of the past, which begins with the claim to recognition of past suffering of the victims and to moral accountability on behalf of the perpetrators with respect to atrocities committed in the past in order to move on to processes of political reconciliation and social integration. Not only punishments but also 'public displays of remorse, no matter whether they stem from instrumental, rhetorical or normative motivations, are central elements of collective conflict resolution and reconciliation processes'.[22]

The last model is again dialogic and relational, this time applied between states (but also possible for groups within one state). Dialogic remembering transforms a traumatic history of violence into an acknowledgement of one's own guilt. On the basis of this shared knowledge two states can coexist peacefully rather than be exposed to the pressure of periodical eruptions of scandals and renewed violence. For the fourth model, however, there are as yet only few illustrations. It is not yet a reality but surely an important new possibility within the European framework.

Memories, to sum up, are dynamic. What is being remembered of the past is largely dependent on the cultural frames, moral sensibilities and demands of the ever-changing present. During the Cold War, the memory of the Second World War was very different from today, the Holocaust has moved from the periphery to the centre of West European memory only during the last two decades, but also other historic traumas went through periods of latency before they became the object of remembering and commemoration. Today, national memories emerge and are presented in a transnational if not in a global arena where they coexist in a web of mutual contiguities, references, imitations, reactions and competitions.

Remembering trauma evolves between the extremes of keeping the wound open on the one hand and looking for closure on the other. We should not forget that it always takes place simultaneously on the separate but interrelated levels of individuals, families, society and the state. It therefore has a psychological, a moral and a political dimension. But there is also a religious dimension when it comes to the proper burying as a prerequisite for the memory of the dead. It is precisely this cultural and religious duty of laying the dead to rest that is so shockingly disrupted after periods of excessive violence. In the case of millions of Jewish victims, there are no graves because their bodies were gassed, burnt and dissolved into air. For this reason this wound cannot be closed. At other places the victims were

22   Daase, 'Apologies and Reconciliation in International Relations'.

'disappeared' or shot and hid in anonymous mass graves. Some of these, relating to the Spanish Civil War, are reopened only now after more than seventy years.[23] While the politicians and the society have still not found a consensus for introducing these victims into a shared memory, it is up to individual family members to recover their dead and to perform these last acts of reverence.

Bibliography

Assmann, Aleida, and Ute Frevert, *Geschichtsvergessenheit, Geschichtsversessenheit. Vom Umgang mit deutschen Vergangenheiten nach 1945* (Stuttgart: DVA, 1999).

Bennett, Christopher, *The Apology Ritual. A Philosophical Theory of Punishment* (Cambridge: Cambridge University Press, 2008).

Bornemann, John, 'Reconciliation after Ethnic Cleansing: Listening, Retribution, Affiliation', *Public Culture* 14/2 (2002), 281–304.

Buschmann, Arno, *Kaiser und Reich. Verfassungsgeschichte des Heiligen Römischen Reiches Deutscher Nation vom Beginn des 12. Jahrhunderts bis zum Jahre 1806 in Dokumenten* (Baden-Baden: Nomos, 1994).

Churchill, Randolph S., ed., *The Sinews of Peace. Post-War Speeches by Winston S. Churchill* (London: Cassell, 1948).

Daase, Christopher, 'Addressing Painful memories: Apologies as a New Practice in International Relations', in Aleida Assmann and Sebastian Conrad, eds, *Memory in a Global Age. Discourses, Practices, Trajectories* (London: Palgrave Macmillan, 2010), 19–31.

——, 'Apologies and Reconciliation in International Relations', <http://www.bundesstiftung-friedensforschung.net/projektfoerderung/forschung/daase.html> accessed 9 December 2010.

Emrich, Hinderk, and Gary Smith, eds, *Vom Nutzen des Vergessens* (Berlin: Akademie, 1996).

---

23 See Paul Ingendaay, 'Der Bürgerkrieg ist immer noch nicht vorbei', *Frankfurter Allgemeine Zeitung* (25 November 2008).

Ganzenmüller, Jörg, *Das belagerte Leningrad 1941–1944. Die Stadt in den Strategien von Angreifern und Verteidigern* (Paderborn: Schoeningh, 2005).

Hazan, Pierre, 'Das neue Mantra der Gerechtigkeit', *Überblick. Deutsche Zeitschrift für Entwicklungspolitik* 43/1+2 (2007), 10–22.

Henne, Thomas, 'Zeugenschaft vor Gericht', in Michael Elm and Gottfried Kößler, eds, *Zeugenschaft des Holocaust. Zwischen Trauma, Tradierung und Ermittlung* (Frankfurt am Main and New York: Campus, 2007), 79–91.

Ingendaay, Paul, 'Der Bürgerkrieg ist immer noch nicht vorbei', *Frankfurter Allgemeine Zeitung* (25 November 2008).

Jahn, Peter, '27 Millionen', *Die ZEIT* (14 June 2007).

Jelin, Elizabeth, *State Repression and the Labors of Memory* (Minneapolis: University of Minnesota Press, 2003).

——, 'Memories of State Violence: The Past in the Present', Ms. 2007.

Judt, Tony, *Postwar. A History of Europe Since 1945* (Harmondsworth: Penguin, 2005).

Loraux, Nicole, *La Cité divisée. L'Oubli dans la Mémoire d'Athènes* (Paris: Payot, 1997).

Maier, Charles S., 'Heißes und kaltes Gedächtnis: Über die politische Halbwertszeit von Nazismus und Kommunismus', *Transit* 22 (2001/2002), 153–65.

Margalit, Avishai, *The Ethics of Memory* (Cambridge, MA: Harvard University Press, 2003).

Meier, Christian, *Das Gebot zu vergessen und die Unabweisbarkeit des Erinnerns. Vom öffentlichen Umgang mit schlimmer Vergangenheit* (Munich: Beck, 2010).

Oz, Amos, 'Israelis und Araber: Der Heilungsprozeß', in Herbert Quandt-Stiftung, ed., *Trialog der Kulturen im Zeitalter der Globalisierung. Sinclair-Haus Gespräche (11. Gespräch 5.–8. Dezember 1998)* (Bad Homburg v.d. Höhe, Herbert Quandt-Stiftung, 1998), 82–9.

Semprún, Jorge, 'Niemand wird mehr sagen können: "Ja, so war es"', *Die ZEIT* (14 April 2005).

Sloterdijk, Peter, *Der starke Grund zusammen zu sein* (Frankfurt am Main: Suhrkamp, 1998).

Smith, Gary, and Avishai Margalit, eds, *Amnestie, oder Die Politik der Erinnerung* (Frankfurt am Main: Suhrkamp, 1997).

SUSANNAH RADSTONE

Trauma Studies: Contexts, Politics, Ethics

Trauma is often associated with the stripping away of agency and the rendering helpless of victims of catastrophe and disaster. The psychologists van Der Kolk and van Der Hart state, for instance, that '[m]any writers about the human response to trauma have observed that a feeling of helplessness, of physical or emotional paralysis, is fundamental to making an experience traumatic [...]: the person was unable to take any action that could affect the outcome of events.'[1] While these attributes are most usually associated with those who have survived catastrophe at first-hand, the sense of there being nothing that could have been done, of impotency, of lack of agency extends to those close-up against, but not immediately imperilled by disaster as well as to those whose witnessing takes place on safer shores. In her essay on documentary films about Hurricane Katrina, Janet Walker, referring to one instance of situated testimony in Spike Lee's *When the Levees Broke* (2006), describes the moment when a survivor 'looks straight into the lens [...] with her remembered helplessness' as she witnessed a neighbour floating in the floodwaters.[2] Much more recently, a searing account from a witness to the shipwreck of a boat carrying asylum seekers from Iran and Iraq to the Australian territory of Christmas Island reported hearing the screams of children as the boat broke up in the crashing waves. Her voice faltering, the unnamed witness related that 'it was terrifying to watch and there was nothing, *nothing*, we could do [...]'.[3]

---

1   Bessel A. van der Kolk and Onno van Der Hart, 'The Intrusive Past: The Flexibility of Memory and the Engraving of Trauma', in Cathy Caruth, ed., *Trauma: Explorations in Memory* (Baltimore: Johns Hopkins University Press, 1995), 158–82, 175.
2   Janet Walker, 'Moving testimonies and the geography of suffering: Perils and fantasies of belonging after Katrina', *Continuum* 24/1 (2010), 47–64, 50.
3   6 O'Clock News, BBC Radio 4. 15 December 2010.

For trauma studies, the term 'witness', once extended to that of the 'secondary witness',[4] comes to describe the position, not of survivors, but of those whose encounters with catastrophe or disaster take place at (at least) one remove. Dominick LaCapra, for instance, understands the practices of interviewers, oral historians and commentators as modes of secondary witnessing.[5] Within literary, film and media studies, the concept of witnessing has been extended still further, to readers of trauma fiction,[6] television audiences confronted with scenes of disaster and suffering,[7] and spectators of what has become known as 'trauma cinema'.[8] Within the frame of trauma studies, these secondary encounters are understood to render their witnesses, like first-hand witnesses, susceptible to symptoms – if perhaps in dilution – of that traumatization provoked by lack of agency and feelings of helplessness and paralysis. Within the humanities, trauma studies, as it has been developed to date, might be understood to be practicing a kind of tertiary witnessing, setting itself the task of bearing witness to culture's extensions of witnessing through media including the visual arts, literature and film, as well as through the practices of historians.

In the watery disasters mentioned already – the devastating floods following Hurricane Katrina and the terrible loss of life in the Christmas Island shipwreck – helplessness and lack of agency on the part of witnesses appear self-evident. Those present on the shore or on dry land could do nothing to save the lives of the drowning. In an essay written in the wake of another maritime catastrophe – the Indian Ocean tsunami of 2004

4   See Dominick LaCapra, *Writing History, Writing Trauma* (Baltimore and London: Johns Hopkins University Press, 2001).

5   *Ibid.*, 98.

6   See, for instance, Anne Whitehead, *Trauma Fiction* (Edinburgh: Edinburgh Univerity Press, 2004).

7   See, for instance, Lilie Chouliaraki, *The Spectatorship of Suffering* (London: Sage, 2006).

8   The term 'trauma cinema' has been carefully developed in Janet Walker, *Trauma Cinema: Documenting Incest and the Holocaust* (Berkeley, Los Angeles and London: California University Press, 1999). For a nuanced elaboration of the use of the concept of the witness in film theory see Joshua Hirsch, *Afterimage: Films, Trauma, and the Holocaust* (Philadelphia: Temple University Press, 2004).

– Suvendrini Perera emphasizes, however, the political obfuscations risked by an accent, in trauma studies, on loss of agency and helplessness.[9] In an excoriating critique of the geopoliticization of the Indian Ocean tsunami and the biopolitics of trauma, Perera shows how helplessness and loss of agency may be ascribed, by Western powers, to those whose lives are deemed to matter little, as those powers disavow their own agency – the agency of their own politics – in the destruction and continued oppression of those they construct as helpless. Perera's essay takes as its impetus and draws the opening words of its title from a line in Alain Corbin's study of the shipwreck in eighteenth-century Europe.[10] The account of shipwreck spectatorship that emerges in Perera's discussion of Corbin contrasts markedly with an emphasis on helplessness and lack of agency on the part of witnesses, foregrounding in its place a focus on performativity, power and agency. Quoting Corbin, Perera details the '"rhetoric of pity" associated with the shipwreck'.[11] 'In the theatre of coastal catastrophe', Perera continues, 'spectators, too, became actors' turning the shore into a theatre 'in which the viewing subject achieves a transcendence over the awe and terror of nature', while engaging in '"torturous dialogues"'[12] with those perishing in the waves. From Perera's perspective, the 'helplessness' of those who watch emerges, rather, as a disavowal of the enshrinement of their 'magisterial' position on the shore.[13] Perera's demonstration of historical continuities between the politics of the eighteenth-century shores and the twenty-first-century tsunami alerts us to the necessity of interrogating the politics of trauma studies,[14] which, as tertiary witnessing, has the potential to partake in or

---

9   Suvendrini Perera, 'Torturous Dialogues: Geographies of trauma and spaces of exception', *Continuum* 24/1 (2010), 31–45.

10   Alain Corbin, *The Lure of the Sea: The Discovery of the Seaside in the Western World 1750–1840*, trans. Jocelyn Phelps (London: Penguin, 1994).

11   Perera, 'Torturous Dialogues', 32.

12   *Ibid.*

13   *Ibid.*

14   For a collection of essays including Perera's that undertake this task in a range of contexts see Mick Broderick and Antonio Traverso, eds, *Interrogating Trauma: Arts and Media Responses To Collective Suffering*, *Continuum* 24/1 (2010).

critique those modes and politics of spectating/witnessing outlined by
Perera. This essay aims to discuss trauma studies from this perspective – as
an active, engaged and agentic practice that intervenes in and practices a
politics and an ethics open to critique, negotiation and transformation.

The Academic Context for Trauma Studies

Trauma studies as it is currently practiced developed, in the main, from
the canonical writings of Cathy Caruth[15] and Shoshana Felman and Dori
Laub.[16] The theory of trauma developed in the writings of Caruth and
Felman and Laub owes much, on the one hand, to deconstruction, poststructuralism and psychoanalysis. But it is also informed by (mainly US-
based) clinical work with survivors of experiences designated as traumatic.
This combination of influences can be traced through the contents of
Caruth's *Trauma: Explorations in Memory* which includes, alongside chapters by Felman and Laub, contributions by the neuroscientists van der Kolk
and van der Hart and the literary theorists Georges Bataille and Harold
Bloom. One definition of the trauma theory developed by these authors
suggests that it includes both work around the experience of survivors of
the Holocaust and other catastrophic personal and collective experiences
and the theoretical and methodological innovations that might be derived
from this work and applied more generally to film and literary studies.[17]
The clinical work that has shaped the trauma studies developed in the

15   Cathy Caruth, ed., *Trauma: Explorations in Memory* (Baltimore and London: Johns
      Hopkins University Press, 1995); Cathy Caruth, *Unclaimed Experience: Trauma,
      Narrative and History* (Baltimore and London: Johns Hopkins University Press,
      1996).
16   Shoshana Felman and Dori Laub, *Testimony: Crises of Witnessing in Literature,
      Psychoanalysis and History* (New York and London: Routledge, 1992).
17   Thomas Elsaesser, 'Postmodernism as mourning work', *Screen* 42/2 (2001), 193–201,
      194.

work of Caruth and her collaborators is informed by a particular and specific type of psychological theory influenced by developments within US psychoanalytic theory and its relation to the categorization of, on the one hand, mental conditions and disabilities, and on the other, the ways in which these categorizations are taken up within the domain of the law.[18] Critical to these developments has been the codification of Post-Traumatic Stress Disorder (PTSD), as demonstrated by the disorder's inclusion and further elaboration in the third and fourth editions of *The Diagnostic and Statistical Manual* of the American Psychiatric Association,[19] a development referred to in Caruth's introduction to Part I of *Trauma: Explorations in Memory*. Critical, too, has been the development, particularly in the United States, of a neuroscientific approach to memory disorders. In this work, a Freudian emphasis on memory's relations with unconscious conflict, repression and fantasy is replaced by an understanding of memory as related to brain functioning.[20]

Within the humanities, deconstruction was one of the theories which, along with these clinical developments, most shaped the emergence of trauma theory. Its influence can be traced through repeated references to the work of Paul de Man (Caruth's erstwhile teacher) throughout Caruth's *Unclaimed Experience* as well as through a chapter devoted to him in Felman

18   Susannah Radstone, 'Screening Trauma: Forrest Gump, Film and Memory', in Susannah Radstone, ed., *Memory and Methodology* (Oxford and New York: Berg, 2000), 79–107, 87–90. See also Ruth Leys, *Trauma: A Genealogy* (Chicago: University of Chicago Press, 2000), especially Chapter 7; Michael Kenny, 'Trauma, time, illness and culture: an anthropological approach to traumatic memory', in Paul Antze and Michael Lambek, eds, *Tense Past: Cultural Essays in Trauma and Memory* (New York and London: Routledge, 1996), 173–98.

19   American Psychiatric Association, *Diagnostic and Statistical Manual of Mental Disorders*, 4th Edition (Washington DC: American Psychiatric Association, 1994).

20   For critical accounts of these developments see Jeffrey Prager, *Presenting The Past: Psychoanalysis and the Sociology of Remembering* (Cambridge, MA, and London: Harvard University Press, 1998); Paul Antze, 'The Other Inside: Memory as Metaphor In Psychoanalysis', in Susannah Radstone and Katharine Hodgkin, eds, *Regimes of Memory* (New York and London: Routledge, 2003), 96–113.

and Laub's *Testimony: Crises of Witnessing in Literature, Psychoanalysis and History*. The development of this theory of trauma aimed to help the humanities move beyond the crises in knowledge posed by poststructuralism and deconstruction – crises associated, in the main, with the bracketing of 'the real' – without abandoning their insights. Trauma studies promises, that is, not a way round the difficulties presented by these theories, but a way through and beyond them. The short sections that follow will critically discuss how the theories developed and now dominant within trauma studies claim to move through and beyond those theoretical difficulties.

Referentiality

If the critiques of referentiality derived from structuralism, poststructuralism, psychoanalysis, semiotics and deconstruction suggest, in their different ways, that representations bear only a highly mediated or indirect relation to actuality, trauma theory moves through and beyond that proposal by suggesting, as Thomas Elsaesser explains, that the traumatic event has 'the status of a (suspended) origin in the production of a representation [...] bracketed or suspended because marked by the absence of traces'.[21] In place of theories that emphasize the conventional, mediated, illusory, deferred or imaginary status of the relation between representation and 'actuality' or 'event', trauma theory suggests that the relation between representation and 'actuality' might be reconceived as one constituted by the absence of traces. For Dori Laub, this absence of traces gives rise to his formulation of the aetiology of trauma as 'an event without a witness'[22] – an absence of witnessing that derives, argues Caruth, from the unassimilable or unknow-

---

21   Elsaesser, 'Postmodernism as mourning work', 194.
22   Dori Laub, 'An Event without a Witness: Truth, Testimony and Survival', in Felman and Laub, *Testimony*, 75–92.

able nature of the traumatic event.[23] In trauma theory, this absence of traces testifies to a representation's relation to (a traumatic) event/actuality. In other words, trauma theory constitutes, in Elsaesser's words, 'not so much a theory of recovered memory as [...] one of recovered referentiality'.[24] This emphasis on the referentiality of traumatic memory emerges in Caruth's introduction to the first section of *Trauma: Explorations in Memory*, which begins with references to the 'war in Bosnia-Herzegovina and the increasing violence in the US'.[25] It is revealed, also, by the centrality accorded by Felman and Laub to Holocaust testimony. This is clearly an interesting and refreshing move that (again, as Elsaesser points out) might be taken up by historians, as well as by media theorists. Yet at the same time, it takes the traumatic event as its theoretical foundation. As we have seen, one of Laub's chapters in *Testimony: Crises of Witnessing* refers to trauma as an event without a witness. An emphasis on the event is also found through- out Caruth's *Unclaimed Experience*, pre-figured by her opening account of Freud wondering, in his *Beyond The Pleasure Principle*, 'at the peculiar and sometimes uncanny way in which catastrophic events seem to repeat themselves'.[26] This raises the question of the meaning and implications of placing trauma at the very heart of a general theory of representation, which would seem to follow from the centrality to Caruth's trauma theory of de Man's general theory of signification. To what extent, that is, are the insights offered by trauma theory generalizable to the whole field of representa- 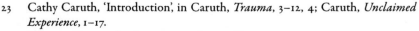 tion? While it might be arguable that language and representation emerge from and bear the mark of that primary break or separation constitutive of subjectivity, to align this break with trauma would constitute, in my view at least, a histrionic manoeuvre resulting in the pathologization of all life lived through language and representation – of all life, that is, beyond very early infancy. Moreover, the generalizability of trauma theory's insights is brought into question by those very theories from which trauma theory

23   Cathy Caruth, 'Introduction', in Caruth, *Trauma*, 3–12, 4; Caruth, *Unclaimed Experience*, 1–17.

24   Elsaesser, 'Postmodernism as mourning work', 201.

25   Cathy Caruth, 'Preface', in Caruth, *Trauma*, vii–ix, vii.

26   Caruth, *Unclaimed Experience*, 1.

is derived. Trauma theory is derived, in part, that is, from de Man's theory of signification in general, and in part from the neuroscientific studies of psychologists including Bessel A. van der Kolk, who have argued, in the words of Ruth Leys, that 'the traumatic event is encoded in the brain in a different way from ordinary memory'.[27] If trauma's encoding is extraordinary, then can that 'encoding' become the foundation for a general theory of representation? These are questions that deserve further elaboration and debate. For is it that theories of trauma are taken to illuminate the relation between actuality and representation in general, or is it that actuality is beginning to be taken as traumatic in and of itself?[28] These questions, crudely stated as they are here, risk becoming obfuscated, I think, as the theory takes on a life of its own.

Subjectivity

A theory of subjectivity is implicit within the theories that have become associated with trauma studies in the humanities. One context for this theory is the constant revising and re-reading of Freud's seminal texts, which has resulted, of course, in a plethora of different schools of psychoanalytic and psychological theory. Over-simplifying somewhat, trauma theory as it informs the humanities has its psychoanalytic foundations in what I'll call the 'postmodernization' of Freud, by which I mean, in particular, an emphasis on actuality over fantasy, and on the interpersonal over the intrapsychical aspects of life. For Caroline Garland, the differences found between varieties of psychoanalytically informed approaches to trauma are

---

27   Leys, *Trauma*, 7. Leys references Bessel A. van der Kolk, Alexander C. McFarlane and Lars Weisaeth, eds, *Traumatic Stress: The Effects of Overwhelming Experience on Mind, Body and Society* (New York and London: Guilford Press, 1996).

28   See Susannah Radstone, 'Trauma and Screen Studies: opening the debate', *Screen* 42/2 (2001), 188–93, 190.

linked with contrasting readings of Freud found particularly within the US, on the one hand and the UK, on the other. In the US, suggests Garland, it is the event that takes precedence over the psychical processes in trauma's aetiology.[29] The impact of neuroscientific research, with its emphasis on the material workings of the brain, has also impacted upon trauma studies.[30] Alongside an emphasis on memory and brain function, this 'postmodern' psychology includes a strand that emphasizes intersubjectivity and the role of the listener or witness in the bringing to consciousness of previously unassimilated memory.[31] The importance of witnessing is illustrated particularly in Felman and Laub's *Testimony: Crises of Witnessing*, which moreover includes the term witness or witnessing in the titles of four of its seven chapters. Though, as Antze has pointed out, an emphasis on narrative, witnessing and the intersubjectivity of memory is at odds with the scientificity of neurobiology,[32] in practice, trauma theory's emphasis on witnessing as well as on pathologies of dissociation demonstrates that it draws on both strands. In debates concerning the model of subjectivity implied by trauma theory and the theoretical difficulties negotiated by that model, this leads to the question of what it is, in other words, that trauma theory moves 'through' or 'beyond' in its construction of a traumatized subject. My response to this question takes as its starting point Ruth Leys's excellent genealogical study of trauma, in which Leys demonstrates that contemporary trauma theory is still struggling to resolve a contradiction that has

29   Writing on clinical approaches to trauma in the work of the Tavistock Clinic in London, Garland explains that 'US work [...] is less central than [...] the work of Freud and Klein, believing that the impact of traumatic events upon the human mind can only be understood and treated through achieving with the patient a deep knowledge of the particular meaning of those events for that individual'. Caroline Garland, *Understanding Trauma: A Psychoanalytic Approach*, Tavistock Clinic Series (London: Duckworth, 1998), 4.

30   See, for instance, Bessel A. van der Kolk and Onno van der Hart, 'Pierre Janet and the Breakdown of Adaptation in Psychological Trauma', *American Journal of Psychiatry* 146/12 (1989), 1530–40. One of the most influential neuroscientific books on trauma has been Judith Herman's *Trauma and Recovery* (New York: Basic Books, 1992).

31   For references to such work see Paul Antze, 'The Other Inside', 110, n. 9.

32   Antze, 'The Other Inside', 97.

underlain the theories of trauma since their inception – the contradiction, that is, between a mimetic and an anti-mimetic theory of trauma. Leys accords a position of centrality, within trauma's genealogy, to *the problem of imitation, defined as a problem of hypnotic imitation*[33] and makes the case that the hypnotized subject provided the template for early psychoanalytic theories of traumatic memory. Leys points out that far from being only a method of research and treatment of the symptoms of trauma,

> Hypnosis [...] played a major theoretical role in the conceptualisation of trauma [...] because the tendency of hypnotized persons to imitate or repeat whatever they were told to say or do provided a basic model for the traumatic experience. Trauma was defined as a situation of dissociation or 'absence' from the self in which the victim unconsciously imitated or identified with the aggressor or traumatic scene in a situation that was likened to a state of heightened suggestibility or hypnotic trance.[34]

Leys goes on to suggest that this tie between trauma and mimesis proved troubling as it threatened the ideal of individual autonomy and responsibility.[35] The notion of subjects absent from themselves and involuntarily mimicking a past traumatic experience threatened to de-stabilize the sovereignty of those subjects. In the mimetic theory of trauma, that is, traumatized subjects are neither fully in control of, nor in charge of themselves. As Leys explains, the unwelcome implications of the mimetic theory of trauma led to the development, alongside that theory, of 'an *anti-mimetic* tendency to regard trauma as if it were a purely external event coming to a sovereign if passive victim'.[36] According to this model, the production of memories is no longer understood to be linked to the unconscious, unbiddable, processes of the inner world. Instead, memories are understood to be the unmediated, though unassimilable records of traumatic events. These memories are understood to undergo 'dissociation', meaning that they come to occupy a specially designated area of the mind that precludes their retrieval. Whereas in the mimetic strand of the psychoanalytic theory

33   Leys, *Trauma*, 8 (original emphasis).
34   *Ibid.*, 8–9.
35   *Ibid.*, 9.
36   *Ibid.*, 10 (original emphasis).

of trauma, traumatization is understood to produce psychical dissociation from the self, in the anti-mimetic strand, it is the record of an unassimilable *event* which is dissociated from memory. Ruth Leys's genealogy of trauma links the rise of an anti-mimetic theory of trauma to the defence of an (ideological) commitment to the sovereignty and autonomy of the subject. This linkage illuminates what may be a problematic aspect of the anti-mimeticism that has come to influence trauma studies within the humanities. For Ruth Leys, the ideological-political implications of the anti-mimetic tendency within early formulations of trauma theory are clear: its advantage was that it allowed the traumatic subject to be theorized as sovereign, if passive. As Leys goes on to argue, it is this anti-mimetic emphasis on the event which 'suppressed the mimetic-suggestive paradigm in order to re-establish a strict dichotomy between the autonomous subject and the external trauma.'[37]

For Leys, mimetic and anti-mimetic tendencies cannot be strictly divided from each other. It is rather that the contradiction between these tendencies has continued to shape psychology and psychoanalysis. Leys argues that 'from the moment of its invention in the late nineteenth century the concept of trauma has been fundamentally unstable, balancing uneasily – indeed veering uncontrollably – between two ideas, theories or paradigms.'[38] Nevertheless, it is possible to read tendencies towards the mimetic or anti-mimetic strands in the theories of trauma that are current within trauma studies. The trauma theory of Caruth and of Felman and Laub emphasizes lack of recall and the unexperienced nature of the trauma. In these senses, it leans towards the mimetic paradigm. However, trauma theory's previously discussed emphasis on the event itself links it clearly with the anti-mimetic theory of trauma. Leys argues that whereas in the mimetic theory, the subject unconsciously imitates or repeats the trauma, in the anti-mimetic theory the subject is 'essentially aloof from the traumatic experience [...]. The anti-mimetic theory is compatible with, and often gives way to, the idea that trauma is a purely external event that befalls

37   *Ibid.*, 9.
38   *Ibid.*, 298.

a fully constituted subject'.[39] This anti-mimetic tendency shapes Caruth's
interpretation of Freud's writings, which return, always, to trauma's relation to an event. Thus, she argues, for instance, that 'the experience that
Freud will call "traumatic neurosis" emerges as the re-enactment of *an event*
that one cannot simply leave behind'.[40] Leys's account of the differences
between the anti-mimetic and mimetic paradigms also draws attention to
the question of the traumatized subject's relation to the aggressor. Whereas
the mimetic paradigm, argues Leys, 'posits a moment of identification with
the aggressor [...] the anti-mimetic theory depicts violence as purely and
simply an assault from without. This has the advantage of portraying the
victim of trauma as in no way mimetically complicitous with the violence
directed against her'.[41] The possibility of an identification with aggression
is markedly absent from the trauma theory of Caruth and Felman and
Laub, thus demonstrating further their theory's alignment with the anti-
mimetic paradigm and the distance between their trauma theory and the
theory that I wish to discuss below.

   Trauma theory's readings of Freud contrast on several points with contemporary re-readings of Freud undertaken by recent interpreters including,
in the UK, those of Object-Relations theorists,[42] and in France, Laplanche
and Pontalis.[43] Whether they follow Object-Relations, or Laplanche, or
post-Freudian theory more generally, the psychoanalytic theories of trauma
that I wish to advocate here all emphasize unconscious conflict and mediation in the formation of neuroses, even where what appears to be at stake

39   *Ibid.*, 299.
40   Caruth, *Unclaimed Experience*, 2 (emphasis mine).
41   Leys, *Trauma*, 299.
42   Object-Relations psychoanalysis developed, mainly in the UK, from the work of
     Melanie Klein and her followers. In place of Freud's tripartite model of ego/id/
     superego, Object-Relations theorizes the inner world as composed of inner objects
     and part-objects constituted through the internalization of encounters with the
     infant's first carers. This school is associated, in particular, with clinicians working
     at the Tavistock Clinic in London.
43   Jean Laplanche and J. B. Pontalis, *The Language of Psychoanalysis* (London: Karnac
     Books, 1988); John Fletcher and Martin Stanton, eds, *Jean Laplanche: Seduction,
     Translation, Drives* (London: Institute of Contemporary Arts, 1992).

is the relation between a neurosis and memory of the past. These alternative approaches to trauma substitute for trauma theory's emphasis on the
dissociation of unassimilated memories a focus on the traumatic nature of
unconscious associations. The topographies of the inner world found in
the trauma theories of Caruth and of Felman and Laub dispense with the
layering of conscious/subconscious and unconscious, substituting for them
a conscious mind in which past experiences are accessible, and a dissociated
area of the mind from which traumatic past experiences cannot be accessed.
In Caruth, and in Felman and Laub, it is the unexperienced nature of the
event, which give rise to PTSD. Caruth argues, for instance, that '[w]hat
returns in the flashback is not simply an overwhelming experience that has
been obstructed by a later repression or amnesia, but an event that is itself
constituted, in part, by its lack of integration into consciousness'.[44] Depth
has no intrinsic value, but trauma theory's revised, depthless topography
of the mind entails the abandonment of Freud's emphasis on the mediating role of unconscious processes in the production of the mind's scenes[45]
and meanings, including those of memory. What is lost – to put this even
more baldly – is that fundamental psychoanalytic assumption concerning
the challenge to the subject's sovereignty posed by the unconscious and
its wayward processes[46] – processes which might include, but should not
be limited to, an identification with the aggressor. In alternative re-inter-
pretations of Freud, it is the unconscious production of associations to a
memory, rather than qualities intrinsic to certain events, that is understood
to render a memory traumatic. These associations have to be understood in
relation to temporality and fantasy. Whereas for Caruth, it is the memory

44   Caruth, *Trauma*, 152.
45   The term 'scenes' – and its relation to and difference from memory – is introduced
      by Paul Antze in his recent discussion of different psychoanalytic understandings
      of memory. See Antze, 'The Other Inside'.
46   Paul Antze quotes from Laplanche, who, he says, 'has coined the term *étrangèreté*
      (literally "strangerness") to capture this dimension of Freud's thought. He equates
      it with what he takes to be truly revolutionary in psychoanalysis, the "Copernican"
      idea of a subject whose centre of gravity lies elsewhere, outside consciousness'. Antze,
      'The Other Inside', 102–3.

of the event itself which arrives belatedly,[47] for Laplanche and Pontalis, it is the meanings conferred on it 'afterwards' that may render a particular memory traumatic.[48] Leys makes a similar point when she argues that 'for Freud traumatic memory is inherently unstable or mutable owing to the role of unconscious motives that confer meaning on it.'[49] In the psychoanalytic theory that has developed in parallel to that drawn on by trauma theory, then, a memory becomes traumatic when it becomes associated, later, with inadmissible meanings, wishes, fantasies, which might include an identification with the aggressor. What I take from this is that it is not an event, which is by its nature 'toxic' to the mind, but what the mind later does to memory. One British Object-Relations psychoanalyst has described this process in the following terms: 'Whatever the nature of the event [...] eventually [the survivor] comes to make sense of it in terms of the most troubled and troubling of the relationships between the objects that are felt to inhabit his internal world. That way the survivor is at least making something recognizable and familiar out of the extraordinary, giving it meaning.'[50] It follows from this, as clinical researchers at the Tavistock Clinic have recently documented, that the traumatization effect does not appear to reside in the nature of the event. Some need no support after a so-called trauma, while others need help.

Trauma studies' sophistication and its associations with radical academic work have become taken for granted. On Leys's account, however, another view emerges. For Caruth's version of trauma implies a 'forgetting' of that radical decentring and de-stabilization of the subject – that emphasis on the *subject's lack of sovereignty* and its unconscious processes of mediation and meaning-making – a forgetting that continues to mark trauma theory in the humanities today.

It hardly needs re-stating that those theories – psychoanalysis, structuralism, poststructuralism, deconstruction – whose aporias trauma theory promises to negotiate, or move through, all problematize, in different ways,

---

47   See, for instance, Caruth, *Trauma*, 4; *Unclaimed Experience*, 17.
48   Laplanche and Pontalis, *The Language of Psychoanalysis*, 467–8.
49   Leys, *Trauma*, 20.
50   Garland, *Understanding Trauma*, 12.

and to different degrees, those very notions of autonomy and sovereignty which lie at the heart of bourgeois constructions of subjectivity. It is paradoxical, then, that contemporary trauma theory's anti-mimetic emphasis on catastrophic events can thus arguably be traced back to a theoretical shift made in defence of a model of subjectivity critiqued by the very theories – structuralism, poststructuralism, psychoanalysis, deconstruction – with which trauma theory in the humanities is explicitly associated and through which, rather than against which, its exponents believe themselves to be travelling.

One of the foundational insights brought to the humanities by psychoanalysis, for instance, concerned the subject's unconscious activities of condensation, displacement and symbolization. This insight enabled the humanities to develop a model of the subject not as passive yet sovereign, but as engaged in processes of desire and meaning-making over which it lacked full conscious control. This model of a de-centred subject caught up in processes of symbolization, desire and fear that lie partly beyond the reach of consciousness has been central to the development of contemporary understandings of the production, negotiation and mediation of culture. The significance of these arguments for any discussion of trauma studies' value for the humanities resides in trauma theory's tendency to abandon any emphasis on the radical ungovernability of the unconscious. As we have seen, in the trauma theory of Caruth, for instance, it is the event rather than the subject, which emerges as unpredictable and ungovernable. I make this point not in the interest of diverting attention from the actuality of historical catastrophes and the suffering caused, but to stress that cultural theory needs to attend to the intra- as well as the inter-subjective processes through which meanings are conferred, negotiated and mediated. The exploration of hidden, unconscious processes of desire- or fear-driven meaning-making have proved immensely valuable in cultural theory's engagement with psychoanalysis to date. An emphasis on trauma's links with the dissociated memory of events retreats from this insight since, in place of those ungovernable processes of the mind that are constitutive of meaning and affect, it substitutes an event's inassimilable nature. In this account of trauma's aetiology, it is the nature of the event itself which prompts its dissociation.

Something else gets lost, too, in trauma theory's retreat from the significance of unconscious process for memory formation and revision. An emphasis on the centrality of unconscious process to all aspects of psychical life has the effect of reminding readers and analysts of two important aspects of that life. First, a fundamental tenet of psychoanalysis is that of a continuum of psychical states. Psychoanalysis avoids any radical differentiation between the 'normal' and the 'pathological'. Trauma theory, on the other hand, does tend to distinguish between the 'normal' and the 'pathological'. One has either been present at or has 'been' traumatized by a terrible event or one has not. Second, whereas psychoanalysis takes the 'darker side of the mind' for granted, emphasizing the ubiquity of inadmissible sexual fantasies, for instance, trauma theory suggests, rather that the 'darkness' comes only from outside. Hence the relevance of Leys's already noted comments concerning the anti-mimetic paradigm's 'depiction of violence as purely and simply an assault from without'.[51] This perspective has recently been challenged by Caroline Garland, who, writing of the difference between perspectives on trauma in the clinical practice found in the US and at the Tavistock Clinic in London, emphasizes that the Tavistock Clinic's view is that '[i]n the internal world there is no such thing as an accident, there is no such thing as forgetting and there is no such thing as an absence of hatred, rage or destructiveness [...] in spite of the urge in survivors to attribute all badness to the world outside them that caused their misfortune'.[52] What I am suggesting, then, is that notwithstanding the sophistication of trauma theory's underpinnings in De Manian or Derridean deconstruction it nevertheless offers a theory of the subject which retreats from psychoanalysis' rejection of a black-and-white vision of psychical life to produce a theory which establishes clear, not to say Manichean binaries of 'inside' and 'outside', 'trauma' and 'normality', and 'victims' and 'perpetrators'.

Ruth Leys explains that the work of Cathy Caruth is informed by that of the deconstructionist theorist Paul De Man, characterizing Caruth's

51   Leys, *Trauma*, 299.
52   Garland, *Understanding Trauma*, 5.

position as a 'deconstructive version of van der Kolk's neurobiological account of trauma [in which] the gap or aporia in consciousness and representation that is held to characterize the individual traumatic experience comes to stand for the "materiality of the signifier"'.[53] Trauma theory, then, arguably moves through and beyond the 'revelation' of the subject's incoherence or 'de-facement'. It moves through and beyond modernity's supposition of a coherent, autonomous, knowing subject, but without simply rendering subjectivity incoherent, unknowing, fragmented. But perhaps it does this (as Leys suggests) while holding, in a relatively hidden way, to a notion of a sovereign yet passive subject. Is this the route through 'post' theories that trauma theory is really producing? And is this a model of subjectivity which, if made explicit, would be followed by those who espouse the theory? And if humanities' theory is beginning to substitute a passive but sovereign subject, for a subject caught up in processes not all of which are available for conscious control, how might that shift best be contextualized and evaluated? These are, I think, questions that invite further consideration.

Subjectivity, Forgetting and Testimony

The subject of trauma theory is characterized by that which it does not know/remember.[54] This is not a subject caught up in desire, but a subject constituted by forgetting. The inner world of the traumatized subject is characterized not by repression of unacknowledgeable fantasies but by dissociated memories – traceless traces. Though the subject of trauma theory cannot be restored to coherence through acts of remembrance, a belated acknowledgement of that which has been forgotten is a possibility.[55]

53   Leys, *Trauma*, 266.
54   Caruth, *Unclaimed Experience*, 4–7; Caruth, *Trauma*, 1–5.
55   *Ibid.*, 4.

The traumatized subject can remember its having forgotten, if you like
– can acknowledge the gaps and absences. Most importantly, this act of
'recovery' takes place in relation to a witness. Testimony, as the title of
Felman and Laub's seminal text confirms and as Caruth demonstrates,[56]
is a term foregrounded in trauma theory. It refers to a relation of witnessing between the subject of trauma and the listener. According to Felman
and Laub, testimony (to trauma) demands a witness and it is only within
the context of witnessing that testimony to trauma is possible. In this relation, some testimony can be made to trauma's 'traceless traces'. What needs
emphasizing here is trauma theory's moving beyond modernity's coherent, autonomous, knowing subject to a model of subjectivity grounded in
the space between witness and testifier within which that which cannot
be known can begin to be witnessed. This may seem to contradict my
earlier argument concerning trauma theory's re-institution of subjective
sovereignty. However, the model of subjectivity inscribed in theories of
testimony conforms to Leys's description: the knowledge this subject lacks
is not that of its own unconscious process, but of an event that cannot be
remembered.

   In trauma theory, then, it is almost as though the topographical
flattening out of the psyche that substitutes dissociation for repression
displaces previously intra-psychical processes of displacement into the space
of the inter-subjective. Processes of dialogic meaning-making between
testifier and witness arguably take the place, that is, of those intra-psychical
yet socially shaped unconscious processes of repression, mediation and
meaning-making foregrounded in psychoanalysis' alternative understanding of traumatic memory.[57]

---

56   See specially Caruth, *Unclaimed Experience*, 108.
57   For a longer discussion of the difference between these two positions see Leys,
     Trauma, 270–92.

History

The foregrounding of questions of testimony and witnessing establish trauma theory's pertinence to the discipline and practice of history. Trauma theory is associated with the 'turn to memory' in history as well as in the humanities more generally. Postmodernism's problematizations of grand narratives, objectivity, universality and totality prompted a turn to memory's partial, local and subjective narratives. Moreover, postmodernism's questioning of history's authoritative truth-claims arose, in part, in relation to a consideration of the Holocaust, the impact of which has been linked to the impossibility of both representation and remembrance. It is telling, therefore, that Shoshana Felman writes towards the beginning of *Testimony* that Adorno's famous dictum concerning poetry after Auschwitz did not imply that poetry could no longer and should no longer be written, but that it must write 'through' its own impossibility.[58] By analogy, trauma theory arguably constitutes one attempt by history to think itself 'through' a post-Auschwitz world. If history was already arguing, that is, that events were always 'without a witness' – in that though events happened, they could only be known 'afterwards' through representation, through language, through the always partial and situated discourses and languages of their telling, trauma theory constituted the 'limit-text' of this position – since, to use Hayden White's problematic term, 'holocaustal' events 'cannot be simply forgotten [...] but neither can they be adequately remembered'.[59] Trauma theory attempts to move through this position in a number of ways: through theories of testimony, as exemplified in the work of Felman and Laub,[60] through reaching for modes of representation better suited to the 'unrepresentability' of trauma than realism,[61] and by deploying psychoanalytic understandings of trauma's belatedness to reveal testimony to trauma's traceless traces 'after' the event.

58   Felman and Laub, *Testimony*, 34.
59   Hayden White, 'The modernist event', in Vivian Sobchack, ed., *The Persistence of History: Cinema, Television and the Modern Event* (New York and London: Routledge, 1996), 17–38, 20.
60   Felman and Laub, *Testimony*.
61   White, 'The modernist event', 22.

History's attempt to think itself through a 'post-Auschwitz' world and the links between this attempt and the challenges posed to history by 'post' theories more generally all led it, then, in the direction of memory – and traumatic memory in particular.[62] The take-up within history of perspectives informed by theories of testimony and trauma arguably evidences that tendency to retain a model of the subject as the sovereign yet passive 'victim' of events found in trauma theory more generally. This is perhaps understandable, given history's primary concerns with deeds and happenings. Yet contemporary history's dominant tendency to link or oppose history to memory, to the near exclusion of other terms including fantasy and the imaginary,[63] does invite some discussion.

Analysts and Readers:
The Ethics and Politics of Trauma Analysis

Theories of trauma, testimony and witnessing are currently informing literary, film and media studies. This work shares in common a drive to engage with and reveal trauma's 'traceless'[64] or absent textual presence. Usually, though not always, taking as their objects texts explicitly concerned with personal or collective catastrophe, trauma analysis aims to demonstrate the ways in which texts may be engaged with the belated remembrance of trauma. There is much that remains to be decided concerning the theories and methods of trauma analysis. For instance, trauma analysis has yet to debate how, given trauma's unrepresentability, the initial choice of texts for analysis is to be made, and whether it can be assumed, as criticism

---

62   Radstone, 'Screening Trauma', 81–90.
63   There are, of course, historians working outside this tendency, as demonstrated by papers given at the long-standing and ongoing London 'Psychoanalysis and History' seminar series, currently organized by Sally Alexander (Goldsmiths College) and Kate Hodgkin and Barbara Taylor (University of East London).
64   Elsaesser, 'Postmodernism as mourning work', 199.

to date seems to have accepted, that it will be texts explicitly concerned with catastrophe that are most likely to reveal trauma's absent traces. Yet, though there is much that remains to be debated concerning every aspect of trauma analysis, the open debate of trauma analysis' grounding theories, and of the readings that it produces are hindered by the nature of the material itself and the contexts – particularly in conferences – within which it is discussed. Criticism and debate can easily appear callous, or even unethical, in a context where an audience is being asked to bear witness to unspeakable sufferings. This can lead, however, to a silencing of discussion which leaves hanging any number of questions about the continuingly problematic nature of academic discussion of trauma and the apparent acceptability of debate only of certain types of material and not others. Yet if self-reflexivity is a *sine qua non* of all cultural analysis, then there are three aspects of trauma analysis that do invite some reflection: first, the construction of and positioning of the trauma text's analyst; second, the fascinations of trauma and, third, the designation of the field to be included by trauma analysis. Though trauma analysis is in its early stages of development, its ethical imperatives do appear to have been accepted: trauma analysis positions itself by analogy with the witness or addressee of testimony to trauma and understands its task as that of facilitating the cultural remembrance and working-through of those traumas whose absent presence marks the analysed text(s). That compassion constitutes a central drive of trauma analysis is beyond dispute. Yet what needs to be reflected upon is the tendency of trauma analysis to foreground the analyst's sensitivity and empathic capacities. In this regard, trauma analysis arguably revises that Leavisite emphasis on fineness of response that was the butt of such extensive critique within the theories from which trauma theory appears to draw breath. Carolyn Steedman's comments on the historical genealogy, particularly in the eighteenth century, of what she calls 'Empathy Theory'[65] provide a timely corrective to the view that the display of empathy, in cultural criticism, is simply to be welcomed:

---

65   Carolyn Steedman, 'Enforced Narratives: Stories of another self', in Tess Cosslett, Celia Lury and Penny Summerfield, eds, *Feminism and Autobiography: Texts, Theories, Methods* (London and New York: Routledge, 2000), 25–39.

> Using [empathy] theory, a sense of self [...] was articulated, through the use of some-
> one else's story of suffering, loss, exploitation, pain [...]. In those moments of vibrat-
> ing reception, when the heart throbs in sympathy and we are sublimely aware of
> the harmony of our reactions with those of the person we are sympathising with, it
> seems necessary, an absolute rock-bottom line of exchange, that he or she who tells
> the harrowing tale, is diminished by having that story to tell; and is subordinated
> in the act of telling.[66]

Steedman's timely remarks invite a greater degree of reflexivity concerning
the ethics of trauma criticism. For what she reveals is that critical 'empathy' is not without its darker aspects. As well as partaking of a discourse of
power that establishes the critic's sensibility as 'finer' than that of nameless
others, the empathetic recovery of the voices of traumatized testifiers and
texts may be at the expense of those for whom trauma criticism claims to
speak. In this context, it is perhaps salutary to be reminded, also (as the
insights of psychoanalysis of any hue would demonstrate), that a focus
on texts of catastrophe and suffering is bound to be inflected, also, by less
easily acknowledgeable fascinations and fantasies concerning victimhood
grounded in aggressivity,[67] or a drive to voyeurism and control.[68] Such
responses have been identified amongst those only indirectly caught up
in actual disasters. As David Alexander, director of the Aberdeen Centre
for Trauma Research, has pointed out, trauma sites and trauma victims
frequently become the objects of voyeuristic, or triumphalist fascination.[69]
Through such manoeuvres, those not directly affected by a catastrophe
shield themselves from the awareness of what might have been by means of
sadistic fantasies of control and/or blame. At the same time, trauma sites,

66   *Ibid.*, 34.
67   For a longer discussion of this point see Susannah Radstone, 'Social Bonds and
     Psychical Order: Testimonies', *Cultural Values* 5/1 (2001), 59–78 (especially 66
     onwards).
68   For a paper that reflects, from a feminist perspective, on the potential of public wit-
     nessing of testimony to invite a powerful voyeuristic gaze see Karyn Ball, 'Unspeakable
     Differences, Obscene Pleasures: The Holocaust as an Object of Desire', *Women in
     German Yearbook* 19 (2003), 20–49.
69   David Alexander, paper presented at the 'Trauma, Therapy and Representation'
     conference, University of Aberdeen, 11–13 April 2003.

victims and texts also proffer the potential for a masochistic identification with victimhood. Trauma analysis might gain from considering the possibility, then, that its impetus to engage with trauma may be shaped, to some degree, by these less easily acknowledgeable fascinations.

There is one sense in which trauma analysis' investment of power in the analyst or reader is explicit. Trauma theory emphasizes the dialogic nature of testimony. Yet notwithstanding its analogous relation to testimonial witnessing, trauma analysis appears to dispense with the insights of contemporary media and literary studies concerning the complex processes of meaning negotiation that take place between texts and their various spectators/readers, and invests the analyst with immensely and conclusively authoritative interpretative capacities. It seems that it is the analyst, and the analyst alone, who is able to discern trauma's absent traces. In this regard, trauma theory seems to return us to an almost Althusserian moment, in which the authoritative analyst alone is invested with the capacity to perceive the truth of representation. This scenario diverges considerably from that of the opening up of texts to multiple, contestable, divergent or contradictory readings that have been bequeathed to the humanities by readings informed by, for instance, psychoanalysis and deconstruction. It diverges, too, from the stress placed by cultural studies on the situated, local and multiple readings of historically specific readers and audiences. To put it this way, for whom, when, where and in what circumstances are particular texts read or experienced as trauma texts? A further and related question that remains hanging, due to the difficulty of debating trauma analysis, hinges on which events, experiences and texts are to be classed as traumatic and which are to be excluded from this category. This is problematic since, to put things at their most stark, trauma criticism arguably constructs and polices the boundary of what can be recognized as trauma – a position made all the more powerful by trauma theory's insistence on the 'tracelessness' or invisibility of trauma to all but the most trained of eyes. It should be obvious by now that the thrust of my argument is not that the boundaries of trauma criticism's reach should be expanded, but rather that questions remain concerning the inclusions and exclusions performed by this criticism. Why is it, for instance, that there has been so little attention, within trauma studies, to the recent sufferings of those in

Rwanda, in comparison to the attention that has been focused on events
in the US on 9/11? The questions of firstly, who it is that gets claimed by
trauma studies, and who ignored, and secondly, which events get labelled
'trauma' and which do not have not been omitted, entirely, from critical
commentary. For example, writing of 9/11, James Berger has recently pointed
out that 'events of comparable and greater devastation in terms of loss of
life happen in other parts of the world quite regularly',[70] yet, he implies,
have not been subject to trauma criticism's empathic attention. Berger
makes the point that while some events get labelled traumatic, others, quite
patently do not. Moreover, it is the sufferings of those categorized, in the
West as 'other', that tend not to be addressed via trauma theory – which
becomes in this regard, a theory that supports politicized constructions
of those with whom identifications via traumatic sufferings can be forged
and those from whom such identifications are withheld. This is not, as I
have already argued, a call to extend trauma's reach – it is rather a call to
attend to this aspect of the politics of trauma theory.

Steedman's essay on the making and writing of the self from the seventeenth century onwards offers some thoughts on testimony that are, in
the context of these questions, both pertinent and potentially salutary. In
Steedman's account, the realist novels of the eighteenth and nineteenth centuries constructed subjectivity – constructed the bourgeois autobiographical 'I' – through two processes of 'colonization'. These novels constructed
subjectivity, using as a template the forced courtroom testimonies of sub-
ordinate others. These testimonies were then 'taken over' in the first-person
writings of the middle classes, who modelled their 'I' on these induced
autobiographies. Further, Steedman suggests, as we have already seen, that
where, in novels of this period, the narrative dwells on the experiences of
an 'other', the narrator and reader place themselves in the position of feeling and displaying the fineness of their response to these tales of suffering.
But if, as Steedman suggests, these autobiographical acts construct their
subjects through a 'colonization' of the stories of others, which also become
the means by which the sensitivity of the narrating and reading subject is

70   James Berger, 'There's No Backhand To This', in Judith Greenberg, ed., *Trauma at
      Home: After 9/11* (Lincoln: University of Nebraska Press, 2003), 51–9.

produced, perhaps contemporary trauma criticism's exclusions reveal that there are some 'others' who are not even worthy of such colonization. In this light, the question of trauma criticism's exclusions and inclusions becomes both more pressing, yet increasingly complex. For to be included within trauma criticism's reach may be to become subject to its drive to construct an empathic listening subject and a subjectivity modelled on those narratives to which it attends. Yet those whose excessive otherness excludes them from trauma criticism's incorporative drives also find themselves beyond trauma criticism's empathic reach.

Trauma criticism has no greater claim to ethical purity than any other critical practice. Like any other intellectual endeavour, it is driven by a complex interweaving of scholarly, academic, political and psychical imperatives. Yet trauma criticism has emerged at a time when the capacity to sustain an awareness of ethical equivocalness in the West, at least, appears attenuated, and when the cultural mood, policies and analyses proffered by politicians and the media verge on Manicheanism. The rule of Manicheanism can be glimpsed, I think, in responses to 9/11. Nancy Miller, commenting on the 'Portraits of Grief' series run post 9/11 in the New York Times, remarked that the stories told in this series were always of fulfilment, happiness and kindness: 'I can't say I cried reading these portraits. On the contrary, I often experienced a powerful sense of disbelief [...]; was it possible that no one who died in the attack on the WTC was ever depressed [...] self-centred [...] without a passion [...] had a career that seemed stalled [...] or sometimes found life not worth living?'[71] Miller points to and critiques that Manicheanism which underpins the culture within which trauma theory has gained ground – a culture of pure innocence and pure evil and of 'the War against Evil'. As Berger has pointed out, in the contemporary West, the framing that follows on from the utter uncertainty produced by catastrophe names the time of that catastrophe as apocalyptic, and heralds a 'world said to be clarified and simplified – a struggle of good versus evil, civilization versus barbarianism [...]. Are you with us or against us'.[72]

71   Nancy K. Miller, 'Reporting the Disaster', in Greenberg, *Trauma at Home*, 39–47, 46.
72   Berger, 'There's No Backhand To This', 56.

Those of us involved in trauma studies, concerned, as we are, with the complex relationships between culture and history, are anything but helpless spectators/witnesses. As this essay has argued, the theories and approaches that we mobilize are implicated *in* politics and the mobilization of power. If trauma studies is to continue to mobilize the concept of witnessing to describe its *own* practices then that concept might best be deployed in the interests of developing a critical trauma studies sustained by an awareness of both ambiguity and the inevitability of ethical impurity.

Bibliography

Alexander, David, paper presented at the 'Trauma, Therapy and Representation' conference, University of Aberdeen, 11–13 April 2003.

American Psychiatric Association, *Diagnostic and Statistical Manual of Mental Disorders*, 4th edn (Washington, DC: American Psychiatric Association, 1994).

Antze, Paul, 'The Other Inside: Memory as Metaphor In Psychoanalysis', in Susannah Radstone and Katharine Hodgkin, eds, *Regimes of Memory* (New York and London: Routledge, 2003), 96–113.

Ball, Karyn, 'Unspeakable Differences, Obscene Pleasures: The Holocaust as an Object of Desire', *Women in German Yearbook* 19 (2003), 20–49.

Berger, James, 'There's No Backhand To This', in Judith Greenberg, ed., *Trauma at Home: After 9/11* (Lincoln: University of Nebraska Press, 2003), 51–9.

Broderick, Mick, and Antonio Traverso, eds, *Interrogating Trauma: Arts and Media Responses To Collective Suffering*, *Continuum* 24/1 (2010).

Caruth, Cathy, *Unclaimed Experience: Trauma, Narrative and History* (Baltimore and London: Johns Hopkins University Press, 1996).

——, ed., *Trauma: Explorations in Memory* (Baltimore and London: Johns Hopkins UP, 1995).

Chouliaraki, Lilie, *The Spectatorship of Suffering* (London: Sage, 2006).

Corbin, Alain, *The Lure of the Sea: The Discovery of the Seaside in the Western World 1750–1840*, trans. Jocelyn Phelps (London: Penguin, 1994).

Elsaesser, Thomas, 'Postmodernism as mourning work', *Screen* 42/2 (2001), 193–201.

Felman, Shoshana, and Dori Laub, *Testimony: Crises of Witnessing in Literature, Psychoanalysis and History* (New York and London: Routledge, 1992).

Fletcher, John, and Martin Stanton, eds, *Jean Laplanche: Seduction, Translation, Drives* (London: Institute of Contemporary Arts, 1992).

Garland, Caroline, *Understanding Trauma: A Psychoanalytic Approach*, Tavistock Clinic Series (London: Duckworth, 1998).

Herman, Judith, *Trauma and Recovery* (New York: Basic Books, 1992).

Hirsch, Joshua, *Afterimage: Films, Trauma, and the Holocaust* (Philadelphia: Temple University Press, 2004).

Kenny, Michael, 'Trauma, time, illness and culture: an anthropological approach to traumatic memory', in Paul Antze and Michael Lambek, eds, *Tense Past: Cultural Essays in Trauma and Memory* (New York and London: Routledge, 1996), 173–98.

LaCapra, Dominick, *Writing History, Writing Trauma* (Baltimore and London: Johns Hopkins University Press, 2001).

Laplanche, Jean, and J. B. Pontalis, *The Language of Psychoanalysis* (London: Karnac Books, 1988).

Leys, Ruth, *Trauma: A Genealogy* (Chicago: University of Chicago Press, 2000).

Miller, Nancy K., 'Reporting the Disaster', in Judith Greenberg, ed., *Trauma at Home: After 9/11* (Lincoln: University of Nebraska Press, 2003), 39–47.

Perera, Suvendrini, 'Torturous Dialogues: Geographies of trauma and spaces of exception', *Continuum* 24/1 (2010), 31–45.

Prager, Jeffrey, *Presenting The Past: Psychoanalysis and the Sociology of Remembering* (Cambridge, MA, and London: Harvard University Press, 1998).

Radstone, Susannah, 'Screening Trauma: Forrest Gump, Film and Memory', in Susannah Radstone, ed., *Memory and Methodology* (Oxford and New York: Berg, 2000), 79–107.

——, 'Social Bonds and Psychical Order: Testimonies', *Cultural Values* 5/1 (2001), 59–78.

——, 'Trauma and Screen Studies: opening the debate', *Screen* 42/2 (2001), 188–93.

Steedman, Carolyn, 'Enforced Narratives: Stories of another self', in Tess Cosslett, Celia Lury and Penny Summerfield, eds, *Feminism and Autobiography: Texts, Theories, Methods* (London and New York: Routledge, 2000), 25–39.

van der Kolk, Bessel A., Alexander C. McFarlane and Lars Weisaeth, eds, *Traumatic Stress: The Effects of Overwhelming Experience on Mind, Body and Society* (New York and London: Guilford Press, 1996).

van der Kolk, Bessel A., and Onno van Der Hart, 'Pierre Janet and the Breakdown of Adaptation in Psychological Trauma', *American Journal of Psychiatry* 146/12 (1989), 1530–40.

van der Kolk, Bessel A., and Onno van Der Hart, 'The Intrusive Past: The Flexibility of Memory and the Engraving of Trauma', in Cathy Caruth, ed., *Trauma: Explorations in Memory* (Baltimore: Johns Hopkins University Press, 1995), 158–82.

Walker, Janet, *Trauma Cinema: Documenting Incest and the Holocaust* (Berkeley, Los Angeles and London: California University Press, 1999).

——, 'Moving testimonies and the geography of suffering: Perils and fantasies of belonging after Katrina', *Continuum* 24/1 (2010), 47–64.

White, Hayden, 'The modernist event', in Vivian Sobchack, ed., *The Persistence of History: Cinema, Television and the Modern Event* (New York and London: Routledge, 1996), 17–38.

Whitehead, Anne, *Trauma Fiction* (Edinburgh: Edinburgh University Press, 2004).

MARÍA JESÚS MARTÍNEZ-ALFARO

Narrating the Holocaust and its Legacy: The Complexities of Identity, Trauma and Representation in Art Spiegelman's *Maus*

Narrativizing the Holocaust is something that raises both aesthetic and moral problems, for historians and not less so for literary writers. According to Hayden White, there is an 'inexpungeable relativity in every representation of historical phenomena'[1] and any event can be emplotted in a number of ways without violating established historical facts. However, tragedies of such magnitude as the Holocaust raise troubling questions as to the limits affecting the kind of story that can responsibly be told about them. As White puts it: '*Can* these events be responsibly emplotted in *any* of the modes, symbols, plot types, and genres our culture provides for "making sense" of such extreme events in our past?'[2] White's answer to this question highlights the difficulty of setting absolute limits between what is acceptable in this context and what is not. As he points out, although a comic emplotment of the history of the Third Reich could be dismissed from the list of adequate narratives by claiming that it is not faithful to the facts – since there is nothing comic about the Holocaust – rejecting such a possibility would amount to embracing a literary decorum of sorts, based on the 'rule that stipulates that a serious theme – such as mass murder or genocide – demands a noble genre – such as epic or tragedy – for its proper representation.'[3] However, a proper representation is still

---

1   Hayden White, 'Historical Emplotment and the Problem of Truth', in Saul Friedlander, ed., *Probing the Limits of Representation. Nazism and the 'Final Solution'* (Cambridge, MA: Harvard University Press, 1992), 37.
2   *Ibid.*, (emphasis in the original).
3   *Ibid.*, 41.

achieved in certain texts where this notion of decorum is subverted, as White acknowledges when he explicitly refers to Art Spiegelman's *Maus* as putting forward

> a particularly ironic and bewildered view of the Holocaust, but it is at the same time one of the most moving narratives of it that I know [...]. It assimilates the events of the Holocaust to the conventions of comic book representation, and in this absurd mixture of a 'low' genre with events of the most momentous significance, *Maus* manages to raise all the crucial issues regarding 'the limits of representation' in general.[4]

White's words belong in an essay entitled 'Historical Emplotment and the Problem of Truth', which focuses on historical writing. My quoting from it here, as well as White's reflections on *Maus* in this context, point to the difficulty of establishing a clear-cut boundary between history and fiction when dealing with a large number of Holocaust texts, which recurrently raise similar problems of taxonomy. *Maus* is no exception in this respect.

Art Spiegelman's *Maus: A Survivor's Tale* was originally published in serialized form (between 1980 and 1991) in successive issues of *Raw*, an avant-garde comic magazine edited by Spiegelman and his wife, Françoise Mouly. It uses hybrid characters – human bodies with animal heads – in order to depict the life and times of Vladek Spiegelman, the author's father and a survivor of Auschwitz. This initially serialized story was later published in two volumes: *Maus I* (1986) tracks the artist's father from the thriving of Jewish culture in pre-war Poland to the gates of Auschwitz, and *Maus II* (1991) finds the old man sicker and crankier as he continues to tell Artie (the author's persona in the book) his story of survival in Auschwitz and Dachau, and, finally, the reunion with his wife Anja after liberation. Wondering whether it was right to use his family's tragic past for his book, Artie appears in this second volume as prey to guilt and remorse over the critical and commercial success of *Maus I*.

Spiegelman's work was classified as 'fiction' on the best-seller list of the *New York Times Book Review*. This led the author to write a letter to the *Times* in which he asked *Maus* to be removed from the fiction list, arguing

4   *Ibid.*, 41–2.

that literature implies a serious aesthetic project, not necessarily fiction. To some extent, one may understand the *Times*'s decision to categorize *Maus* as fiction given the author's choice to depict various groups of people as animals: Jews are mice, Germans are cats, Poles are pigs, North-Americans are dogs, Swedes are reindeer, French are frogs, and Gypsies are bees/moths. On the other hand, it is also true that there is a huge amount of research behind the book, which contains a wide variety of materials – including maps, graphics and real photographs – and which is, after all, an unconventional history that combines biography (the father's) and autobiography (the son's). Two distinct but intertwined narratives unfold in *Maus*: a) a wartime narrative taking place in the late 1930s and early 1940s, which comprises Vladek's story of suffering and survival in the past, and b) the complicated relationship of Artie with his father in the present, which the reader has access to as the son regularly visits and interviews Vladek in order to write a comic book about the old man's experiences shortly before, during and immediately after the war. Consequently, the vignettes alternate the past and the present, 'then' and 'now', the latter including self-referential depictions of Artie in the act of drawing and also his doubts about the aesthetically and ethically appropriate ways of presenting his subject. *Maus* emerges in this way as the testimony of a real survivor of the Nazi genocide transmitted by his artist son, who can thus be said to bear witness to the problematics of Holocaust representation and also to the fact that survivors' descendants cannot extricate themselves from the traumatic experiences gone through by their parents.

The interconnection between the father's past in Eastern Europe and his life as well as that of his son in modern-day New York becomes apparent from the very beginning. The subtitle of *Maus I* is *My Father Bleeds History*, thus suggesting a wound that is both personal and historical. No matter how long ago it was inflicted, the wound still bleeds. It bleeds into the present, spilling suffering all over and creating ripple effects that seep through the years and through generations. As Spiegelman himself points out: 'for a child a father can be a very threatening figure, and the fact that

he carried so much pain with him, well, that spilled over.'⁵ Or, as he said in
a National Public Radio interview about being a child of survivors: 'You
grow up as a survivor's kid – it seems to be a common denominator – that
as a kid, you're playing baseball or whatever and you break a window and
then your mother or father says, "Ach, for this I survived?" And that's a
heavy load for breaking a window with a baseball – or less.'⁶

Maus opens with a two-page preface of sorts which significantly illustrates Spiegelman's words in the quotations above. The events portrayed in
these vignettes – the only part of the book in which Artie appears as a child
in intercourse with his father – take place in 1958, in Rego Park, Queens,
where the Spiegelmans settled after the war. The child Artie is playing
with friends when he breaks his roller skate. His friends run along, leaving
him behind, and he walks back home in tears. On hearing of the incident,
Vladek tells his son: 'Your friends? ... If you lock them together in a room
with no food for a week ... then you could see what it is, friends!'⁷ This
short exchange is enough for the reader to see Artie as someone growing
up in the shadow of the Holocaust, thus illustrating the typical plight of
survivors' descendants which Marianne Hirsch explains in the light of what
she calls 'postmemory'. She uses the term to describe the relationship of
survivors' children to the events that inhabit their parents' memories, and
which are grasped only indirectly by the second generation. Postmemory
'is distinguished from memory by generational distance and from history

5   Quoted in Michael G. Levine, The Belated Witness. Literature, Testimony, and the
     Question of Holocaust Survival (Stanford: Stanford University Press, 2006), 23.
6   Quoted in Michael E. Staub, 'The Shoah Goes On and On: Remembrance and
     Representation in Art Spiegelman's Maus', MELUS 20/3 (1995), 33–46, 40.
7   Art Spiegelman, The Complete Maus (London: Penguin, 2003), 6 (emphasis in the
     original). All quotations from Maus are taken from The Complete Maus, which opens
     with the two-page preface mentioned above and brings together Maus. A Survivor's
     Tale I: My Father Bleeds History and Maus. A Survivor's Tale II: And Here My Troubles
     Began. The information after each quotation indicates the volume (Maus I or Maus
     II) and the page. It should be noted in this respect that pagination is consecutive in
     The Complete Maus, that is, it does not begin anew in the second volume.

by deep personal connection.'[8] Resorting to Kaja Silverman's concept of 'heteropathic identification' as a model for the second generation seeking resolution with respect to their parents' (or guardians') traumas, Hirsch emphasizes that being responsive to other people's traumas is productive only if the experience and feelings of the other are not subsumed in an 'appropriative identification' in which 'the viewer can too easily become a surrogate victim.'[9] Thus, the second generation must negotiate their implication in their parents' traumas with a distance that leaves room for empathy.[10] In the case of second-generation writers, this endeavour tends to produce what Hirsch defines as a 'hybridised narrative', whose success depends on the author's ability to claim the Holocaust without claiming to have experienced it.[11]

That the past of Artie's parents has left its indelible mark on the son's life becomes more than evident throughout the narrative, the two-page preface referred to earlier being just a prologue to what is to come. From his very birth, Artie's life has been shadowed by his elder brother, Richieu, who did not survive the war. He died at the hands of his aunt Tosha, who poisoned herself, Richieu and her two children rather than be sent to the camps. On the frontispiece of the second volume we can see the picture of a child that we assume is Richieu. The caption above the picture reads 'For Richieu', and below it, 'And for Nadja', who is Art Spiegelman's daughter.

8   Marianne Hirsch, 'Family Pictures: *Maus*, Mourning, and Post-Memory', *Discourse* 15/2 (1992–3), 3–29, 8.

9   Marianne Hirsch, 'Projected Memory: Holocaust Photographs in Personal and Public Fantasy', in Mieke Bal, Jonathan Crewe and Leo Spitzer, eds, *Acts of Memory: Cultural Recall in the Present* (Hanover: Dartmouth University Press, 1999), 2–23, 17.

10   Empathy as a form of virtual, not vicarious, experience is also at the core of Dominick LaCapra's 'empathic unsettlement'. LaCapra himself relates his notion of 'empathic unsettlement' to Silverman's 'heteropathic identification' as both concepts are grounded on the premise that 'emotional response comes with respect for the other and the realization that the experience of the other is not one's own.' Dominick LaCapra, *Writing History, Writing Trauma* (Baltimore and London: Johns Hopkins University Press, 2001), 40.

11   Hirsch, 'Projected Memory', 16.

The coupling of the dead brother and the living daughter throws light on Spiegelman's claiming his place in a family that lost much in the past but some of whose members survived, though maimed, to go on living and create new life. There is a past full of losses, represented by Richieu, but there is also a present and a future, represented by Nadja.

Talking to his wife Françoise at the beginning of the second volume, Artie refers to his sibling rivalry with his 'ghost' brother. As he points out, Richieu was 'mainly a large blurry photograph hanging in my parent's bedroom ... The photo never threw tantrums or got in any kind of trouble. It was an ideal kid, and *I* was a pain in the ass. I couldn't compete. They didn't *talk* about Richieu, but that photo was a kind of *reproach*. *He*'d have become a *doctor*, and married a wealthy Jewish girl ... The creep' (II, 175, emphasis in the original). On the whole, Artie has always felt unable to compete with his father, too. As he himself admits, no matter what his professional and even personal achievements are, they will never be enough. 'No matter what I accomplish,' he complains to his psychiatrist in Volume II, 'it doesn't seem like much compared to surviving Auschwitz' (II, 204). And so, he tells his wife that, insane as it may sound, he somehow wishes he had been in Auschwitz with his parents (II, 176). It is this lack of first-hand experience of the pogroms, the war and the camps that makes him feel estranged from his own family. Significantly, Vladek is not portrayed as a survivor who needs to talk about the past; it is rather the son, Artie, who needs to listen. By listening to his father's story and 'translating' it into a comic book afterwards, Artie finds a way of getting engaged with his family's past, coping with this feeling of estrangement while maintaining the distance required by heteropathic identification: his parents' traumas are not his own, he does not lay claim to them, but he does lay claim to their after-effects.

The interconnection between the past and the present is revealed not only through words, but also through images. As has been pointed out, the vignettes alternate between the time of Vladek's story and the time of its narration, but the reader should pay attention not only to what happens within each vignette, each frame, but also to what happens between the frames. As Spiegelman observes, comics are 'a gutter medium; that is, it's what takes place in the gutters between the panels that activates the medium.'[12] If, as the subtitle of Volume I states, Vladek 'bleeds history', the past can also be said to bleed into the present through the very medium of vision. The past and the present are superimposed on some occasions, but there is also what Levine refers to as 'the hemorrhaging of *visual images*, which literally burst out of their pictorial frames'.[13] Thus, for instance, in the third chapter of *Maus I* Vladek tells Artie about his circumstances in 1939, when he became a prisoner of war. Artie is on the floor of his father's home in Queens, pencil in hand, but panels are disposed as if Artie's body was bridging decades, overlapping and joining a panel depicting 1939 and the next panel, depicting his conversation with Vladek in the present (I, 47). Later on, we will see Vladek beginning to describe the operation of the gas chambers in Auschwitz. Father and son are sitting together, the father holds a cup of tea in his hand, while Artie, as usual, is smoking. In the vignette below there appears one of the chimneys at the concentration camp, but the top of the chimney intrudes into the panel above and so part of it appears between father and son to the point that the smoke from the cigarette Artie is smoking almost seems to emerge from the top of the chimney (II, 229). Repeatedly, the past and the present break into one another in this very visual way, but there are also vignettes which literally spill over. Vladek drops his pills while he is talking to his son about the past and they fall not only onto the table but also outside the frame (I, 32). Or, on other occasion, Vladek shows Artie the pictures of family members, many of whom did not survive the Holocaust. The photographs are taken out of a box and then thrown onto the floor, laying in a heap which will not stay in place: their size is maximized in a kind of close-up, they surround father and son, and they flow over the bottom part of the frame, invading the page margins (II, 275). It is as if frames could not hold the story that is being told. As Vladek tells Artie at the very beginning: 'It would take *many* books, my life, and no one wants anyway to hear such stories' (I, 14, emphasis in the original).[14] Later on, faced with obvious

---

12   Quoted in Levine, *The Belated Witness*, 25.

13   *Ibid.*, 23 (emphasis in the original).

14   Thomas Doherty refers to the unobtrusive modulation of Vladek's voice as Spiegelman's 'most impressive literary achievement.' Devoid of 'oratorial flourish

problems of representation, Artie complains to his wife: 'There's so much
I'll never be able to understand or visualize. I mean, reality is too complex
for comics ... so much has to be left out or distorted' (II, 176). No representation can contain the Holocaust, which is too traumatic to be put in
words or images. This is a story that resists being contained by frames, as
is suggested by vignettes spilling over; and also a story that has no end and
whose effects are felt in the present, as is highlighted by vignettes breaking
into one another or superimposing different temporal planes.

Interestingly, the story that is told is framed by a conspicuous absence,
the absence of the mother, Anja, missing entirely except through her husband's and son's memories. In Vladek's story, Anja appears as a loving though
weak woman, who survives mainly thanks to her husband's resourcefulness
and unflinching protection. Before getting married, Vladek discovers her
propensity to nervous disorders when he sees the pills she takes inside a
wardrobe in Anja's bedroom. Then, she has a depression after the birth
of their first son, Richieu, which requires a short period of internment.
Although Anja survives Birkenau while Vladek is sent to Auschwitz and
the couple is miraculously reunited after the war, Anja will never overcome
the extreme experiences and the suffering she went through. Anja Spiegelman committed suicide in May 1968, shortly after her son Art, then twenty
years old, returned home after a brief but intense nervous breakdown. She
left no note.

Anja kept a diary during the first stages of the war and so, in *Maus*, she
is several times depicted in the process of writing. Although this diary was
lost, Anja rewrote what she remembered after the war and kept a second
diary which Artie insistently asks his father to search for in the course of the
interviews. Vladek recurrently finds excuses and changes subject whenever
the question of Anja's notebooks comes up, but he eventually confesses
to his son that he burned them in a fit of anger and despair after his wife's
suicide. He tells Artie that he never read them, although he remembers
Anja saying that one of the reasons for writing them was that she hoped

or self-pity', this voice is infused with 'the music of second-language English and
Yiddish syntax.' Thomas Doherty, 'Art Spiegelman's *Maus*: Graphic Art and the
Holocaust', *American Literature* 68/1 (1996), 69–84, 80.

her son would be interested in her story when he grew up. Artie angrily responds to his father with a 'God damn you! You – you murderer! How the hell could you do such a thing!' (I, 161). And so, Anja's diaries and Anja herself, her story, become a very much present absence throughout the narrative, the silence imposed on her by the burning of her notebooks being regarded as a second death.

Just as the story told in *Maus* speaks not only through the frames but also through what happens between the frames, it can equally be said to speak not only through what is told but also through the silences it contains. In fact, one of the author's challenges is not to erase this silence, that of the mother in particular and that of those who died in the Holocaust in general. As Nancy Miller puts it, we should 'understand [...] the question of Anja as that which will forever escape representation and at the same time require it.'[15] For each story that is told there are many that have been lost, for each thing that can be portrayed about Holocaust experience and Holocaust trauma, there are many that are unavoidably left out. Anja's radical silence and Vladek's selective gaps incorporate into *Maus* what Sara R. Horowitz refers to as 'the trope of muteness' – predominant in Holocaust narratives of all sorts – and the related motif of the untold or truncated story. As she puts it:

> Muteness expresses not only the difficulty in saying anything meaningful about the Holocaust, it also comes to represent something essential about the nature of the event itself. The radical negativity of the Holocaust ruptures the fabric of history and memory, emptying both narrative and life of meaning. [...] For this reason, Holocaust literature enacts a kind of muteness in the very midst of an ongoing narrative. The absent, truncated, incomplete telling helps unfold the ambivalences and ambiguities that shape not only the way we read Holocaust literature but also the way we think about the Holocaust itself.[16]

15   Nancy K. Miller, 'Cartoons of the Self. Portrait of the Artist as a Young Murderer. Art Spiegelman's *Maus*', in Deborah R. Geis, ed., *Considering Maus: Approaches to Art Spiegelman's 'Survivor's Tale' of the Holocaust* (Tuscaloosa: University of Alabama Press, 2003), 44–62, 49.
16   Sara R. Horowitz, *Voicing the Void. Muteness and Memory in Holocaust Fiction* (New York: State University of New York Press, 1997), 38–9.

Two years after his mother's suicide, Art Spiegelman published a short comic connected with this tragic event in his life – 'Prisoner on the Hell Planet: A Case History' – which is interestingly included in *Maus*. Thus, on arriving at his father's home one day, Vladek's second wife Mala tells Artie that his father will not see him as he is very much upset after reading 'Prisoner on the Hell Planet'. A friend of Mala gave her a copy of the book in which it was published, and although she did not show it to Vladek then and kept it hidden, he somehow found it by chance. As Artie is depicted holding the book in the last panel of one page, the four following pages reproduce it, Artie's hand still visible in one of the page's pitch black margins. These four pages are disruptive in many respects. Not only do they break the chronological development of the story, but they also introduce a marked contrast with the rest of the work. 'Prisoner' uses human figures instead of humanized animals, the style is highly expressionistic and it portrays past events that Artie did actually witness, thus presenting his mother (for the first and last time) through his eyes, not through Vladek's eyes. As Spiegelman himself has explained: 'it's important in these pages to think of them as complete pages. In the book there's a black border around the whole page which actually bleeds off the page. It acts as a funereal border. When the book is closed, on the edges you actually see that as a separate section inside the book.'[17] Thus, the author wants us to view this text-within-the-text as a discrete, self-contained subsection of *Maus*. Paradoxically, though, he uses the same 'bleeding' metaphor in the quotation above as in *My Father Bleeds History* and he does so in order to refer to the rendering of this part of his mother's story, a traumatic event that soaks through and pervasively invades the narrative. If this bleeding can figuratively be connected with the wounds of trauma, this time, however, it is a personal trauma the author is dealing with, one which, unlike the Holocaust, he has first-hand experience of, one he can lay claim to. In line with this, Sheng-Mei Ma argues that the stylistic contrast between 'Prisoner' and the rest of the book reveals the diametrically opposed approaches adopted by the author when it comes to dealing with personal tragedy and

---

17   Quoted in Levine, *The Belated Witness*, 42.

mass destruction: it is as if the intense agony ensuing from the suicide of one's mother had to be articulated in its full horridness, while Holocaust mass destruction is so overwhelming, so collectively acknowledged and so pervasively present in our culture that it can be rendered much more telegraphically, in the austere and simple way of the crude comic strip panels which characterize *Maus*.[18]

Despite these different approaches, though, there is a clear connection between both traumas, which is also represented visually. At the beginning of 'Prisoner', Artie is informed of his mother's suicide by a doctor wearing a conspicuous Hitler's moustache. All throughout, Artie is depicted in a black and white striped uniform, typical of a prisoner (on the Hell Planet) but, obviously, also strikingly similar to the clothes worn by camp inmates. As the Spiegelmans are visited by friends willing to present their condolences, Artie guesses what some of them think and so one bubble reads 'It's his fault, the punk!', referring to Artie being blamed for and also feeling guilty about his mother's death. As he searches for a reason, contradictory thoughts are conveyed by captions that crowd around the character's head. One of them reads 'menopausal depression', while another one – 'Hitler did it!' – appears close to a heap of dead bodies and a forearm with a tattooed number (I, 106). It is telling, in this respect, that it was the trauma of his mother's suicide that first prompted Spiegelman to engage explicitly with the related trauma of the Holocaust.

'Prisoner' should also be regarded as one of the many strategies that Spiegelman resorts to in order to question the animal imagery in *Maus*. The epigraph to *Maus I* provides a first explanation for Spiegelman's aesthetic choices and his use of animal images.[19] It reproduces a passage from Hitler's inflammatory speech: 'The Jews are undoubtedly a race, but they are

---

18 Sheng-Mei Ma, 'Mourning with the (as a) Jew: Metaphor, Ethnicity, and the Holocaust in Art Spiegelman's *Maus*', *Studies in American-Jewish Literature* 16 (1997), 115–29, 116.

19 See Thomas Doherty for an insightful discussion of the most relevant intertexts when it comes to analysing Spiegelman's artistic style: the two graphic media whose images make up the visual memory of the twelve-year Reich – cartoons and cinema – and the animation legacy of US popular culture.

not human.' Fascist thought simplified something as complex as identity
and then equated this simplification with disease-carrying vermin. *Maus*,
which means mouse in German, *relies on* this fabrication as it casts humans
as animals based on ethnic difference, but the author also *deconstructs* such
a representation. At first, it is far from clear whether mice are mice because
they are so, in essence so, or because they see themselves as such, or because
that is the way they are seen.[20] Then the reader realizes that Spiegelman's
stylistic choices serve precisely as a vehicle for dealing with the complexities of ethnic categories. As Michael E. Staub points out:

> The choice to turn people into animals, as the Hitler quote that opens the first volume
> [...] makes clear, can be read as a straightforward metaphor for the dehumanization
> of victims that allows genocide to occur. But it also points up the obverse: that it was
> the Nazis who acted like animals. Simultaneously, *Maus*'s reliance on increasingly
> banal associations – especially in the second volume where French frogs, Swedish
> reindeer and Gypsy moths all make an appearance – works to expose the hollowness
> of 'racial' theories of all kinds. Ultimately *Maus* illustrates (literally) how irresponsible
> the assignment of 'race' is as a method for disaggregating people, and how utterly
> destructive it has been.
>
> Yet at the same time, and held in tension with this point, *Maus* also takes seriously
> the way marginalized peoples not only often rely on group identity to survive, but
> also have every right to celebrate their specialness and differences from the dominant
> culture. But – and this is the key issue – *Maus* suggests that that identity can never
> be understood as self-evident.[21]

Maus makes the reader reflect on the construction of Jewishness. There is
no denying that the Holocaust has become a cornerstone of Jewish identity
and, precisely for that reason, the passing of the first generation (that of
Holocaust survivors) and other factors like assimilation and intermarriage

20   As Spiegelman reflects, 'one thing that fascinated me, and it was a horrible fascination
     that I suspect I share with many non-religious Jews, was the fact that the people sent
     to their slaughter as Jews didn't necessarily identify themselves as/with Jews; it was up
     to the Nazis to decide who was a Jew. As Sartre pointed out in *Anti-Semite and Jew*,
     a Jew is someone whom others call a Jew.' Art Spiegelman, *Comix, Essays, Graphics,
     and Scraps: From MAUS to Now to MAUS to Now* (New York: Raw, 1998), 15.
21   Staub, 'The Shoah Goes On and On', 37–8.

can be seen as threatening to severe the community ties to a most important source of identity. Thus, new ways of connecting with the Holocaust and establishing identity links have been sought for. Amy Hungerford refers to them as 'technologies of connection,' which include movies, books, classes, and museums that tell the Holocaust story, as well as the separate efforts of the Yale's Fortunoff Archive and of director Steven Spielberg to collect videotaped testimonies of survivors. As these new connections 'remain independent of the life of individual survivors for their future existence, they promise to remain available to all for all time.'[22]

We live in the post-Holocaust era and what the many representations of the Holocaust seem to convey is that it affects us all. The Holocaust has become a global phenomenon, and so, many representations of it are aimed at the reader/viewer getting closer – not so much, or not only, intellectually, but also emotionally – to the events and to those that went through it. When it comes to *Maus*, the first impression may be that the hybrid characters, their animal faces, have an estranging effect on the reader, creating a distance between them and us. Yet one should also consider the effects of Spiegelman's *minimalist* style. In 'Prisoner on the Hell Planet' characters are human, but the style is so intense, so excessive, that these four pages emerge as a private nightmare with which the reader may find it more difficult to connect than with the rest of the book. There, we are not really dealing with mice, cats, pigs, dogs, etc., but with schematic animals, especially schematic mice. Ian Johnston draws on Scott McCloud to explain how these schematic characters affect the reader's rapport with them and their story:

> For the most part all we see of the mouse is the outline of a head, the eyes and the mouth (and occasionally the tail). We are confronting the cartoon outline of an animal. [...] Why is this important? To get a sense of this I'd like to borrow an idea from Scott McCloud's book *Understanding Comics*. He talks about a spectrum of art from the fully subjective to the fully objective. What he means is that an image can insist upon its factual reality apart from us (i.e., invite us to treat it objectively) or it can invite us to identify with the image (i.e., draw us into the subjective experience

---

22   Amy Hungerford, *The Holocaust of Texts. Genocide, Literature, and Personification* (Chicago and London: University of Chicago Press, 2003), 78

of being inside the image). McCloud argues that the simpler and more schematic
the representation of an image, the more subjective it becomes and, thus, the more
easily and quickly we can identify with it.[23]

Although Johnston admits that the schematic portrayal of faces is often a
common technique of comic books, he emphasizes that the experience of
reading Spiegelman's *Maus* puts the reader under a subtle and continuing
artistic pressure to place him/herself in the position of the mice. This agrees
with the implications of Spiegelman comparing the mouse heads with the
empty look of the classic US comic book character Little Orphan Annie
(and her blank eyeballs) and his figuratively referring to both as 'a screen
the reader can project on.'[24]

Moreover, precisely because the Holocaust is still very much present
in our culture, and because the present as post-Holocaust age can be said to
be defined by the past, characters in *Maus* who have their identities determined by Holocaust events remain unchanged in the vignettes depicting
present-day North America. In the two-page prologue referred to earlier
– telling about an incident that took place in Rego Park, New York, in the
late 1950s – a New Yorker cycling in the park where Artie and his friends
are playing is drawn with a dog's head, while the children and Vladek are
mice. At this stage, the reader does not know yet about the animal identity
of each group, but it soon becomes clear that the identities defined by the
role of each ethnic group in the war and the Holocaust remain unaltered
in the present. In other words, present-day identities still go back to the
Holocaust. This is the case not only for mice/Jews, and, for that matter, this
is not only the case for characters/people. Thus, Vladek spends his holidays
in the *Catskill* Mountains of Upstate New York, and so, place names can
also be said to bear, in the present, a connection with the Holocaust past.
As Hungerford explains regarding this point, the 'technologies of connection' we see in *Maus* convey the message that 'all important aspects of the
present take their identity from the past event'.[25]

23   Ian Johnston, 'On Spiegelman's *Maus I* and *II*, <http://records.viu.ca/~johnstoi/
      introser/maus.htm> accessed 3 December 2010.
24   Spiegelman, *Comix, Essays, Graphics, and Scraps*, 17.
25   Hungerford, *The Holocaust of Texts*, 86.

Interesting too is the case of Artie's wife, Françoise, who is a French Gentile but who converted to Judaism before marrying. At the beginning of Volume II, Artie is depicted contemplating different possibilities as he does not know how to draw her in his comic book: as a frog, because she is French, as a mouse, because she is a Jew, etc. Françoise is a mouse, but not because of her religious commitment to Judaism (she admits that she converted only to make Vladek happy), but because in being connected by marriage with Artie, a survivor's son, she is also connected with the Holocaust. This is also why Artie is a mouse. Art Spiegelman is far from being very Jewish in religion, in art, in marriage, or in any other matter. With the exception of *Maus*, his works do not specially deal with the subject of Jewishness at all, the author being a product of the 1960s counterculture movement in North America, married to a Frenchwoman. That his religious beliefs are problematically related to his Jewish inheritance is made clear when, in 'Prisoner on the Hell Planet', he depicts himself reading from *The Tibetan Book of the Dead* – instead of reciting the *Kaddish*, the traditional Jewish mourning prayer – during his mother's funeral. And in spite of all this, Artie the character is, unmistakably, a mouse.

The second chapter in Volume II opens with Artie wearing a mouse mask that hides a human face. He is sitting at his drawing table, in the midst of a writer's block, overwhelmed and full of doubts on account of the success of *Maus I*. For the first time in *Maus*, words are not written in capital letters but in lower case, as if to match the way Artie feels. A reporter wearing a dog's mask asks him, microphone in hand, about the message he wanted his work to convey. Another reporter, wearing a cat's mask, angrily remarks that *Maus* may cause feelings of guilt in German readers, who have already had enough of the burden of the past. Still another character proposes a business deal to Artie, who receives an offer to turn *Maus* into a TV special or movie, as well as another offer to mass-produce the vest Artie always wears in the book.[26] These vignettes constitute just

26　This points to just another side of the Holocaust: its having become part of the consumerist market. Nazism enjoys an enormous selling potential, as Susan Sontag already made clear and somehow advanced in her 1975 essay 'Fascinating Fascism' [republished as: Susan Sontag, 'Fascinating Fascism', in *Under the Sign of Saturn* (New York:

one example of the several instances in which characters in *Maus* appear
wearing masks. The various uses of masks in Spiegelman's work are open
to manifold interpretations, one of them being the self-constructedness
of ethnicity. According to Werner Sollors,

> ethnicity is not so much an ancient and deep-seated force surviving from the histori-
> cal past, but rather the modern and modernizing feature of a contrasting strategy
> that may be shared far beyond the boundaries within which it is claimed. It marks
> an acquired modern sense of belonging that replaces visible, concrete communi-
> ties whose kinship symbolism ethnicity may yet mobilize in order to appear more
> natural. The trick that it passes itself off as blood, as 'thicker than water', should
> not mislead interpreters to take it at face value. It is not a thing but a process and it
> requires constant detective work from readers, not a settling on a fixed encyclopedia
> of supposed cultural essentials.[27]

Masks in *Maus* are often clues for the reader to carry out such detective
work.

In order to cope with his troubling feelings and his writer's block,
Artie decides to visit his psychiatrist, Paul Pavel, who is, like his father, a
survivor. At this stage in the narrative, Artie has informed the reader that
Vladek died of congestive heart failure four and a half years earlier. The
son's interviews to the father were completed before, and Vladek's story is
recorded, but Artie still has to finish his comic book. Curiously, Paul Pavel
is also wearing a mouse mask that covers a human face, like Artie, but his is
a mask that makes him look very much like Vladek. Artie feels sunk – he
is literally diminished in size, like the letters in captions and bubbles – due
to the weight of what he still has to tell in his book, but also on account of
all the commercial fuss brought about by *Maus I*. He discusses with Pavel

Farrar, Straus and Giroux, 1980), 73–105]. Among other things, the Holocaust is
much of a business nowadays and *Maus* critically reflects on the commercialization
of the *Shoah* in contemporary society. At the same time, Spiegelman has also participated himself in this commodification of the Holocaust: the serialized issues in
Raw generated a printed book, a CD ROM package, a museum exhibition, and a
lot of interviews and publicity.

27   Werner Sollors, 'Introduction. The Invention of Ethnicity', in Werner Sollors, ed., *The
Invention of Ethnicity* (New York: Oxford University Press, 1991), ix–xx, xiv–xv.

some of the problems related to his work and also talks about his complex relationship with his father. When Artie explains that he always felt inferior when faced with Vladek's great feat of survival, Pavel remarks: 'But you weren't in Auschwitz, you were in Rego Park.' And yet, he goes on: 'Maybe your father needed to show he was always right – that he could always *survive* – because he felt *guilty* about surviving. And he took his guilt out on *you*, where it was safe ... on the *real* survivor' (II, 204, emphasis in the original). These words lead us to think of the work's subtitle – *A Survivor's Tale* – in a new light. The survivor of the title emerges now as possibly referring not only to the father, but also to the son.[28] However, the view of Artie as a survivor is both put forward *and* questioned in this exchange between the character and his psychiatrist. As Pavel says, Artie was not in Auschwitz, but in Rego Park. Moreover, although Pavel theorizes that Vladek might be suffering from survivor's guilt, when asked by Artie if he himself felt any guilt about surviving the camps, Pavel answers: 'No ... just sadness' (II, 204). Be it as it may, Artie leaves Pavel feeling well again. From one vignette to the next we see him regaining the size of an adult as he walks back home. We assume also that his writer's block is over, as the following pages resume the narrative of his father's story. Once again, words are written in capitals.

Among the 'technologies of connection' dealt with by Amy Hungerford, special attention is paid to 'the belief in specifically intergenerational transmission of trauma [as] a powerful technology for recruitment of Jewish identity'.[29] Artie's mask is somehow related to a feeling of inauthenticity, as if the passing of time, his father's death, and the commercial success of his work had disturbed or weakened his Jewish identity. This is based, as

28 Volume II's subtitle – *And Here My Troubles Began* – already advances this merging of father and son, as the possessive 'my' may well refer to both. *Maus I* closes with Vladek's arrival at Auschwitz, so Volume II covers the hardest part of his story: his stay first in Auschwitz and then in Dachau after being separated from Anja. Vladek uses this sentence himself but, given the fact that we find Artie in the midst of a crisis at the start of the second volume, the sentence may refer to him as well as to his father.

29 Hungerford, *The Holocaust of Texts*, 92.

explained earlier, on his connection with the Holocaust and represented in the story by his organic mouse head. If, as Sollors puts it in the quotation above, ethnicity can be said to be not a thing but a process, this process may well go through different stages. The strategies to attain what Sollors refers to as a modern sense of belonging may not be themselves authentic – given the fact that there is much of constructedness about ethnicity – but *they must make one feel so*, that is, they must make one feel authentic. Thus, the session with Pavel works well with Artie because what he needs at this critical moment is not to close the chapter of the family's Holocaust past, but to reinforce his own connection with it.

Critics like Dominick LaCapra forcefully warn against the conflation of certain key concepts and subject positions in the field of trauma theory in general and Holocaust trauma in particular. Thus, LaCapra argues that although there is an important sense in which the after-effects of extreme traumatic events like the Holocaust may be said to affect practically every-body, the indiscriminate generalization of the category of survivor has the effect of obscuring crucial historical distinctions.[30] Being affected by the Holocaust does not automatically turn one into a survivor or a victim. From this perspective, then, Artie is not a survivor. On the other hand, an author as relevant in the field of Holocaust studies as Elie Wiesel is surely voicing a widespread opinion when he asserts: 'No Jew can be fully Jewish today, can be fully a man today, without being a part of the Holo-caust. All Jews are survivors. They have all been inside the whirlwind of the Holocaust, even those born afterwards, even those who heard its echoes in distant lands.'[31]

In sum, what Artie is or is not in this respect is a debatable question, but what is relevant here is the fact that Pavel saying that he is a survivor – his arguing that Vladek transferred his guilt on him and, by extension, his traumas, too – has the effect of reinforcing Artie's connection with the

---

30   LaCapra, *Writing History, Writing Trauma*, xi.
31   Quoted in Alan L. Berger, 'Bearing Witness: Theological Implications of Second-Generation Literature in America', in Efraim Sicher, ed., *Breaking Crystal. Writing and Memory after Auschwitz* (Urbana and Chicago: University of Illinois Press, 1998), 252–75, 253.

Holocaust. His link with it thus re-established/strengthened, he can go on writing about it, which will in turn reinforce the said link even further.[32] On the one hand, the effect of Pavel's words may seem to collapse the crucial distinctions that LaCapra insists should be maintained. On the other, Spiegelman self-consciously problematizes all these issues and, despite all ambiguities, or rather on account of them, the author can equally be said to keep the required distance with something – the Holocaust, Holocaust trauma, ethnic identity – which is presented (and which the reader is intended to perceive) as always open to manipulation.

This possibility of manipulation is precisely what the third and last real picture inserted in *Maus* suggests.[33] When, after his liberation from the camps, Vladek discovered the whereabouts of Anja, he sent her a picture of him to show that he had not died. In one vignette, we see Anja holding the picture and expressing her surprise and happiness as she finds out that Vladek is alive and well. In the following vignette, the real picture – slightly slanted, as if refusing to stay within the panel's frame – is reproduced. On the one hand, the picture is authentic and, as Anja's words emphasize, it unquestionably proved that Vladek had survived the camps. On the other

32 'The wish to forget prolongs the exile, and the secret of redemption is to be found in remembrance.' This sentence – attributed to the Ba'al Shem Tov, mystic and founder of the Hassidic movement – reflects the relevance of memory in the Hebrew tradition and cosmovision. The task of bearing witness is a normative element of Jewish existence, which accounts for views such as the one put forward by Alan L. Berger when he argues that, although in *Maus* Art does not embrace 'traditional Jewish narrative as constituting his identity [...] the survivor father and his son express themselves as Jews by sharing the father's Holocaust story' (Berger, 'Bearing Witness', 262). Thus, there can be said to be something unmistakably Jewish in the author's decision to embrace the covenant of bearing witness by listening to Vladek's testimony and then transmitting it. It can equally be argued, though, that if bearing witness somehow amounts to Art expressing himself as a Jew, then this Jewishness may not be the cause of his fulfilled duty as a witness to the Holocaust past. One can also approach it the other way round: his Jewishness is *constructed* by his role as listener and writer.

33 The three real photographs in *Maus* are: 1) that of Art and his mother – taken during a holiday in Trojan Lake, New York, in 1958, when Art was ten – included at the beginning of 'Prisoner on the Hell Planet', in Volume I; 2) that of Richieu, on the frontispiece of Volume II; and 3) that of Vladek at the end of the second volume.

hand, there is something odd about this picture which makes it feel unreal. Vladek appears wearing a camp uniform but he does not look like a camp inmate at all. What the reader sees is a healthy handsome round-faced man in a clean uniform, carefully buttoned up, and with a cap slightly slanted in a way that seems as studied as the expression on his face. As Vladek explains to Artie: 'I passed once a photo place what had a camp uniform – a new clean one to make souvenir photos ...' (II, 294). So this is the genesis of Vladek's picture, which makes it both real and fake. As Marianne Hirsch puts it:

> this photograph is particularly disturbing in that it *stages, performs* the identity of the camp inmate. [...] This photograph both is documentary evidence (Vladek was in Auschwitz) and isn't (the picture was taken in a souvenir shop). This picture may look like a documentary photograph of the inmate – it may have the appearance of authenticity – but it is merely, and admittedly, a simulation, a dress-up game. [...] [A]nyone could have had this picture taken in the same souvenir shop [...]. Breaking out of the frame, looking intently at the viewer/reader, Vladek's picture dangerously relativizes the identity of the survivor.[34]

Just as Vladek's picture was staged in a souvenir shop, so Spiegelman's cartoons constitute an artistic distortion, a performance, and, like the photograph, are both real and contrived. The hybrid characters call attention to the artificiality of representation, but they are also the vehicle for telling an authentic story. When Spiegelman was asked 'Why mice?', he answered, 'I need to show the events and memory of the Holocaust without showing them. I want to show the masking of these events *in* their representation.'[35] And so, both the picture and the book are grounded on the same principle: to show reality without showing it. Like Vladek's photograph, *Maus* is fraught with ambivalence and contradiction, refusing to separate one man's life and memories from the predicament of representing them in the present. The photograph evokes what once was but cannot

34 Hirsch, 'Family Pictures', 25 (emphasis in the original).
35 Quoted in James E. Young, 'The Holocaust as Vicarious Past: Art Spiegelman's *Maus* and the Afterimages of History', *Critical Enquiry* 24/3 (Spring 1998), 666–99, 687 (emphasis in the original).

be reproduced: Vladek wearing a camp uniform in a souvenir shop evokes the Vladek as a camp inmate that the picture does not capture. After all, and as pointed out by, among others, Roland Barthes in *Camera Lucida* and Susan Sontag in *On Photography*, photographs simultaneously confer presence and absence. *Maus* is both effective in narrating the story behind this picture, in presenting it to the reader (in the sense of making it present, almost as a photograph does) while simultaneously calling attention to what escapes the narrative, to what is irretrievable because it is lost, left unsaid or distorted by memory.[36]

Vladek finishes his story with his joyous meeting with Anja: 'More I don't need to tell you. We were both very happy, and lived happy, happy ever after.' The last two panels of *Maus* show Vladek in bed and Artie beside him. 'Let's stop, please, the tape recorder,' Vladek says, 'I'm *tired* from talking, Richieu, and it's enough stories for now' (II, 296, emphasis in the original). These last frames may prompt the reader to approach them – and through them the work as a whole – in the light of Saul Friedlander's distinction between what he terms 'common memory' and 'deep memory' of the Holocaust.[37] Common memory tends to restore or establish coherence, closure, and possibly a redemptive stance, while deep memory remains essentially inarticulable and unrepresentable, pointing to that which continues to exist as unresolved trauma just beyond the reach of meaning. That is to say, every common memory of the Holocaust is to some extent haunted by what it necessarily leaves unstated, its coherence a necessary but ultimately misleading evasion. Thus, Vladek's 'happy, happy ever after' imposes a closure that is questioned not only by the reader's knowledge of Anja's suicide (and the gap left by the destruction of her notebooks) but also by Vladek mistaking his living son Artie for his dead son Richieu, thus suggesting that there are unresolved traumas, wounds which are still very much open and which remain unnarrated.

36 As James E. Young explains, what 'may appear as historical errors of fact in *Maus*, such as the pictures of Poles in Nazi uniforms and of others saying "Heil Hitler" [...] are accurate representations of his [Art's] father's possibly faulty memory'. *Ibid.*, 697.

37 Saul Friedlander, 'Trauma, Transference, and "Working Through" in Writing the History of the *Shoah*', *History and Memory* 4/1 (1992), 39–59, 41.

Maus dexterously navigates in this way between the need to tell and the need to acknowledge that not everything can be told. In the course of Artie's session with his psychiatrist, the latter sadly remarks that perhaps it would be better not to tell any more Holocaust stories. Then Artie quotes Beckett as saying once: 'Every word is like an unnecessary stain on silence and nothingness.' After a marked silence in a vignette with no words, Artie resumes, in the following vignette: 'On the other hand, he *said* it' (II, 205, emphasis in the original). And so did Spiegelman himself, by narrating a story that bears the silences of (personal and collective) history and that makes the reader reflect on the paradoxes and dilemmas of representing what can be told, through words and images.[38]

Bibliography

Barthes, Roland, *Camera Lucida: Reflections on Photography*, trans. Richard Howard (New York: Hill, 1981).
Berger, Alan L., 'Bearing Witness: Theological Implications of Second-Generation Literature in America', in Efraim Sicher, ed., *Breaking Crystal. Writing and Memory after Auschwitz* (Urbana and Chicago: University of Illinois Press, 1998), 252–75.
Doherty, Thomas, 'Art Spiegelman's *Maus*: Graphic Art and the Holocaust', *American Literature* 68/1 (1996), 69–84.
Friedlander, Saul, 'Trauma, Transference, and "Working Through" in Writing the History of the *Shoah*', *History and Memory* 4/1 (1992), 117–37.
Hirsch, Marianne, 'Family Pictures: *Maus*, Mourning, and Post-Memory', *Discourse* 15/2 (Winter 1992–3), 3–29.
——, 'Projected Memory: Holocaust Photographs in Personal and Public Fantasy', in Mieke Bal, ed., *Acts of Memory: Cultural Recall in the Present* (Hanover: Dartmouth University Press, 1999), 3–23.

38   The research carried out for the writing of this essay is part of a research project financed by the Spanish Ministry of Science and Innovation and the European Regional Development Fund (code HUM2007–61035).

Horowitz, Sara R., *Voicing the Void. Muteness and Memory in Holocaust Fiction* (New York: State University of New York Press, 1997).

Hungerford, Amy, *The Holocaust of Texts. Genocide, Literature, and Personification* (Chicago and London: University of Chicago Press, 2003).

Johnston, Ian, 'On Spiegelman's *Maus I* and *II*', <http://records.viu.ca/~johnstoi/ introser/maus.htm> accessed 3 December 2010.

LaCapra, Dominick, *Writing History, Writing Trauma* (Baltimore and London: Johns Hopkins University Press, 2001).

Levine, Michael G., *The Belated Witness. Literature, Testimony, and the Question of Holocaust Survival* (Stanford: Stanford University Press, 2006).

Ma, Sheng-Mei, 'Mourning with the (as a) Jew: Metaphor, Ethnicity, and the Holocaust in Art Spiegelman's *Maus*', *Studies in American-Jewish Literature* 16 (1997), 115–29.

Miller, Nancy K., 'Cartoons of the Self. Portrait of the Artist as a Young Murderer. Art Spiegelman's *Maus*', in Deborah R. Geis, ed., *Considering Maus: Approaches to Art Spiegelman's 'Survivor's Tale' of the Holocaust* (Tuscaloosa: University of Alabama Press, 2003), 44–59.

Silverman, Kaja, *The Threshold of the Visible World* (New York: Routledge, 1996).

Sollors, Werner, 'Introduction. The Invention of Ethnicity', in Werner Sollors, ed., *The Invention of Ethnicity* (New York: Oxford University Press, 1991), ix–xx.

Sontag, Susan, 'Fascinating Fascism', in *Under the Sign of Saturn* (New York: Farrar, Straus and Giroux, 1980), 73–105. First published in the *New York Review of Books* (6 February 1975).

——, *On Photography* (New York: Doubleday Anchor, 1990).

Spiegelman, Art, *Comix, Essays, Graphics, and Scraps: From MAUS to Now to MAUS to Now* (New York: Raw, 1998).

——, *The Complete Maus* (London: Penguin, 2003).

Staub, Michael E., 'The Shoah Goes On and On: Remembrance and Representation in Art Spiegelman's *Maus*', *MELUS* 20/3 (1995), 33–46.

White, Hayden, 'Historical Emplotment and the Problem of Truth', in Saul Friedlander, ed., *Probing the Limits of Representation. Nazism and the 'Final Solution'* (Cambridge, MA: Harvard University Press, 1992), 37–53.

Young, James E., 'The Holocaust as Vicarious Past: Art Spiegelman's *Maus* and the Afterimages of History', *Critical Enquiry* 24/3 (1998), 666–99.

BETTINA BANNASCH

Zero – A Gaping Mouth: The Discourse of the Camps in Herta Müller's *Atemschaukel* between Literary Theory and Political Philosophy[1]

/ rushword
title !

I.

In *Atemschaukel* (Breathing to and fro),[2] the latest novel by the Romanian-German author Herta Müller, the first-person narrator, who is interned in a labour camp and suffering acute hunger, leaves his body from time to time. He undergoes an exchange with objects which 'are not living, but undead', which is to say that, as we expect of undead creatures, they need the blood of human beings to bring them to life.[3] The first-person narrator gives life to objects, and in exchange they give him the ability to endure. This exchange, in which the narrator perceives his salvation, his survival strategy, continues until 'the worst is past'. 'The worst' is the zero point.

and so this is
of limited usefulness to curre-
readly ?

1   I am grateful to David Midgley for his sensitive and incisive translation of this article from the original German, particularly for his brilliant translation of Müller's hitherto untranslated German texts.

2   Translator's note: No English translation of this work has yet appeared. The title adopted for the French edition is *La bascule du souffle* (2010). The German *Schaukel* is used to denote a swing or a rocking cradle.

3   The act of transfusion described in *Atemschaukel* differs from that in traditional vampire stories, however, in several respects. Firstly, it is not the desire of the undead that is directed at the living, but the other way round; secondly, giving life to the undead serves the preservation of human life or its conversion into an enduring (undead) existence, and not its termination; and this outcome is not a final and irreversible state of affairs, but a provisional way of coping with circumstances.

The zero point is ineffable. On this we agree, the zero point and I: it is not something we can talk about. At best we can talk round about it. The gaping mouth of the zero can eat, but not speak. The zero encompasses you in its delicate stranglehold. The saving exchange cannot be compared with anything. It is as direct and compelling as '1 shovelful = 1 gram of bread'.

(A 249[4]: Der Nullpunkt ist das Unsagbare. Wir sind uns einig, der Nullpunkt und ich, dass man über ihn nicht sprechen kann, höchstens drumherum. Das aufgesperrte Maul der Null kann essen, nicht reden. Die Null schließt dich ein in ihre würgende Zärtlichkeit. Der Rettungstausch duldet keine Vergleiche. Er ist zwingend und direkt wie: 1 Schaufelhub = 1 Gramm Brot.)

These few sentences are the only comments we find in the entire novel on the subject of what can and cannot be said. In German-language discussions of the literary depiction of the camps, which for understandable reasons have focused primarily on writings about the Nazi concentration camps, this has always been a central issue, at least since the debates that arose from Adorno's publications on the subject.[5] There is more to this issue than the question of the legitimacy of storytelling after Auschwitz. It is also associated with questions of narrative technique, which link reflection about narrative forms to the psychoanalytical scenario of a talking cure and derive from it such forms of 'traumatic narration' as fragmentary narration, incomplete narration, etc. In terms of its narrative composition, *Atemschaukel* pursues a fundamentally different question, namely that of a *politically relevant ethic*.

---

4   Herta Müller, *Atemschaukel* (Munich: Hanser, 2009) (subsequently abbreviated to A).
5   The texts by Theodor W. Adorno that have provided an abiding focus for debate in this area are the radio talk 'Was bedeutet: Aufarbeitung der Vergangenheit' first published in *Eingriffe: Neun Kritische Modelle* (Frankfurt am Main: Suhrkamp, 1963) translated into English as 'The Meaning of Working Trough the Past', in *Critical Models: Interventions and Catchwords*, trans. Henry W. Pickford (New York: Columbia University Press, 1998) and 'Kulturkritik und Gesellschaft' in *Prismen. Kulturkritik und Gesellschaft* (Munich: DTV, 1963) translated as 'An Essay on Cultural Criticism and Society', in *Prisms* (London: Spearman, 1967).

The impossibility of speaking about the zero point is as self-evident to the narrator in *Atemschaukel* as the fact that it is possible to talk round about it. In adopting this point of view, he is not appealing to positions that have been formulated in recent Shoah literature and the discussions about it, which have shifted since the early 1990s from the question of representability to the question of forms of representation. Rather, the first-person narrator of Herta Müller's novel appeals to his *own* highly individual and intimate acquaintance with the zero point. It is his accord with this that legitimates his concise and somewhat apodictic utterance. Since I draw below on Roland Barthes's, essay collection *Writing Degree Zero* when I discuss the poetics of Müller's writings, in particular those of *Atemschaukel*, I should like to show here that it is no coincidence that Müller's first-person narrator uses the word 'zero'.

The narrator's certainty, which appears to be nourished solely by his personal experience, is recognizably constructed as an attitude informed by Shoah discourse as it has developed since 1945 and situated within it in a quite deliberate way. On the one hand, the talk of a zero point here has nothing to do with the debate about a 'zero hour' that developed in Germany after 1945, which was associated with the hope that literary writing might be able to leave the past in the past and start afresh. On the other hand, Müller's novel can be read as a critical engagement with the discourse about the literary depiction of the camps, which arose largely in response to Adorno, has continued since 1960, with variations, and has been substantially determined by Paul Celan's theme of the 'breathturn' (Atemwende).[6] But whereas Celan's breathturn is something momentary (the poet draws himself in to the confines of his inmost space, and then liberates himself from it with his work), Müller's term 'Atemschaukel' emphasizes the living process and the interminability of the artistic attempt to give expression to the memory of the camp. Correspondingly, the zero point referred to in Herta Müller's novel is also something other than the date that Paul Celan meant in his famous acceptance speech for the Büchner Prize in 1960.

6   See Paul Celan, 'Der Meridian', in *Gesammelte Werke*, vol. 3, ed. Beda Allemann, Stefan Reichert and Rolf Bücher (Frankfurt am Main: Suhrkamp, 1983), 187–202, 195 and 200; 'The Meridian', in *Collected Prose*, trans. Rosemarie Waldrop (Manchester: Carcanet, 1986), 37–55, 47 and 52.

Celan had a very specific date in mind, 20 January 1942, the date of the Wannsee conference at which the systematic mass murder of the Jews was determined; and his implication is that the Shoah as an event can never be expunged, and should therefore henceforth be inscribed into every poem written. This perception predominated in the literature of the 1970s and continued to do so right up to the Shoah literature of the recent past. Oskar Pastior's little essay about the 'withdrawal poem', with its ironic tone, can perhaps be understood as a reply to the notion of the 'breathturn' in Celan's Büchner Prize Speech, and to the 'discreet narration' of the texts that were to follow it. Pastior describes the way these texts proceed as follows:

> The withdrawal poem is not able to perform any action, however, and therefore cannot withdraw itself either; so with this little linguistic trick, which does not amount to a precise description, at least we come a little closer to the possibility of description that we achieve when, by switching the negative in the DESCRIP- TION OF INDESCRIBABILITY that we seem to be conducting, we derive the NON-DESCRIPTION OF DESCRIBABILITY. The subjective factor in the first element is an extra-literary one, and by extrapolation we arrive at bare DESCRIB- ABILITY. That is what we hold on to. We are still at a point in time where we pre- tend to omit the description, but we are already working with describability. That is quite something.[7]

If we read the term 'Atemschaukel' as – amongst other things – a reply to Celan's 'Atemwende' in his Büchner Prize Speech, then in contrast to Celan it is the processual nature of poetry, its living, 'breathing', 'rocking' character that receives a stronger emphasis. The decision to use the word 'Atemschaukel', which Müller and Pastior jointly adopted as the work- ing title of the novel, was evidently influenced not only by this apparent intertextual allusion, but also by the existential dimension of breathing. Like food, breathing is a necessity of life; in this way, the 'Atemschaukel' can be seen as a counterpart to the 'angel of hunger' (Hungerengel) that hovers over everything.

---

7   Oskar Pastior, *Jetzt kann man schreiben was man will*, Werkausgabe, vol. 2, ed. Ernest Wichner (Munich: Hanser, 2003), 22.

Müller responds to Celan's demand that the date of the Wannsee conference should be inscribed in *any* poem written after Auschwitz by making a different kind of claim to universal validity. Müller's narrator-protagonist in *Atemschaukel* is not talking about the concentration camp, but a different kind of camp – even if this does not of course exclude the possibility that intertextual allusions also establish an unmistakable connection to relevant examples of Shoah literature. This extended claim to universal validity is, however, also to be distinguished from those tendencies to universalization that are characteristic of current discussions about the camps, as in Giorgio Agamben's *Homo Sacer* and those who have taken their cue from it.[8] The figure zero in *Atemschaukel* is specific in a different way, and it lays claim to a general validity that reaches beyond the Shoah. Its poetic and political relevance arises through the simple, sensually direct image of the figure zero, of its gaping mouth – although this is something we have to imagine, it is not depicted in the text itself.

The zero sign is hunger, that ever-present and all-powerful hunger of which the novel has to tell. In order to describe it, the first-person narrator adopts the clarity of mathematical expressions. The equals sign ($=$) describes precisely the relation between the single shovelful (denoted by an Arabic numeral) and the single gram of bread (also denoted by an Arabic numeral). By choosing a mathematical form of representation the narrator refuses to engage in the debate about the question of the necessity and admissibility of comparisons that continues to determine the discourse about Shoah literature to this day. The equation is immediately preceded by the comment, 'The saving exchange cannot be compared with anything.' This text works with *equations*, not with comparisons.

In recent German, and particularly Austrian Shoah literature, including the secondary literature, the debate about comparisons has been conducted in a careful and differentiated way. The dilemma that underlies it – the dilemma between making use of suffering for the purposes of a story from

<hr>

8   On this issue, see the early critique by Astrid Deuber-Mankowsky: 'Homo Sacer, das bloße Leben und das Lager. Anmerkungen zu einem erneuten Versuch einer Kritik der Gewalt', *Die Philosophin* 25 (2002), 95–115.

which it might be possible to learn and simultaneously insisting that the
sacrifices involved were senseless, or the danger that Ingeborg Bachmann
noted at an early date of indulging in 'the most feeble and thoughtless
poeticization' of sacrifice[9] – cannot be resolved simply by naming it. The
narrator in *Atemschaukel* evidently recognizes this problem and is not prepared to dwell on it. The narrative procedure adopted might be described
in Roland Barthes's terms as the ideal case of narration, namely a narration in which literature has been vanquished and the human problematics
are recognized and presented without any added colouring, a narration
in which the writer has once more become 'honest'. In Barthes's chapter
on 'Writing and Silence' there is indeed a remark about writing in equations which can be directly applied to the mode of narration in Müller's
Atemschaukel:

> If the writing is really neutral, and if language, instead of being a cumbersome and
> recalcitrant act, reaches the state of a pure equation, which is no more tangible than
> an algebra when it confronts the innermost part of man, then literature is vanquished,
> the problematics of mankind is uncovered and presented without elaboration, the
> writer becomes irretrievably honest.[10]

With the 'translation' of the mathematical equation into spoken language,
the existential quality of the narration in *Atemschaukel* becomes apparent.
The German verb 'ist' (is), which is how the equals sign might be spoken,
sounds just like the verb 'isst' (eats), and thereby denotes what is always
and exclusively at stake in the camp: hunger, the emaciation of the inmates
through under-nourishment.

In *Atemschaukel* hunger is personified as an overwhelmingly powerful
angel, which lies in wait for the first-person narrator to give himself up. The
angel of hunger repeatedly invites him to 'let go'. But the narrator does not
succumb to the angel's wiles, and unmasks him as a deceiver.

---

9   Ingeborg Bachmann, *Werke*, vol. 4, ed. Christine Koschel, Inge von Weidenbaum
     and Clemens Münster (Munich: Piper, 1978), 335.
10   Roland Barthes, *Writing Degree Zero & Elements of Sociology*, trans. Annette Lavers
     and Colin Smith (London: Jonathan Cape, 1984), 65. Cf. also Barthes's remarks in
     the chapter 'Is there any Poetic Writing?', *ibid.*, 35–43, esp. 37–8.

You are deceiving me with my own flesh. My flesh has fallen victim to you. But I am not my flesh. I am something else, and I won't let go. It is no longer a question of who I am, but I won't tell you what I am. What I am eludes your scales.

(A 87: Du betrügst mich mit meinem Fleisch. Es ist dir verfallen. Aber ich bin nicht mein Fleisch. Ich bin etwas anderes und lasse nicht locker. Von Wer bin ich kann nicht mehr die Rede sein, aber ich sag dir nicht, was ich bin. Was ich bin, betrügt deine Waage.)

In its resistance to the angel of hunger, personal identity can no longer achieve an integral sense of identity, all that remains is the sheer will to survive. The only possibility of reaching an accord with the angel of hunger is by starving to death.

The distinction the narrator makes between *who* I am and *what* I am seems to correspond to a motif in Giorgio Agamben's *Homo Sacer*.[11] Agamben's thinking starts with Aristotle and his separation of human identity into social being (*bios politicos*) and bare life (*nuda vita*). Ostensibly following Foucault, Agamben argues that, by aiming to reduce human identity to a biological zero, biopolitics makes naked life the true subject of modernity. By contrast, the passage cited from *Atemschaukel* makes it clear that Herta Müller's view differs fundamentally from Agamben's in this crucial respect: in *Atemschaukel*, the *who* that has been reduced to a *what* remains the subject of the narration. The trope of personification – in this case the personification of the angel of hunger – enables the 'I' to retain its dignity, its ethical composure, in spite of everything.[12]

11 Giorgio Agamben, *Homo Sacer: Sovereign Power and Bare Life*, trans. Daniel Heller-Roazen (Stanford: Stanford University Press, 1998).

12 It was in this sense that, when she gave a reading from her novel in Munich on 12 November 2009, Herta Müller expressly said that Oskar Pastior had succeeded in preserving his dignity in the camp by personifying things. Similarly, the narrative sovereignty of the narrator figure who recalls his personal history from a distance of sixty years is founded upon the harmonious relation in which he stands to the personified zero point: the survivor in the camp and beyond the camp is broken, and yet he remains in command of the situation.

It is also questionable whether Agamben's writings about the concentration camps are really consistent with Foucault's thinking about discourses
of power or whether Agamben is not rather extrapolating in his own terms
– terms which Foucault did *not* pursue for good reasons. It is indicative that
Foucault did not conclude his analyses of discourses of power with reflections on the (concentration) camps, but instead concerned himself in his late
writings with distinctly ethical issues.[13] At the same time, Foucault emphasizes that he does not wish these reflections to be seen as a new turn in his
philosophical thinking.[14] Rather, he speaks of his thoughts on care for the
self as a pendant to his earlier analyses. Asked about the relation between his
reflections on care for the self and his analysis of power, Foucault answers:

> It [liberty] is political in the measure that non-slavery with respect to others is a condi-
> tion: a slave has no ethics. Liberty is then in itself political. And then, it has a political
> model in the measure where being free means not being a slave to one's self and to one's
> appetites, which supposes that one establishes over one's self a certain relation of domi-
> nation, of mastery, which [in ancient Greece] was called arché – power, authority.[15]

Herta Müller expresses a similar view in her essay on Ruth Klüger's *weiter
leben* (Still Alive) when she speaks of 'free' and 'arbitrary' as antitheses:

> Almost incidentally, Ruth Klüger teaches us *that freedom is always the opposite of arbi-
> trariness*. She does not need to add a single word to the concrete process of events. Her
> choice of words is a matter of attitude and inseparable from ethical considerations.
> The book shows that morality shapes the way we deal with language as unfailingly
> as it does the way we deal with everyday events.[16]

13   See, for example, Michel Foucault, *Ästhetik der Existenz. Schriften zur Lebenskunst*,
      ed. Daniel Defert and Francois Ewald (Frankfurt am Main: Suhrkamp, 2007). Cf.
      also Michel Foucault, *The Hermeneutics of the Subject: Lectures at the Collège de
      France, 1981–1982*, ed. Frédéric Gros, trans. Graham Burchell (New York: Palgrave
      Macmillan, 2005).
14   On this aspect, see Frédéric Gros, 'Course Context', in Foucault, *The Hermeneutics
      of the Subject*, 507–50.
15   Michel Foucault, 'The ethic of care for the self as a practice of freedom', in James
      Bernauer and David Rasmussen, eds, *The Final Foucault* (Cambridge, MA: MIT
      Press, 1988), 1–20, 6.
16   Herta Müller, 'Sag, dass du fünfzehn bist – *weiter leben* von Ruth Klüger', in *In der
      Falle. Drei Essays* (Göttingen: Wallstein, 2009), 25–40, 27.

II.

Atemschaukel tells of the deportations of Romanian Germans by the Soviet Union early in 1945.[17] The narrator is seventeen years old when he arrives in the camp; so he is about the same age as the first-person narrator of Imre Kertész's novel *Fateless*[18] when he is taken to a concentration camp. Their youthful naïvety means that these two narrators have much in common. But there is one important respect in which Müller's narrator differs from Kertész's: he is already familiar with his own sexuality. He is homosexual, and that means that, already in the life he leads *before* his deportation, the threat of torture and death hangs over him if this fact were to be discovered.[19] Müller's narrator is thus *not* confronted with a fundamentally new situation when he arrives in the camp; now as before, mistrust of others is of the essence. All that is new is that this mistrust is now something that all the inmates of the camp share – although, in the nature of mistrust, it is not something that can provide any sense of community amongst them:

> The mistrust grows higher than any wall. In the melancholy atmosphere of this build-ing site, everyone is suspicious of everyone else, that he is carrying the lighter end of the sack of cement, that he is exploiting you and making it easier for himself. [...]

17   Between 70,000 and 100,000 people aged between seventeen and forty-five were affected by these deportations. The estimates vary (cf. Alfred-Maurice de Zayas, *Anmerkungen zur Vertreibung der Deutschen aus dem Osten* (Stuttgart: Kohlhammer, 1986)). Around 60 per cent of those deported were women. The first returned home in 1949, the last in 1952, except for a few who only returned in 1956; a third of them died in the camps.

18   Imre Kertész, *Fateless*, trans. Christopher C. Wilson and Katharina M. Wilson (Evanston: Northwestern University Press, 1992). For the discussion of this text below, cf. also the title adopted for Kertész's screenplay, in which the series of steps evoked in the final chapter of the novel is emphasized: Imre Kertész, *Schritt für Schritt* (Frankfurt am Main: Suhrkamp, 2002).

19   This threat is intensified in the camp. But in his innocence the first-person narrator nevertheless peceives it initially as a liberation from the narrow circumstances of the society he comes from – from the false intimacy with his mother, with whom he cannot discuss his homosexuality, and from the tormenting proximity of his father, an enthusiastic supporter of National Socialism.

On the way home every evening, when you had to get away from the cement, and with my back to the building site, I knew that it was not us deceiving each other, but that we were all being deceived by the Russians and their cement. But the suspicion came back the next day, despite this knowledge, suspicion of everyone. And everybody sensed it. And they were all suspicious towards me. And I sensed that. The cement and the angel of hunger are in league with each other.

(A 38–9: Höher als jede Wand wächst das Misstrauen. In dieser Baustellenschwermut verdächtigt jeder den anderen, dass er am Zementsack das leichtere Ende zu tragen hat, dass er einen ausnützt und sich schont. [...] Jeden Abend auf dem Heimweg, in der nötigen Entfernung vom Zement, mit dem Rücken zur Baustelle, habe ich gewusst, dass nicht wir uns gegenseitig betrügen, sondern alle betrogen werden von den Russen und ihrem Zement. Aber am nächsten Tag kam wieder der Verdacht, gegen mein Wissen und gegen alle. Und das haben alle gespürt. Und alle gegen mich. Und das habe ich gespürt. Der Zement und der Hungerengel sind Komplizen.)

In the theme of mistrust we may recognize what this text has in common with the other novels and stories by Herta Müller: they all tell of lives threatened by totalitarian circumstances, in the small and sharply controlled social units of the village, the school, the factory, the town, the dictatorship. Like the first-person narrator in *Atemschaukel*, all her protagonists lead solitary lives because of the mistrust that is essential to their survival. Herta Müller's novels tell of life under dictatorship, of escape to Germany and the continuation of terror there, with the result that no new homeland – or any kind of homeland – can be found in Germany either.[20] The life of the narrator of *Atemschaukel before* his deportation – a life forever threatened by torture and murder – resembles that of figures in earlier novels by Herta Müller who rebelled against dictatorship.

The new experience for the first-person narrator is that of hunger. Both aspects are important for a proper understanding of this novel within the context of Müller's oeuvre and of its claim to universality beyond the narrow context of its subject-matter. We need to understand, firstly, that the camp

20   The extent to which Müller's novels draw on authentic experience is documented by the record of the surveillance and persistent terrorization to which Herta Müller was subjected by the Romanian secret service, the *Securitate*, which is contained in the 'Cristina files'.

represents the continuation of a totalitarian system composed of smaller and larger 'camp' units, and secondly that the experience of hunger in the camp creates a state of emergency, which is what fundamentally distinguishes the experience of the camp and the memory of the camp from the experience of dictatorship and memories of life under dictatorship.[21]

Atemschaukel is an homage to Oskar Pastior, the German-language poet who was born in Siebenbürgen (Transylvania). In many respects it is his story that is told. The novel was indeed conceived jointly by him, the eyewitness, and Herta Müller. Together they sought out further eyewitnesses, and together they visited the site where the camp had stood. Herta Müller's decision to maintain the first-person perspective and to complete the novel on her own after the death of Oskar Pastior in 2007 attracted criticism when the work appeared in 2009. It is true that this criticism was subsequently muted when the public estimation of her work, and of the newly published novel *Atemschaukel* in particular, had been rendered sacrosanct, so to speak, by the announcement that Herta Müller had been awarded the Nobel Prize for Literature. But such criticism might have been anticipated, because it draws on a long and by no means defunct tradition in the discourse about the literary representation of the camps. Until well into the 1990s, this discourse largely refused to acknowledge other literary works about the camps than those written by eyewitnesses. This strong association between literary writing about the concentration camps and eyewitness accounts was only broken by the writings of the so-called 'second generation'. From the point of view of literary and historical scholarship, this break with the assumption that autobiography was the sole criterion of authenticity in Shoah literature was long overdue. But what was often overlooked was that it is only to a limited extent that we can speak of a break with tradition here. For most of the recent Shoah literature only fits the category of 'second generation' (which is not exactly a category of

---

21   On this point, compare the many comments of the first-person narrator on the self-alienation that takes place in the camp, as the inmates themselves recognize, as well as on the problem that the narrator confronts when he looks back and reflects that he is a 'false witness'.

literary analysis) by virtue of the fact that the texts in question were written by authors who were themselves children or grandchildren of eyewitnesses. So what we are dealing with is rather a *second degree* legitimation – a notion that is in itself not unproblematic – to which nearly all authors of the relevant texts can appeal.

Precisely this 'second degree' legitimation has been claimed for Herta Müller, too. It was emphasized that the author's mother had been among the deportees.[22] In this way, the accusation that the author had appropriated and 'exploited' someone else's story for the purposes of their own literary work was defused by pointing to the fact that in this instance the people concerned were mother and daughter. This legitimation strategy was powerfully reinforced by the way it was presented in print and visual media: the Nobel Prize-winner was presented to the public gaze as a dark, melancholic, fragile and broken figure. In the way it deals with the incorporation of biographical material and with the viewpoint of the male narrator that it adopts, however, the novel works against this kind of legitimation strategy. It emphasizes instead the relationship in which it stands to the life of Oskar Pastior and, no less importantly, to the literary work of Oskar Pastior.

III.

For all the suffering that can be recognized as 'genuine', as we find it represented in the stories and novels of Herta Müller, her texts are always also concerned with putting up resistance through narration, with making narration itself recognizable as an act of resistance against the totalitarian structures of dictatorship and the camps.

---

22   This fact is mentioned in the afterword to the novel, albeit briefly. When Herta Müller was awarded the Nobel Prize for Literature, *Bild* was among the first newspapers to take it upon itself to 'investigate' this connection by calling on her mother in the privacy of her own home.

One characteristic of such narration has already been pointed out: Müller's novels are full of personifications of abstract and inanimate objects. Just like the first-person narrator in *Atemschaukel*, who speaks with the zero-point, unmasks the angel of hunger as a deceiver, or denounces the snow as a traitor because it shows the persecutors the traces that lead to the hideaways of the persecuted, so too do the first-person narrators in Müller's earlier stories and novels maintain a special relationship with inanimate objects. There is no world of objects in the works of Herta Müller. To assume a world in which things appear as things would mean accepting the notion of a world in which human beings, too, are perceived as objects, in which power is exerted over human beings as over objects. It would mean using the pretext of preserving 'objectivity' to elude those claims to respect for others that one's own humanity, individuality and subjectivity bring with them.

Another characteristic of Herta Müller's narration is one that she herself, in one of her poetological texts, calls working with 'the index finger in our heads'.[23] The index finger points to things and words, which the narration highlights and often detaches from their context in order to make their true significance apparent, and thus to lend them a new significance. This procedure, which is characteristic of all Herta Müller's novels, is recognizably one that she learned from structuralism. Narration with 'the index finger in our heads' is reminiscent in many respects of the 'structuralist activity' described by Roland Barthes. This is also true, in a particularly striking way, of Herta Müller's lyric poetry, of the collage poems she makes by cutting out words and pasting them together.[24]

23   Herta Müller, 'Wie Wahrnehmung sich erfindet', in *Der Teufel sitzt im Spiegel. Wie Wahrnehmung sich erfindet* (Berlin: Rotbuch, 1991), 7–31, 7.

24   Müller's first collection of poems, which was printed on index cards, bears the delightful and indicative title, 'The Watchman Picks up his Comb. Of Departures and Evasions' (*Der Wächter nimmt seinen Kamm. Vom Weggehen und Ausscheren*, 1993). In order to keep the collage character of the poems visible, they are photographically reproduced. In this way it becomes apparent that all the words she uses have been *found*, that they have all been extracted from other contexts and newly assembled, and finally that, as an image and sign, each word possesses its own optically transmitted aesthetic quality – just as the zero in *Atemschaukel* first appears as an image and sign.

The importance that Müller herself attaches to Oskar Pastior's work as an inspiration for her own early writing suggests that he also shared with her some of his own early attempts at storytelling in a structuralist vein.[25] As far as the novel *Atemschaukel* is concerned, our understanding of the zero-point is enhanced by a further, distinctly poetologic level of signification, as Roland Barthes describes it in *Writing Degree Zero*, where he sets out his thinking about an author's mode of writing as the site of his social engagement.[26] This engagement is articulated as a 'morality of form'. As Barthes puts it, the mode of writing is a form of literary expression transformed by its social determination:

> A language and a style are blind forces; a mode of writing is an act of historical solidarity. A language and a style are objects; a mode of writing is a function: it is the relationship between creation and society, the literary language transformed by its social finality, form considered as a human intention and thus linked to the great crises of history.[27]

For Barthes, the zero-point marks the centre from out of which this engagement writes itself; it should not be understood so much as the zero-point of literature, but rather as that of narration.[28] The gaping mouth of the

---

25   At the same time, Müller emphasizes that she always saw Pastior's (post-)structuralist way of writing as entirely 'realistic', as a way of looking at reality that corresponded to her own view of things. In this connection, Müller decidedly opposes the notion that Pastior's works are just surrealistic language games.

26   Barthes distinguishes the mode of writing (*écriture*) from 'fascist' speech on the one hand and from style, which is tied to the 'personal and secret mythology of the author', on the other: 'But language – the performance of a language system – is neither reactionary nor progressive; it is quite simply fascist; for fascism does not prevent speech, it compels speech'. Roland Barthes, 'Inaugural Lecture, Collège de France', in Susan Sontag, ed., *A Barthes Reader* (New York: Hill and Wang, 1982), 457–78, 461.

27   Barthes, *Writing Degree Zero*, 15. In her comments on Pastior's works, Müller emphasizes the aspect of form precisely in relation to the subject matter of the camp, noting that, while he hardly ever deals with this directly, his work is moulded by the experience of the camp. It contains a number of 'code words'. And Müller places these 'found' words from her reading of Pastior as exhibits in her novel, such as the word 'Hasoweh', which stands, without further commentary, at the end of the short chapter about the hare (German: *Hase*).

28   The zero-point for Barthes is not a zero-point in any chronological sense, nor does it relate to literature arriving at or departing from a zero-point. Rather it refers to

zero, the memory of the experience of hunger, is the ethical centre of the novel *Atemschaukel*, or – as Müller puts it in her essay on Ruth Klüger's autobiographical text *weiter leben* (Still Alive) – the 'ethical claim' that remains 'constant in all its aspects' and is 'the point of orientation for this writing'.[29] It is a kind of writing that does not aim for emotive empathy, but at intellectually guided precision: 'The author [...] does not set any dead person up on a pedestal. She sets them up at an appropriate height for precise inspection. Maintaining this height, which all the senses can reach, is difficult.'[30] Such precision aspires first and foremost to deal scrupulously with words: 'Survivors are broken people. And goodness only comes from intact people. What broken people require is sympathy through precision, with the intellect. By contrast with intact people, they have an ear for any verbal dissimulation.'[31] Herta Müller's use of metaphors, which the critics have always praised, corresponds to this demand for precision. They always prove to be particularly precise descriptions, rather than particularly effective images: they are equations, not comparisons. A particularly striking example from *Atemschaukel* is the image of a white hare that accompanies those who are dying. It is the white down that forms on the cheeks of the starving.

By exhibiting found words as if they were found objects, the text resists the construction of a beautiful world of art that promises refuge from an ugly reality. Precisely because there is this relation to reality, some words cannot be used, however beautiful they may be. It is this precision in dealing with language that distinguishes the poetic work that goes into Müller's writings. Accordingly, the first-person narrator in *Atemschaukel* explains his narrative strategy of selection with reference to a plant called 'Meldekraut' (a type of wild spinach). This plant is of immense significance in the lives of all the inmates of the camp because it provides them with nourishment

---

a different level of signification, that of *écriture*. Cf. Ottmar Ette, *Roland Barthes. Eine intellektuelle Biographie* (Frankfurt am Main: Suhrkamp, 1998), 62–4.

29   Müller, 'Sag, dass du fünfzehn bist', 27.

30   *Ibid.*, 31.

31   *Ibid.*, 36.

in the spring; for this reason a whole page of the novel is dedicated to a description of it.[32] And yet,

> 'the name MELDEKRAUT is a bit much. It doesn't say anything. For us, MELDE was a word without any particular associations, a word that left us in peace. It wasn't called MELDE DICH,[33] it wasn't a roll-call kraut, it was a wayside word.'

> (A 26: Der Name MELDEKRAUT ist ein starkes Stück und besagt überhaupt nichts. MELDE war für uns ein Wort ohne Beiklang, ein Wort, das uns in Ruhe ließ. Es hieß ja nicht MELDE DICH, es war kein Appellkraut, sondern ein Wegrandwort.)

IV.

In her works, Herta Müller presents us with the anarchic and politically potent explosive force of a way of writing that works with 'the index finger in our heads'.[34] It is a way of writing that articulates the refusal to reconstruct totalitarian structures in the act of narration. This refusal is not limited to the poetic work that goes into the writing. It extends to any form of narration, above all to the narration of the self.[35]

---

32 It is only in the course of the summer that the leaves of the Meldekraut become increasingly woody and are no longer edible – the plant loses its use value in proportion as it gains in beauty, putting out a glorious radiant flower.
33 Translator's note: in the context of the camps, the most likely connotation of this phrase would be a command to report to someone.
34 This is true of the early stories, which evoke the comprehensive control to which the life of a child in her Transylvanian German village is subjected, and it is true of the novels that describe the continuity of terror in German exile as well as those that are dedicated to the ever-present surveillance and the threat of death under the Romanian dictatorship. The closed world of the camp in which the Romanian-German deportees find themselves represents an existential intensification of these scenarios.
35 In *Kritik der ethischen Gewalt* (Critique of ethical Power), the published version of her Adorno lectures of 2002, Judith Butler also speaks of an abandonment of the

In *The Course of Recognition*, Paul Ricoeur distinguishes between two sorts of first-person narration. One offers a coherent story of an 'I' that takes its story upon itself and accepts responsibility for its story: this is the 'idem'. Ricoeur places it in a dialectical relation of tension to the 'ipse', to the historically conditioned 'I', the 'I' that is entitled to movement and change.[36] It is precisely this entitlement on which the figures in Herta Müller's novels insist, in the face of all circumstances.[37] In her 1997 novel *Heute wär ich mir lieber nicht begegnet* (The Appointment), the security service man yells at the 'I' during her interrogation, 'You see, everything is connected,' and she replies, 'In your mind they are, in my mind they aren't.'[38]

---

demand for self-identity ('Aussetzung der Forderung nach Selbstidentität'): Judith Butler, *Kritik der ethischen Gewalt* (Frankfurt am Main: Suhrkamp, 2003), 36. By contrast with Müller, who always thinks in (socio-) political terms (and this is of particular interest in connection with her reflections on the theory of narration), Butler derives her arguments from psychoanalytical trauma-theory. Butler departs from the generality of research on the concentration camps, however, in that she draws no distinction between structural and historical trauma.

36 Paul Ricoeur, *The Course of Recognition*, trans. David Pellauer (Cambridge, MA, and London: Harvard University Press, 2005), 89–149.

37 By comparison with earlier texts of Müller's, the situation of the 'I' in *Atemschaukel* is intensified to the extent that a starving person cannot oppose the totality of the camp with a resistant identity, but only with a resistant will to survive. A sense of identity is a luxury item in *Atemschaukel*, it is predicated on the assuaging of hunger.

38 Herta Müller, *The Appointment*, trans. Michael Hulse and Philip Boehm (New York: Metropolitain Books, 2001), 20. Cf. Oskar Pastior's little text 'Geschichte, Poesie' (History, Poetry), where he writes: 'History happens; historiography is done by somebody; poetry happens and is done. [...] I am horrified by what the fundamental and purposive logic of my own words can perpetrate, however charming and historically disturbed that logic might appear. By writing against the automatism of the fear of automatism, I am publicly playing with the history of automatism. My interest in saying "I" seems to be general; that is the basis on which I calculate the chances of achieving anything. I don't know what poetry is. I ascribe a meaning to sentences, and that meaning might contain me, but I don't know how to measure that meaning. Then there are disjunctures. And then there are no more disjunctures. In retrospect poetry degenerates into history'. Oskar Pastior, 'Geschichte, Poesie', in *"... was in der Mitte zu wachsen anfängt"*, Werkausgabe, vol. 4, ed. Ernest Wichner (Munich: Hanser, 2008), 306.

But at the same time, the resisting figures in Müller's novels are characterized above all by reliability. More than that, the absence of reliability separates those figures in her novels who work with totalitarian systems from those who refuse to collaborate.[39] And yet the demand for reliability does not fall together with the demand for a coherent and conclusive narrative of the self in Müller's novels; if that were the case, then things would link up and conspire in their totality against the protagonists. When asked about offers to work with the Romanian secret service, the *Securitate*, Herta Müller sometimes answers, in a succinct and lapidary fashion, that she never considered anything like that, that she is 'not that sort'. The same goes for the figures in her novels. Without pathos, but with an all the more decisive normative stance, they insist on this 'basic form' of first-person narration, the 'sort' that cannot be used for collaboration with totalitarian systems. The figures in Herta Müller's novels are rooted in this conception of themselves.

This is not true of the first-person narrator in *Atemschaukel*. He has had the experience of losing the ability to link the act of saying 'I' with an awareness of who he is. It is true that this experience was of limited duration. But the *memory* of this experience is not. Even sixty years later, the gaping mouth of the zero is the centre from which he narrates. Even sixty years later he therefore leads an existence that has lost its centre, an existence round about the gaping mouth of the zero. *Atemschaukel* does *not* pose the question whether this memory of the zero, of the loss of identity and social reliability, can be reintegrated into the construction of a socially acceptable 'I'. Rather, the novel shows *that* this occurs as soon as money is circulating again and hunger can be assuaged; in the novel this is the case in the last year of the camp. But it also shows that the damage done to the 'I' remains. It is in the light of this lasting damage that the novel formulates its question about justice and injustice, about morality and ethics in relation to the experience of a state of emergency.

---

39   All of Herta Müller's novels, from *Der Fuchs war damals schon der Jäger* (1992) to *Heute wär ich mir lieber nicht begegnet* (The Appointment, 1997), tell of this gulf between human types. It is a gulf that Herta Müller also frequently notes in discussions.

V.

This question is not posed from a position external to that of the characters in *Atemschaukel*, it is presented from a first-person perspective. More than that, Herta Müller designates this novel, in which her material is for the first time *not* predominantly drawn from her own biography, as an 'autofictional' text, just like her earlier works.[40] The use of the term 'autofictional' is just as revealing for the earlier novels as it is for *Atemschaukel*. It makes it clear that Müller's conception of 'autofictionality' is not limited to denoting the freedom of a writer in dealing with autobiographical material. It is to be

40 The term 'autofiction' was first used by the French Jewish author Serge Doubrovsky to describe the construction of a fiction out of real events and facts that he had achieved in his work *Fils* (1977), and has subsequently been applied to a wide variety of quasi-autobiographical writings. Müller used this expression in a conversation with Jürgen König on 'Deutschlandradio Kultur' on 13 August 2009 ('"Es war ja eine ganze Generation". Herta Müller im Gespräch mit Jürgen König. Die Schriftstellerin Herta Müller über Deportationen von Rumäniendeutschen nach dem Zweiten Weltkrieg durch die Sowjets und ihr Romanprojekt *Atemschaukel*'). The exchange runs as follows: 'Müller: "I always have to emphasize this: the first-person narrator is not Oskar Pastior. I can't be Oskar Pastior, so after Pastior's death I had to make a decision. And I can't behave as if I were Oskar Pastior and myself. That would be wrong." König: "So it's an autofiction." Müller: "It's an autofiction, and I think that when you have experienced something traumatic it's natural to want to isolate yourself, that happens a lot earlier, that sense of not being able to endure a relationship or not wanting to get close to someone as a relationship demands. This vicious circle you are subjected to, precisely when you most need a relationship you no longer have a way of sustaining that relationship, the fact that the two things exclude each other, that's what I was after."' In the context of Herta Müller's work to date, the narrative procedure adopted in *Atemschaukel*, i.e. the recognizable incorporation of biographical material, is by no means new. In the early stories as well as Müller's previous novels, characters are demonstrably and unmistakably endowed with a variety of features from her own biography. Statements by Herta Müller in interviews and on the occasion of public readings, as well as the afterword she wrote for the novel, indicate that she used these opportunities to draw attention to Pastior's life and works after his death.

understood in a broader sense as taking responsibility for the biographical material that is used.[41]

What makes the adoption of a first-person perspective in *Atemschaukel* remarkable, however, is the fact that the biographical material in question is that of someone else. It brings with it the adoption of a fundamentally new perspective towards the ethical interest in a 'state of emergency', and for this reason I should like to reinforce here the distinction I drew earlier between Müller's way of looking at the matter and Giorgio Agamben's. Agamben begins his reflections on the *homo sacer* with a discussion of Carl Schmitt's definition of a 'state of emergency' (in German more literally a 'state of exception': *Ausnahmezustand*). According to Schmitt, 'sovereign is he who decides on the state of exception.' What Herta Müller does in her literary work sets up an opposition to the political and juridical discussion that Agamben develops in response to Schmitt in *Homo Sacer*. She departs from the external perspective that Schmitt and Agamben adopt in developing their argument from the point of view of a sovereign power that determines the 'state of emergency', and she adopts the internal perspective of the person who *experiences the emergency situation* and who subsequently has to live with this experience. This person is allowed to speak as the 'I' in the text. This shift of perspective on the 'state of emergency' is, I believe, one of the main achievements of the novel *Atemschaukel*.

41   Beyond this, the concept of 'autofictionality' implies that the characters in Müller's novels, like the words in her texts, are *found* in the realm of 'reality', they are not invented. The notion of 'autofictionality' also points to the sense in which the characters are not exhibited; they are imagined and presented in the text. This is what distinguishes the way she works with language from the way she works with biographical material.

VI.

Atemschaukel shows us figures who suffer the loss of their sense of identity, and along with it the shattering of civilities that had previously been self-evident to them. In the camp, even love, which under normal circumstances would promise a maximum of mutual commitment, is not protected from this effect. Thus the first-person narrator remembers the lawyer Paul Gast, who consumes the daily ration of his wife in the camp until one day she starves to death. The other inmates, the narrator amongst them, look on. Nobody protests. A little later we encounter the lawyer with Toni Mich, who is wearing the coat of his newly dead wife. Nobody passes comment on this event, nobody permits himself a moral condemnation. The narrator, too, withholds any judgement. But at this moment the novel cites a pertinent passage from Imre Kertész's novel *Fateless*. There, the first-person narrator, who has just returned from the concentration camp and is asked by a journalist about 'the hell' he has presumably experienced, tries to explain his view of things. It is not hell that he has experienced, Kertész's first-person narrator replies, but the camp, and there everything that happened had appeared quite normal; over time, he had accustomed himself, step by step, to this normality. And this was a good thing. For had it not been for this sequence of steps in time, he goes on, 'then it's possible neither your brains nor your heart could bear it. [...] "On the other hand," I continued, "there is the unfortunate disadvantage that you somehow have to pass away the time."'[42]

---

42   Kertész, *Fateless*, 182. The passage as a whole runs like this: 'I tried to explain how fundamentally different it is, for instance, to be arriving at a station that is spectacularly white, clean, and neat, where everything becomes clear only gradually, step by step, on schedule. [...] And while you come to understand everything gradually, you don't remain idle at any moment: you are already attending to your new business; you live, you act, you move, you fulfil the new requirements of every new step of development. If, on the other hand, there were no schedule, no gradual enlightenment, if all the knowledge descended on you at once right there in one spot, then it's possible neither your brains nor your heart could bear it. [...] "On the other hand,"

In *Atemschaukel* the story of the two wives of the lawyer Paul Gast
follows Kertész, not least by adopting the calm sobriety of his language, as
a story that arises out of the sheer passage of time and for which ultimately
no-one carries the responsibility:

> thus the days couldn't help the fact that they were a chain of causes and consequences,
> any more than the causes and consequences could help the fact that they were the
> naked truth, although a coat was at stake.
> That was the way things went: because there was nothing anyone could do about it,
> nobody could do anything about it.

> (A 230: so konnten auch die Tage nichts dafür, dass sie eine Kette von Ursachen und
> Folgen waren, so wie auch die Ursachen und Folgen nichts dafür konnten, dass sie
> die nackte Wahrheit waren, obwohl es um einen Mantel ging.
> So war der Lauf der Dinge: Weil jeder nichts dafür konnte, konnte keiner was
> dafür.)

Alluding to Kertész in this way, Müller's *Atemschaukel* describes the dilemma
that results on the one hand from the necessity of accommodating to the
normality of the everyday life of the camp, i.e. to the continued existence
of the state of emergency, in order to survive, and on the other hand from
the associated abandonment of moral and ethical values. This description,
let us emphasize once again, is tied, in Kertész's case as in Müller's, to the
perspective of the camp *inmates*.

It is no coincidence that Herta Müller attributes the story of the man
who steals his wife's food to a professional-class person. In her essay on

---

I continued, "there is the unfortunate disadvantage that you somehow have to pass
away the time. [...]" Because he was silent, I added: "You have to imagine it this
way." He [...] then said in a somewhat more subdued, duller voice: "No, you can't
imagine it." I, for my part, thought to myself: "That's probably why they say 'hell'
instead."' (*ibid.*, 181–2). – Müller aligns herself with Kertész in her writing about the
world of the camp by foreswearing 'poetic' metaphors of terror, which distort the
state of affairs instead of illuminating it. But whereas Kertész opts for a decidedly
sober description of the sequence of events that will, in retrospect, constitute the
path taken by his innocent first-person narrator, Müller opts for a mode of narration
that is full of metaphors.

Ruth Klüger – in which Müller, moreover, displays her familiarity with works of concentration camp literature from Primo Levi to Paul Celan and Jorge Semprún – she also cites Oskar Pastior at one point. She tells how Pastior had observed that the collapse of civilities in the camp began with the intellectuals:

> But there was one precept that the so-called simple people never forgot: 'We don't do that sort of thing.'
> This short and perhaps questionable sentence is enough to keep someone responsible towards others in all situations. For this sentence contains an image of the difference between justice and injustice, one that is not ideological. Where this sentence is ready to be levelled at people, they have already made themselves unforgivably guilty.
>
> (Die sogenannten einfachen Leute aber behielten einen Satz im Kopf: 'Sowas tut man nicht.'
> Dieser kurze, vielleicht sogar fragwürdige Satz reicht jedoch, um verantwortlich zu bleiben gegenüber anderen in allen Situationen. Der Satz hat nämlich ein Bild vom Unterschied zwischen Recht und Unrecht, eines, das nicht ideologisch ist. Wo dieser Satz bereit ist, gegen Menschen vorzugehen, haben diese sich vorher bereits unverzeihlich schuldig gemacht.)[43]

Atemschaukel is about this question of the possibility and the limits of responsibility towards others in all situations.

VII.

As in many other examples of the literature of the camps, there is also a moment of compassion in *Atemschaukel* that defies the logic of camp life. *Atemschaukel* depicts this moment as what Emmanuel Levinas calls

---

43 Müller, 'Sag, dass du fünfzehn bist', 28. The intellectuals on the other hand, who were used to maintaining social appearances, had no means of countering the 'dissolution of society in death by work, starvation and hypothermia'.

the encounter with the other. For if on the one hand the inmates look on passively when Heidrun Gast is dying, on the other hand they intervene decisively and in harmony with each other when the deranged Planton-Kati is about to be deprived of her bread ration.

> But Planton-Kati lives, though she does not know where she is. We know this, and we treat her as if she belongs to us. With her we can compensate for what we do to others. As long as she lives among us, we might be capable of all sorts of things, but we are not capable of anything. The fact that this is so probably counts for more than Planton-Kati herself.

> (A 122: Aber die Planton-Kati lebt, auch wenn sie nicht weiß, wo sie ist. Wir wissen es und behandeln sie wie unser Eigentum. An ihr können wir gutmachen, was wir einander antun. Solang sie zwischen uns lebt, gilt für uns, dass wir zu allerhand, aber nicht zu allem fähig sind. Dieser Umstand zählt wahrscheinlich mehr als die Planton-Kati selbst.)[44]

According to Levinas, the claim that the face of the other makes on me, and to which I unconditionally submit, stands in an antithetical relationship to the claim of a third party – and this is what we see in Müller's *Atemschaukel*.

---

44   At this point in the text, Planton-Kati is expressly identified as the 'placeholder' of an ethic that is pledged to unconditional responsibility for the other. Her madness, which places her beyond all attempts to categorize her, predestines her for this role. This is the sense of Emmanuel Levinas's remark with reference to Wassilij Grossmann that 'the "small goodness" from one person to his fellowman is lost and deformed as soon as it opts for doctrine, a treatise of politics and theology, a party, a state, or even a church. Yet it remains the sole refuge of the good in being. Unbeaten, it undergoes the violence of evil, which, as small goodness, it can neither vanquish nor drive out.' Emmanuel Levinas, 'The Other, Utopia, and Justice', in *Entre nous. Thinking-of-the-Other*, trans. Michael B. Smith and Barbara Harshav (London and New York: Continuum, 2006), 193–202, 199. *Atemschaukel* hints at the other, endangered and dangerous side of 'small goodness', without making it explicit. For the deranged Planton-Kati could easily forfeit her function as 'placeholder' if she were to become in the least a burden to the others: 'The madness of Planton-Kati was always confined to forgiveable proportions. She didn't cling to you, and she didn't reject you. All through the years she retained the naturalness of a domestic animal at home in the camp. There was nothing strange about her. We liked her' (A 105).

This claim demands the establishment of a form of jurisdiction, as a guarantee of social co-existence.[45] In Herta Müller's *Atemschaukel* the jurisdiction exercised by the community of inmates forms the necessary counterpart to the particular relationship in which the community of inmates stands to the deranged Planton-Kati. In the face of hunger, which usually makes any form of sociability among the inmates impossible, only one kind of crime is recognized by this community, and that is the stealing of bread. Whoever commits such a crime is punished with a severity that corresponds to the overriding importance that food has in the camp. One of the forced labourers, Karli Halmen, is almost beaten to death by the fellow inmates of his hut for this reason. If the lawyer Paul Gast had not intervened at the last minute, Karli Halmen would have been killed – killed, moreover, by the first-person narrator. Here, too, the novel withholds any judgement, since 'ordinary morality has no answer to bread-justice' (A 114).

But since it is the first-person narrator who nearly kills Karli Halmen, *Atemschaukel* brings the question of morality as close as it can to the protagonist with whom the reader is invited to identify – even if that morality has no answer to bread-justice. And by having that protagonist repeat this story retrospectively to a third person, the novel does ultimately permit itself – through the medium of a listener – something like a moral judgement. The listener in question is a figure that we find in virtually every novel by Herta Müller, namely a hairdresser. The hairdresser is a receptor for other people's stories; for him they are not associated with any expectation in particular, nor do they enter into any kind of functional nexus.[46]

45   'In the meeting with the face, it was not one's place to judge: the other, being unique, does not undergo judgment; he takes precedence over me from the start; I am under allegiance to him. Judgment and justice are required from the moment the third party appears. In the very name of the absolute obligations towards one's fellow man, a certain abandonment of the absolute allegiance he calls forth is necessary. Here is a problem of a different order, for which institutions and a politics – the entire panoply of a state – are necessary. But a liberal state: always concerned about its delay in meeting the requirement of the face of the other.' Emmanuel Levinas, 'Dialogue on Thinking-of-the-Other', in *Entre nous. Thinking-of-the-Other*, 173–8, 174–5.

46   Together with the seamstresses, the hairdresser is the *epitome* of the listener in Herta Müller's works. The hairdresser sweeps people's stories into a bag as he does the hair

They are stories that are always told while looking into the mirror, and
thus they are told with an aspect of self-reflection.[47] And this is the case
in *Atemschaukel*, too:

> The barber laid his hairy hands on Karli's shoulders and asked, 'When did we lose
> those two front teeth?' And Karli Halmen replied, not to the barber, but to his hairy
> hands, 'On the occasion of the bread theft.'
> When his beard had been shaved off I took my place on the chair. It was the only
> time that Oswald Enyeter whistled a kind of serenade while shaving someone, and
> that a little drop of blood oozed through the foam. Not bright red like sealing-wax,
> but dark red like a raspberry in the snow.

> (A 114: Der Rasierer legte seine pelzigen Hände auf Karlis Schultern und fragte: Seit
> wann fehlen uns vorn die zwei Zähne. Weder zu mir noch zum Rasierer, nur zu den
> pelzigen Händen sagte Karli Halmen: Seit dem Kriminalfall mit dem Brot.
> Als sein Bart abrasiert war, setzte ich mich auf den Stuhl. Es war das einzige Mal,
> dass Oswald Enyeter beim Rasieren eine Art Serenade pfiff und aus dem Schaum
> ein Fleckchen Blut quoll. Nicht hellrot wie Siegellack, sondern dunkelrot, wie eine
> Himbeere im Schnee.)

The shaving 'accident' is taken by the first-person narrator to connote an
unspoken moral judgement. Unspoken because, in the camp, before you
can utter a moral judgement you first have to be able to afford it. The hairdresser in *Atemschaukel* can afford it for two reasons. For one thing, as a
privileged prisoner whose hunger is more or less assuaged, he can afford the
luxury of a moral judgement. For another, he can permit himself a moral
judgement in accordance with the ethical orientation of storytelling in this
novel. For what distinguishes him from the other privileged prisoner in this
novel, Tur Prikulitsch, whom everybody hates, is that he is not someone
who takes advantage of the camp system. In the contrast that is established
between these two prisoners, each with their particular function, we find,
once again, that characterization of figures as collaborators and objectors

---

that he has cut from their heads; and when the bag is full, the people die. Herta Müller,
Der Fuchs war damals schon der Jäger (Frankfurt am Main: Fischer, 2009), 19.
47 On the metaphor of the mirror, cf. Müller, 'Wie Wahrnehmung sich erfindet',
esp. 25–7.

that fundamentally determines the character of Müller's works, and in this instance, too, the gulf between the two is unbridgeable.

It is noticeable that in this scene, which I believe to be crucial for an understanding of the novel, Herta Müller devotes much care to the precise description of the blood. We note at the beginning of this paper that blood is needed to bring undead objects to life by telling about them. Here, in the hairdresser scene, the constituency of this blood is described more precisely. It is 'not bright red like sealing-wax, but dark red like a raspberry in the snow'. As I should like to demonstrate by way of a conclusion, this image can be understood as an allusion to the work of the Russian poet Ossip Mandelstam. Mandelstam's work is devoted to the description of life under dictatorship, and he, too, spent many years of his life in Stalin's camps. What triggered his persecution was the famous epigram he wrote to Stalin, in the last two lines of which he says of the dictator that he consumes the deaths of those who have fallen foul of him with as much relish as if he were eating raspberries. The raspberry is a recurrent motif in Mandelstam's poetry, most often taking the form of the raspberry glow of the lamps that hang in front of pharmacies. In his well-known prose text 'The Egyptian Stamp' the raspberry colour stands for the feverish delirium of the poet figure, which also cures and saves him.[48] There, too, the glow of the pharmacy lamps in the snow is described once again. It is a snow that tries, as in many other texts by Mandelstam, to cloak the crimes of the dictatorship with silence and oblivion.

In Herta Müller's novel *Atemschaukel* we again encounter the snow as an accomplice of tyranny.[49] And in *Atemschaukel* we again encounter the raspberry, or more precisely the raspberry colour. By using these motifs

---

48 On the connection between the delirium in 'The Egyptian Stamp' and the journey to Malina, cf. Charles Isenberg, *Substantial Proofs of Being. Ossip Mandelstams Literary Prose* (Columbus: Slavica Publishers, 1987), 129–30. On the *malina* motif generally, cf. Omry Ronen, *An Approach to Mandelstam* (Jerusalem: Magnes Press, 1983), 269–70. [Translator's note: The word *malina* is commonly used in Slavonic languages to denote various kinds of dark soft fruit.]

49 For the poetological level of significance here, cf. Roland Barthes's discussion of *écriture blanche* in *Writing Degree Zero*, esp. 66–9.

which establish a relation between her text and Mandelstam's writings, Herta Müller expands the intertextual resonance of her novel beyond the narrow corpus of texts about concentration camps to other instances of literature about camps. In this way her novel lays claim to a universalization of the questions that present themselves to the first-person narrator with his recollection of the experience of the camp: whether and how, in view of the emergency situation that this experience represented for the inmates, right and wrong can still be distinguished, or whether, as Agamben put it, 'the essence of the camp consists in the materialization of the state of exception and in the subsequent creation of a space in which bare life and the juridical rule enter into a threshold of indistinction'.[50] *Atemschaukel* vouches for the conviction that distinctions between right and wrong, between objectors and collaborators, between democracy and dictatorship, between state of emergency and normality can be maintained.[51] It is the task of literature to stand up for this conviction. Not through a literature that freezes the traces of the personal into a seal with its totalising coldness. But through a literature as it appears to Ossip Mandelstam's fevering poet figure in a truly wonderful image: as a raspberry bush bearing fruit in the snow.

50   Agamben, *Homo Sacer*, 174.
51   A distinction should be made between the emergency situation of a starving person in the camp and life in totalitarian circumstances, between dictatorship and democracy. Müller would scarcely subscribe to the notion of an 'inner solidarity between democracy and totalitarianism', as Agamben promotes it in the introduction to *Homo Sacer* (*ibid.*, 10, cf. also the closing pages of *Homo Sacer*). We should maintain the distinction between right and wrong, even if this presents itself in its most rudimentary forms as a 'senseless' act of charity (as 'bread justice'), and between those who are complicit in the totalitarian system and profit from it and those who resist such a system. Dictatorship and democracy, the forced labourer and the patient in a coma, are not the same thing. They do not even come near to being the same thing.

Bibliography

Agamben, Giorgio, *Homo Sacer: Sovereign Power and Bare Life*, trans. Daniel Heller-Roazen (Stanford: Stanford University Press, 1998).

Bachmann, Ingeborg, *Werke*, vol. 4, ed. Christine Koschel, Inge von Weidenbaum and Clemens Münster (Munich: Piper, 1978).

Barthes, Roland, 'Inaugural Lecture, Collège de France', in Susan Sontag, ed., *A Barthes Reader* (New York: Hill and Wang, 1982), 457–78.

——, *Writing Degree Zero & Elements of Sociology*, trans. Annette Lavers and Colin Smith (London: Jonathan Cape, 1984).

Butler, Judith, *Kritik der ethischen Gewalt* (Frankfurt am Main: Suhrkamp, 2003).

Celan, Paul, 'Der Meridian', in *Gesammelte Werke*, vol. 3, ed. Beda Allemann, Stefan Reichert and Rolf Bücher (Frankfurt am Main: Suhrkamp, 1983), 187–202.

——, 'The Meridian', in *Collected Prose*, trans. Rosemarie Waldrop (Manchester: Carcanet, 1986), 37–55.

Deuber-Mankowsky, Astrid, 'Homo Sacer, das bloße Leben und das Lager. Anmerkungen zu einem erneuten Versuch einer Kritik der Gewalt', *Die Philosophin* 25 (2002), 95–115.

Ette, Ottmar, *Roland Barthes. Eine intellektuelle Biographie* (Frankfurt am Main: Suhrkamp, 1998).

Foucault, Michel, 'The ethic of care for the self as a practice of freedom', in James Bernauer and David Rasmussen, eds, *The Final Foucault* (Cambridge, MA: MIT Press, 1988), 1–20.

——, *The Hermeneutics of the Subject: Lectures at the Collège de France, 1981–1982*, ed. Frédéric Gros, trans. Graham Burchell (New York: Palgrave Macmillan, 2005).

——, *Ästhetik der Existenz. Schriften zur Lebenskunst*, ed. Daniel Defert and Francois Ewald (Frankfurt am Main: Suhrkamp, 2007).

Gros, Frédéric, 'Course Context', in Michel Foucault, *The Hermeneutics of the Subject: Lectures at the Collège de France, 1981–1982*, ed. Frédéric Gros, trans. Graham Burchell (New York: Palgrave Macmillan, 2005), 507–50.

Isenberg, Charles, *Substantial Proofs of Being. Ossip Mandelstams Literary Prose* (Columbus: Slavica Publishers, 1987).

Kertész, Imre, *Fateless*, trans. Christopher C. Wilson and Katharina M. Wilson (Evanston: Northwestern University Press, 1992).

——, *Schritt für Schritt* (Frankfurt am Main: Suhrkamp, 2002).

Levinas, Emmanuel, 'Dialogue on Thinking-of-the-Other', in *Entre nous. Thinking-of-the-Other*, trans. Michael B. Smith and Barbara Harshav (London and New York: Continuum, 2006), 173–8.

——, 'The Other, Utopia, and Justice', in *Entre nous. Thinking-of-the-Other*, trans. Michael B. Smith and Barbara Harshav (London and New York: Continuum, 2006), 193–202.

Müller, Herta, 'Wie Wahrnehmung sich erfindet', in *Der Teufel sitzt im Spiegel. Wie Wahrnehmung sich erfindet* (Berlin: Rotbuch, 1991), 7–31.

——, *The Appointment*, trans. Michael Hulse and Philip Boehm (New York: Metropolitain Books, 2001).

——, *Atemschaukel* (Munich: Hanser, 2009).

——, '"Es war ja eine ganze Generation". Herta Müller im Gespräch mit Jürgen König. Die Schriftstellerin Herta Müller über Deportationen von Rumäniendeutschen nach dem Zweiten Weltkrieg durch die Sowjets und ihr Romanprojekt *Atemschaukel*', *Deutschlandradio Kultur* (13 August 2009).

——, *Der Fuchs war damals schon der Jäger* (Frankfurt am Main: Fischer, 2009).

——, 'Sag, dass du fünfzehn bist – *weiter leben* von Ruth Klüger', in *In der Falle. Drei Essays* (Göttingen: Wallstein, 2009), 25–40.

Pastior, Oskar, *Jetzt kann man schreiben was man will*, Werkausgabe, vol. 2, ed. Ernest Wichner (Munich: Hanser, 2003).

——, 'Geschichte, Poesie', in *"...was in der Mitte zu wachsen anfängt"*, Werkausgabe, vol. 4, ed. Ernest Wichner (Munich: Hanser, 2008), 306.

Ricoeur, Paul, *The Course of Recognition*, trans. David Pellauer (Cambridge, MA, and London: Harvard University Press, 2005).

Ronen, Omry, *An Approach to Mandelstam* (Jerusalem: Magnes Press, 1983).

de Zayas, Alfred-Maurice, *Anmerkungen zur Vertreibung der Deutschen aus dem Osten* (Stuttgart: Kohlhammer, 1986).

HUBERT ZAPF

Trauma, Narrative and Ethics in American Literature

1. Trauma Studies and Literature

The present volume brings together two different but interconnected questions. One is the question of trauma and the possibility and limits of its representation in language and narrative. The second is the question of the ethical implications of depicting 'other people's pain,' which is on one level a very general feature of literature and art. I am trying to comment on these interconnected questions here with a special focus on narratives of trauma in American literature.

Trauma studies have become a vast field of interdisciplinary research characterized by a broad diversity of subjects, approaches, and directions, and by the contributions of various disciplines such as medicine, psychiatry, law, political science, history, and cultural studies. Trauma is defined in Webster's Dictionary as '1. An injury or wound to a living body caused by the application of external force or violence. 2.a) a psychological or emotional stress or blow that may produce disordered feelings or behaviour (trauma of being left by mother; trauma of Civil War; b) the state or condition of mental or emotional shock produced by such a stress or by a physical injury.' Important aspects of trauma are then its original meaning as a 'wound;' the differences as well as the interconnections between physical and psychological, individual and collective, everyday and extreme forms of trauma; the disruptive effects of trauma on emotions, behaviour, values, and personal identity; and the potentially long-term consequences of the initial traumatic moment or experience for individuals as well as for cultures. Trauma involves experiences of fear, terror and disempowerment that overwhelm the defences and threaten to paralyze vital functions of a person or community, leading to states of disillusionment, disorientation, and loss of meaning and control. Trauma invalidates habitual categories of order and sense-making systems, representing a non-integrated and non-integratable part of personal and collective memory that at once demands and resists integration and verbal-narrative representation.

For my discussion of literary narratives of trauma, I take as a starting-point a much-cited example in trauma studies, the Italian Renaissance writer Torquato Tasso's epic *Jerusalem Liberated*, which Freud summarizes in *Beyond the Pleasure Principle* in the following way:

> Its hero, Tancred, unwittingly kills his beloved Clorinda in a duel while she is disguised in the armour of an enemy's knight. After her burial he makes his way into a strange magic forest which strikes the Crusader's army with terror. He slashes with his sword at a tall tree; but blood streams from the cut and the voice of Clorinda, whose soul is imprisoned in the tree, is heard complaining that he has wounded his beloved once again.[1]

This is something like a *locus classicus* of trauma studies, which is mentioned by Freud to demonstrate the repetition compulsion that goes along with trauma, and which has been taken up by recent trauma theorists to position themselves in continuity with but also in distinction from Freud. Cathy Caruth, in her *Unclaimed Experience*, proposes that 'the literary resonance of Freud's example goes beyond this dramatic illustration of repetition compulsion, and exceeds, perhaps, the limits of Freud's conceptual or conscious theory of trauma.' She extends his theory by specifically emphasizing the voice of the speaking wound as an aspect of traumatic narrative, 'the moving and sorrowful voice that cries out [...], a voice that is paradoxically released *through the wound*.'[2] Laura DiPrete in turn expands Caruth's reading of this scene by adding the aspect of *the corporeality* of the traumatic experience. 'This relationship [between trauma and voice] could be rethought and revised, expanded and complicated, once we add to the

---

1   As quoted in Cathy Caruth, *Unclaimed Experience: Trauma, Narrative, and History* (Baltimore: Johns Hopkins University Press, 1996), 2.
2   *Ibid.*

binary – voice and trauma – the element of corporeality.'[3] Referring to a remark by Freud in *Moses and Monotheism* on trauma as a 'Fremdkörper', a 'foreign body' in the individual's consciousness and memory, DiPrete contends that traumatic memories escape mental representation and instead are written in and onto the body. 'For a number of writers, bearing witness to traumatic experience means to articulate the complicated process from traumatic memory to conscious memory by attending not only to verbal signs but also to that nonverbal, sensorial, and perceptual experience that remains locked within the body.'[4] DiPrete convincingly substantiates this insight in analyses of novels such as Toni Morrison's *Beloved*, to which we will return later.

The aspect I would especially highlight here is that the textual example these theorists are relying on to elucidate the nature of trauma is an example from imaginative literature, which appears to provide an especially rich source of knowledge for trauma studies. I agree with Laurie Vickroy here, who in her exemplary study *Trauma and Survival in Contemporary Fiction* argues that fictional trauma narratives 'have taken an important place among artistic, scholarly, and testimonial representations in illuminating the personal and public aspects of trauma and in elucidating our relationship to memory and forgetting within the complex interweavings of social and psychological relationships.'[5] Vickroy focuses not only on the subject of trauma as textual content but also on the various fictional techniques through which it is mediated. In her book, trauma narrative is viewed as a relatively recent historical phenomenon responding to the socio-political upheavals and the mass catastrophes of the modern and postmodern era. But if we look again from here at the example of Tasso's epic, we see that perhaps the literary representation of trauma goes much further back in literary history. If we take this epic seriously as a textual source, we first of all would have to notice that the story of Tancred and Clorinda only

---

3   Laura DiPrete, *'Foreign Bodies': Trauma, Corporeality, and Textuality in Contemporary American Culture* (London and New York: Routledge, 2006), 9.

4   *Ibid.*, 10.

5   Laurie Vickroy, *Trauma and Survival in Contemporary Fiction* (Charlottesville: University of Virginia Press, 2002), 1.

represents a subplot in the long verse poem consisting of twenty lengthy books, in which the crusade with its aim of reconquering Jerusalem for the Christian world is portrayed in all its cultural-ideological force in a series of minutely described bloody battles that contrast with highly personal and even intimate scenes of human encounters between melancholic sensibility and passionate love. The cognitive richness and suggestive power of Tasso's epic is thus clearly linked to its status as imaginative literature, which only functions as a complex representation of trauma because of its fictionalizing, metaphorical and mythopoetic mode of textualizing experience. The story opens up an imaginative space of multiple conceptual blendings and metamorphoses[6] that enable Tasso's narrative to represent and interrelate the aspects of repetition compulsion, of giving voice to voiceless suffering, and of the corporeality of the traumatic experience that are described by trauma theorists. The text blends heterogeneous domains into one storyline in which the strange and the familiar, violence and love, self and other, subject and object, soul and body, the living and the dead, conscious and unconscious forces, culture and nature, anthropomorphic and biomorphic forms are brought together in unexpected ways. What appears ethically relevant in this example is the interdependence between the relational and the self-reflexive aspects of trauma, since the fate of the agent of traumatization, the crusading knight, is existentially interrelated with the fate and voice of the victim, and the apparent enemy of the hero turns out to be vitally connected to his innermost self. Human action is contextualized in the light of its unintended and unpredictable consequences. The experience of trauma that Freud and his later commentators identified in this episode represents a counter-discourse within the text to the affirmative depiction of heroic battle-scenes, and therefore constitutes an ethical corrective to the triumphalist ideology and mentality of the crusade. A psychoanalytical or psychocultural theory of trauma, it seems to me, would thus have to be

6   For the notion of multiple conceptual blendings within the framework of a cognitive
     poetics, see Mark Turner, 'The Art of Compression', in Mark Turner, ed., *The Artful
     Mind. Cognitive Science and the Riddle of Human Creativity* (New York: Oxford
     University Press, 2006), 93–114.

supplemented by a literary theory and poetics of trauma, which involves all elements of the textual system from narrative perspective, character, plot, time, space, imagery, and symbolism to the role of the implied reader, but also the generic, historical, and intertextual signatures that make up the narrative matrix of the text. What is moreover remarkable in Tasso's epic is that the traumatizing event affects not only the cultural but the natural world, which in the image of the bleeding tree is shown to be violated here as well. Thus one further ethical implication of the scene seems to be that human acts and experiences of traumatization are, in a significant way, connected to the violation of a fundamental biophilic embeddedness of human beings in the vital force-fields and ecological interrelatedness of all life. A literary poetics of trauma, the example seems to suggest, would thus have to be connected on some significant level with a cultural ecology of trauma.[7]

If we look from here into literary history, the scene from Tasso's epic represents no absolutely exceptional case, since in a broad sense, much of literary narrative has always been a post-traumatic form of narrative. Some notable examples – and I have to be highly selective here of course – would be biblical narratives of captivity, sacrifice, and redemption; ancient mythological stories of monstrous origins as the Minotaur myth, which has as much been a source of imaginative literature as the myth of the Medusa as a death-in-life figure in which erotic traumatization is transformed into a paralyzing power over the gaze of others that can only be endured in the indirect reflection of the mirror, i.e., of fictional mimesis; then of course the medieval pagan-Christian Grail myth of the wounded king and the corresponding wasteland motif which became such an influential topos in modern literature; dramas of oedipal traumatization and melancholia as in Shakespeare's *Hamlet*, the post-traumatic story-telling of Coleridge's

---

7   For the approach of cultural ecology as a transdisciplinary paradigm of literary studies, see Hubert Zapf, 'New Directions in American Literary Studies: Ecocriticism and the Function of Literature as Cultural Ecology' in Ansgar Nünning and Jürgen Schlaeger, eds, *English Studies Today. Recent Developments and New Directions* (Trier: WVT, 2007), 139–64; Hubert Zapf, ed., *Kulturökologie und Literatur. Beiträge zu einem transdisziplinären Paradigma der Literaturwissenschaft* (Heidelberg: Winter, 2008).

ecological apocalypse *The Rhyme of the Ancient Mariner*, the traumatizing
effects of modernization and science in the gothic romanticism of Shelley's
Frankenstein; and then at the beginning of the twentieth century the traumatic alienation of Kafka's protagonists, both in the anonymous labyrinths
of modern bureaucracies and in the grotesque deformities of personal family
traumas. Kafka's *Metamorphosis, Die Verwandlung*, is an especially instruc-
tive case in point. In the story, Gregor Samsa's monstrous self-alienation is
visualized not only in his metamorphosis into a giant cockroach, but very
pointedly in the painful and never-healing wound in his back caused by an
apple that his angry father threw at him and that keeps sticking in his body,
a psychosomatic symptom of the broken father-son-relationship and, more
generally, of the victimizing forces that determine Gregor's life 'behind his
back.' We have the repetition compulsion in the repeated scenes of Gregor's
victimization, we have the voice of the victim in the narrative perspective,
we have the corporeality of trauma in the never-healing wound, and we
have the perverted relationship to and abuse of nature in the apple thrown
at Gregor, which points to the alienated form of civilizational existence
from which Gregor's trauma has originated.

2. Trauma and American Literature

Even within American literature, which is often considered as fundamentally more affirmative and optimistic than its European counterpart, trauma
has been an important point of reference for its fictional scenarios. Already
in Hawthorne's *The Scarlet Letter*, the legacy of puritanism appears as a
traumatizing prison-house of culture, which produces symptoms of depression and self-alienation in all major characters; in Melville's surreal 'Bar-
tleby, the Scrivener,' the protagonist is deeply traumatized by the capitalist
world of nineteenth century Wall Street; in their different ways, Poe's
and Dickinson's thanatographic poems are clearly shaped by traumatic
experiences; in the twentieth century, the wasteland motif of T. S. Eliot's
eponymic poem recurs not only in Hemingway's wounded heroes but also

quite prominently in Fitzgerald's novel about the American Dream, *The Great Gatsby*, in which the hectic pursuit of happiness in the Jazz Age is contrasted with and undermined by the industrial wasteland and symbolic underworld of the Valley of the Ashes. One particularly impressive example of literary trauma writing, I think, is the fiction of William Faulkner, especially his novel *The Sound and the Fury*, in which the first chapter is narrated by a thirty-three-year-old mentally retarded character with the brain of a three-year-old, who is unable to speak and who is traumatized not only by his castration but by the loss of his beloved sister Caddy, for whom he keeps waiting at the garden door even decades after she has been forced to leave the family. Benjy's brothers, too, are traumatized by the loss of meaning and shared values, and even though these are traumas of everyday life, they are also symptoms of a deeper crisis of Southern culture, which manifests itself on the levels of individual consciousness and personal communication.

Faulkner's novels invite readers to share experiences with fictional characters that they couldn't share in other modes of discourse, to feel empathy or, as Dominick LaCapra has it, 'empathetic unsettlement'[8] towards social outsiders like Benjy, whose unarticulated bellowing is a leitmotiv of the text and, as it were, a speaking wound of trauma as the undecipherable 'grave hopeless sound of all voiceless misery under the sun.'[9] Through Faulkner's experimental technique of simultaneously disrupting and rearranging the flow of language and the text, readers are enabled to follow the fragmented, achronological stream of Benjy's unarticulated sensations and emotions, in other words to participate symbolically in the pain of another, without being able to distance themselves into illusionary linguistic or intellectual control or to escape into melodramatic voyeurism. The visible intertextual signature of Shakespeare's *Macbeth* in the title and narrative conception of *The Sound and the Fury* nevertheless testifies to the presence of a transhistorical and transcultural repertoire and poetics of trauma on which even such highly experimental novels can draw.

---

8   Dominick LaCapra, *Writing History, Writing Trauma* (Baltimore: Johns Hopkins University Press, 2001), xi.

9   William Faulkner, *The Sound and The Fury* (New York: Vintage, 1984 [1929]), 366.

3. Trauma and Recent American Literature: Two Exemplary Cases

Thus trauma has been a surprisingly widespread topic in American literature, reflecting disruptions in cultural history and a radical critique of the
American Dream as a shaping myth of American culture in which there
seemed to be no place for historical and personal trauma. Nevertheless,
one can still distinguish this cultural-critical function of trauma from the
prominent role that trauma gains in the later twentieth century in writings
about World War II and the Holocaust in particular, but also in the postcolonial literatures of cultural minorities within the US, in which trauma
became a defining aspect of the ways in which these minorities rediscovered and reinterpreted their history and their cultural self-concept. The
historical traumas of the displacement of the indigenous people, as well
as the long years of black slavery, came to be seen as shaping events of the
histories and cultures of Native Americans and African Americans respec-
tively, which provided a narrative source and paradigm for the imaginative
reconstruction of long-term experiences of humiliation, victimization, and
disempowerment, but also for processes of rediscovery, re-empowerment,
and personal and cultural regeneration.

3.1. Leslie Marmon Silko, Ceremony

In Leslie Marmon Silko's *Ceremony*, several traumatic experiences are interconnected, taking as a starting point the situation of the protagonist Tayo,
who has returned from World War II:

> Tayo didn't sleep well that night. He tossed in the old iron bed, and the coiled springs
> kept squeaking even after he lay still again, calling up humid dreams of black night
> and loud voices rolling him over and over again like debris caught in a flood. Tonight
> the singing had come first, squeaking out of the iron bed, a man singing in Spanish,
> the melody of a familiar love song, two words again and again, '*Y volveré.*' Sometimes
> the Japanese voices came first, angry and loud, pushing the song far away, and then
> he could hear the shift in his dreaming, like a slight afternoon wind changing its

direction, coming less and less from the south, moving into the west, and the voices would become Laguna voices, and he could hear Uncle Josiah calling to him, Josiah bringing him the fever medicine when he had been sick a long time ago. But before Josiah could come, the fever voices would drift and whirl and emerge again – Japanese soldiers shouting orders to him, suffocating damp voices that drifted out in the jungle steam, and he heard the women's voices then; they faded in and out until he was frantic because he thought the Laguna words were his mother's, but when he was about to make out the meaning of the words, the voice suddenly broke into a language he could not understand; and it was then that all the voices were drowned by the music – loud, loud music from a big juke box, its flashing red and blue lights pulling the darkness closer.[10]

This opening passage of the novel, which shows the protagonist in a hospital bed, describes characteristic symptoms of post-traumatic stress disorder – sleeplessness, severe anxiety, stress, fragmented perception and self-perception, a breakdown of psychological defences in an uncontrolled flood of memories, and an inability to interpret and understand the meaning of what has been happening to him. It conveys a subjectivity disintegrating under the pressure of overwhelming memories, and exposed to chaotic feelings of disorientation and powerlessness, which are expressed in the imagery of breaking waves and near-drowning. The scene resembles in its blurred and shifting focus of fragmented sounds, visions and memories the effect of 'white noise' in the brain, suggesting a disturbing breakdown of the boundary between past and present, internal and external world, the conscious and the unconscious self. Mixed with Tayo's war memories of Japanese soldiers is the memory of his uncle Josiah and of his mother's voice – who has left him orphaned as a child – a memory which is finally extinguished by the juke box with its red and blue lights as an empty metonymic signifier of a trivialized American Dream of happiness. Different traumas are interconnected in this initial scene: the loss of his mother, the crisis of the Laguna community, and his war trauma, which is a central catalyst and motivating shock for the narrative process. The most painful of his insistently recurring memories is the shooting of captured Japanese soldiers, one of whom Tayo believes to be his own uncle Josiah:

10   Leslie Marmon Silko, *Ceremony* (Harmondsworth: Penguin, 1977), 5–6.

When the sergeant told them to kill all the Japanese soldiers lined up in front of the cave with their hands on their heads, Tayo could not pull the trigger. The fever made him shiver, and the sweat was stinging his eyes and he couldn't see clearly; in that instant he saw Josiah standing there; the face was dark from the sun, and the eyes were squinting as though he were about to smile at Tayo. So Tayo stood there, stiff with nausea, while they fired at the soldiers, and he watched his uncle fall, and he knew it was Josiah; and even after Rocky [his brother, who is much more patriotic than Tayo and is wounded and killed soon afterwards] pushed him toward the corpses and told him to look, look past the blood that was already dark like the jungle mud, with only flecks of bright red still shimmering in it. Rocky made him look at the corpse and said, 'Tayo, this is a *Jap*! This is a *Jap* uniform!' And then he rolled the body over with his boot and said, Look, Tayo, look at the face,' and that was when Tayo started screaming because it wasn't a Jap, it was Josiah, eyes shrinking back into the skull and all their shining black light glazed over by death.[11]

In the chaotic flow of his semi-unconscious stream of memories, Tayo repeatedly returns to this scene which he desperately tries to avoid, a scene in which his 'madness' began as a shock reaction to the horrors of war, a mental disturbance and hallucination in which the unknown Japanese soldier is blending into Tayo's beloved uncle Josiah, who has initiated him into the beauty and the mysteries of nature and of Indian traditions – and who, as Tayo learns later, has indeed died at home while Tayo was away in the war. Symbolically speaking, then, the killing of the Japanese soldier means the killing of Tayo's own life and culture, it is a self-destructive act which leads him into the death-in-life situation in which he finds himself, after his return from the war, at the beginning of the novel. In his madness and his hypersensitive 'misunderstanding' of the situation, Tayo in fact reacts to a signal from the unconscious and displays a deeper understanding of the interconnections between the foreign war scene and his own cultural identity. Two apparently separate events – the shooting of the Japanese soldier in the Pacific, and the traumatic experience of Indians on reservations in America, are brought together here in such a way that the destructive forces of the war and the destructive forces which lead to the loss of Indian identity and traditions are linked to each other. Since Tayo's reactions are at first primarily unconscious and uncontrolled, he does not fully realize this connection before he is dismissed from hospital,

11   *Ibid.*, 8–9.

and starts on his journey of a quest for the lost Laguna traditions in the unfolding healing ceremony which constitutes the process of the novel. After a time of aimless and futile existence, in which he spends his life as an alcoholic, jobless drifter with other war veterans in bars, Tayo first consults a traditional healer, who however is unable to help him, and then the modern shamanistic figure of Bretonie, who advises him to search for a new ceremony that does not simply repeat the past but must combine the virtues of tradition with the experiences of modernity to be effective. As Tayo performs this ceremonial journey, which opens up to him a whole new universe of ancient Indian myths, songs and rituals of nature and the landscape, of love and eros, and of the imaginative power of story-telling, his paralyzed vital functions are gradually restored.

But his personal therapy and healing through the ceremony of story-telling, which in painful steps transforms the initial death-in-life state of the protagonist into a new sense of self and communal responsiveness, remains linked to the more general themes of war, trauma, and violence which are introduced at the novel's beginning. The vicious circle of violence can only be broken by tracing it back to the exploitation of natural resources by the technological war machinery of white civilization, and by a renewed vision of nature, humanity, and civilization that considers everything to be connected to everything else in the shared ecosemiotic space of a global ethics and consciousness. As Tayo is approaching the uranium mines in Los Alamos, the site of the development and first testing of the atomic bomb, which was then used against the Japanese, he recognizes the connection he has made in his traumatized unconscious:

> There was no end to it; it knew no boundaries, and he had arrived at the point of convergence where the fate of all living things, and even the earth, had been laid [...]. He walked to the mine shaft slowly, and the feeling became overwhelming: the pattern of the ceremony was completed there [...]. He cried the relief he felt at finally seeing the pattern, the way all the stories fit together – the old stories, the war stories, their stories – to become the story that was still being told. He was not crazy; he had never been crazy. He had only seen and heard the world as it always was: no boundaries, only transitions through all distances and time.[12]

12   *Ibid.*, 246.

The process of the protagonist's quest, which culminates in this moment
of insight, is reflected and communicated in the narrative structure of the
novel, which starts out in the chaotic, disruptive, achronological mode
of a trauma narrative and then gradually shifts towards a more coherent
mythopoetic rhythm of story-telling as it is prefigured in the metatextual
frame of the novel, the myth of the spiderwoman as aboriginal story-teller
and creator of the world. Her narrative power precedes the writing of the
modern novel, signifying a mythopoetic source of the imagination and of
narrative that brings forth always new worlds, including the world of the
novel and the reality that it depicts:

> Thought-Woman, the spider,
> named things and
> as she named them
> they appeared.
> She is sitting in her room
> thinking of a story now
> I'm telling you the story
> she is thinking.[13]

The generative power of traditional story-telling is brought together in
the novel with modern and postmodern techniques of self-reflexivity, of
intertextual webs of signification and associative stream-of-consciousness
writing to convey the complexities of an ecocultural trauma narrative that
is also a narrative of therapy and regeneration. The fictional representation
of trauma thus helps to achieve several things: the mimesis of a complex,
life-threatening phenomenon of human experience; the contextualiza-
tion of this experience as culturally representative; the generalization of
this local and personal experience for a globalized ethics; the imaginative
sharing of this experience by the reader, which implies the paradox of a
transpersonal and transcultural openness and translatability of the fundamentally untranslatable trauma narrative; and the process of imaginative
regeneration and cultural self-renewal into which the initial state of traumatization is symbolically transformed in the search for a new beginning
within a new global ecological ethics.

13   *Ibid.*, 1.

3.2. *Toni Morrison, Beloved*

Toni Morrison's *Beloved*, a much-discussed text in trauma studies, is about the historical experience of slavery, which is explored in its various manifestations. Its plot is partially based on the so-called *Black Book*, a collection of documents about American slavery on which Morrison drew in her research for the novel, and particularly on the historical case of Margaret Garner, a fugitive slave who killed one of her children when she was about to be recaptured into slavery. Morrison is taking up this case in her neo-slave-narrative and turns it into the central focus and starting point for the novel's narrative process. The historical material is fictionalized in order to convey the interiority of the characters, without which trauma could not be represented, and to reconstruct the voices of people who had no voice in the historical process. The single self becomes part of a multivoiced discourse and of polyphonic, achronological storytelling, which reflects the disruptions of the traumatic experiences that it confronts. The killing by the protagonist Sethe of her own two-year-old daughter in order to prevent her being taken back into slavery is the core event of the text, the result of her earlier traumatization in slavery, but also an ethical challenge as an outrageous act of protective violence, which continues the cycle of destruction and becomes the source of new, even deeper traumatization for herself and for others. Sethe has to spend six years in prison and, after she is released, is excommunicated from the black community, living with the suppressed memory of the murdered child in a haunted house on the outskirts of Cincinnati. She lives for years in a traumatized state of numbness, of paralyzed emotions and communicative abilities. A bodily sign of her traumatization already before the killing of her child is the scar on her back, a horrible wound which is the result of a cruel whipping during her time as a slave. As a visible trace and sign of violence and humiliation, this 'revolting clump of scars'[14] on her back represents the bodily signature of traumatization by slavery, which affects different characters in the novel in different ways. Denver, Sethe's daughter, for example, who is the only one to stay with Sethe after the brothers have left, becomes deaf for two

---

14   Toni Morrison, *Beloved* (Harmondsworth: Penguin, 1991 [1987]), 26.

years after she first hears about the killing of her sister, and is haunted by
recurring nightmares in which her mother cuts off her head and subsequently braids her hair.

The most conspicuous fictional device of the novel, of course, is the
return of the ghost of the dead daughter into the life of the survivors, a representative not only of Sethe's individual child but of all the victims of slavery. That way, the act of 'rememory,' as Morrison calls it, is more and more
traced back to the initial scene of historical traumatization in the Middle
Passage, as becomes manifest in Beloved's stream-of-consciousness:

> I am Beloved and she is mine [...] All of it is now   it is always now   there will
> never be a time when I am not crouching and watching others who are crouching
> too   I am always crouching   the man on my face is dead his face is not mine   his
> mouth smells sweet but his eyes are locked   some who eat nasty   themselves   I
> do not eat   the men without skin bring us their morning water to drink   we have
> none   at night I cannot see the dead man on my face   daylight comes through the
> cracks and I can see his locked eyes [...][15]

The experience of the Middle Passage is remembered here by the imaginary consciousness of Beloved, which becomes the narrative medium of
a traumatic experience that transcends time, space, and individuality. It
conveys the inescapable imprisonment on the slave ship, the omnipresent
experience of anonymity, starving, rape, and death, and the internalized
patterns of compulsory repetition and self-paralyzing behaviour resulting
from it ('I am always crouching'). The stream-of-consciousness of an infant,
the rhythm of the sea waves, and the fragmented nightmare scenes of a collective unconscious are brought together here in a reintegrative discourse
which reflects the collective in the individual consciousness, the past in
the present, the working through of the painful rememory in a distorted
kind of blues rhythm.

Again, however, trauma is not only represented as the mimesis and
memory of past suffering and victimization, but also from a perspective
of survival and regeneration. This regenerative counter-discourse starts
with Paul D's search for Sethe, whom he finds following the tree blos-
soms in spring; it is somatically inscribed into the body of Sethe in the

---

15   *Ibid.*, 259 [Editors' note: spacing in the original].

metamorphosis of the scar on her back into the shape of a tree; it manifests itself – somewhat comparable to Silko's *Ceremony* – in the new spiritual ritual and ceremony that Sethe's mother-in-law Baby Suggs performs, and in which she preaches passionate love and acceptance of their long-abused bodies to the Black community; and it culminates in the temporary reappearance and eventual exorcism of the ghost of Beloved, a trickster figure from African American myth and folklore, which helps both to reenact and finally to overcome the trauma; and, last but not least, in the reintegration of Sethe and Denver into the community from which they had been excluded. The vision of Beloved as a young pregnant woman at the end, before she magically disappears into the water from which she had emerged – 'a naked woman with fish for hair'[16] – clearly points to the new beginning that seems to be possible after the painful processes of remembering and slow distancing of the trauma. As in the case of Silko, this is an ecocultural counterdiscourse which is associated with images of nature, the body, community, and creativity, and finally also links up with the narrative process itself. As in Silko, this doesn't mean any easy solution to the problems raised in the book. The instability of the new beginning is obvious, since the memory of trauma and its forgetting are both necessary and impossible. The memory of slavery, which structures the novel as an ethical and imaginative act, is both preserved and suspended, and the necessity and impossibility of the story it tells becomes an explicit paradox that is repeated like a refrain at the end: 'This is not a story to pass on.'[17] The ethical problem of trauma narratives, the problem of 'how not to betray the past'[18] by transforming it into fictional story-telling, is concretely addressed here and embodied in the self-cancelling gesture at the end of the novel.

Morrison is here exploring a collective trauma in African American history in the light of an extreme ethical borderline situation, and again the individual forms of traumatization are made to be representative of a historical experience which has had a long-term effect not only on the African American community.

16   *Ibid.*, 328.
17   *Ibid.*, 337.
18   Caruth, *Unclaimed Experience*, 27.

4. American Trauma Narratives in the Twenty-First Century

In the early twenty-first century, trauma continues to be a conspicuous focus of American literature, which on the one hand seems to respond to and to co-evolve with the development in trauma studies in science, medicine, and psychology, and on the other hand to reflect the deeply felt impact of the terrorist attacks of 9/11 on the American imagination. One characteristic feature of these novels is that several traumas – public and private, extreme and everyday, physical and psychological – are interconnected and explored in their mutual effects in the narrative process. In Philip Roth's *The Human Stain*, multiple traumas structure the novel's plot and the psychology of the characters, from racial identity problems in the male protagonist Coleman Silk to childhood abuse, domestic violence, and the loss of her children in a fire in the female protagonist Faunia Farley, to veritable PTSD in her husband and Vietnam War veteran Lester Farley. All of the characters respond to their trauma by adopting the roles of invented, other selves as strategies of self-protection and survival: Coleman Silk the role of the Jewish intellectual, Faunia Farley the role of the illiterate underclass woman, Lester Farley the role of a mad war victim and bizarre Thoreauvean natural man. In the crisis of these roles, the continuing divisions and ideological fault lines of American society are revealed. But again this crisis is also a chance for an at least temporary revitalization of the characters' quietly desperate lives, which is primarily expressed in the love affair of Coleman Silk with Faunia Farley, who not only in her name reminds us of the nature spirits of Greek mythology, but also in her erotic power and her intimate contact to nature and animals represents an inspirational dionysian energy and ecotherapeutic counterforce to the brutal experiences of mutual aggression and traumatization in civilization, which are depicted in the book with manifold allusions to the genre of classical tragedy.[19]

---

19   For a cultural-ecological analysis of *The Human Stain*, see Michael Sauter, 'Ethische Aspekte des kulturökologischen Literaturmodells am Beispiel von Philip Roths *The*

In Richard Powers's, *The Time of Our Singing*, too, multiple traumas of the main characters become the focal points of plot construction, character development, and cultural-historical analysis. The novel's microcosmic interracial family consists of the exiled German-Jewish father David Strom, a physicist who has escaped Nazi Germany but has lost most of his family in the Holocaust, of the black American mother Deliah, who had to abandon her dreams of a musical career because of the deep-rooted racism in American society, and who dies in a fire which may well have been a racist terrorist attack, of their two sons Jonah and Joseph, who follow a musical career in the no man's land of the racial divide which determines their identities, and of their youngest daughter Ruth, who has directly witnessed her mother's death and needs decades to overcome this experience. Again, historical and personal traumas are interconnected and blended in complex ways, illuminating in powerful emotional scenarios central political, ethical, and psychological catastrophes of modern civilization. Once more, however, the traumas are also a starting point for processes of intense personal remembrance, communication, and creativity, as is most vividly expressed in the singing and the musical activities of all the protagonists, who bring together the culturally separated spheres of life and society in their improvised performances and their fusion of classical European with black American jazz music.

In his novel *The Echo-Maker*, Powers consults insights from contemporary neuroscience when he deals with the victim of a truck accident, who after waking from his coma is a split personality, suffering from a special brain disorder which lets him only remember factual information but no emotions, with the result that all personal relations appear in an entirely depersonalized light, and that the radical strangeness of the familiar becomes a starting point for a redefinition of reality and the self. The process of therapy, however, remains painful and difficult, and the attempts of the neurologist to cure the trauma are, significantly, unsuccessful.

Human Stain' in Zapf, *Kulturökologie und Literatur*, 309–21. For a detailed analysis of *The Human Stain* in the context of trauma studies see Rudolf Freiburg's article in this volume.

The human difference remains, and the radical defamiliarization of the familiar presents not only a therapeutic challenge to the characters, but an ethical challenge to the readers of Powers's novel.

The dialogue with psychoanalysis, trauma studies, psychiatry and neuroscience characterizes the ways in which Siri Hustvedt deals with trauma in her novels. Her emphasis is very much on personal and psychological trauma, even though the larger context of modern history is, often inconspicuously, worked into the plot and the characters' fates. In *What I Loved*, the central trauma around which the novel's action revolves, is the death of the eleven-year-old son of the narrator Leo Hertzberg, who is killed in an accident during a summer vacation in a youth camp. As a result, Leo's marriage breaks apart and he remains traumatized for years, and even much later at the time of the writing of the novel, this loss is still a wound that hasn't healed. But a more quiet form of traumatization goes back into his own early childhood, when he was a boy in the Jewish community of Berlin, who had been driven from the country at the age of five and who has lost most of his relatives in the Holocaust.

> I have the formal wedding portrait of my Uncle David and Aunt Marta, and a picture of the twins in short wool coats with ribbons in their hair. Beneath each girl in the white border of the photo, Marta wrote their names, to avoid confusion – Anna on the left, Ruth on the right. The black-and-white figures of the photographs have had to stand in place of my memory, and yet I have always felt that their unmarked graves became a part of me. What was unwritten then is inscribed into what I call myself.[20]

His memories constitute his self, which is a plural rather than a single coherent and individualistic self. 'The longer I live the more convinced I am that when I say "I", I am really saying "we".'[21] His attempt of narrating his multiple, incoherent, and contradictory memories within the horizon of these traumas, is always cautious, tentative, and highly self-reflexive, but it is authenticated by the crisis of radical self-exposure that he risks. The interaction of the two traumas becomes obvious in the 'game of mobile objects' that he plays with objects he has faithfully collected over time.

20   Siri Hustvedt, *What I Loved* (London: Hodder and Stoughton, 2003), 22–3.
21   *Ibid.*, 23.

His mobile collection of personal memorabilia contains, as the narration itself a double, negative *and* positive energy, which both destroys and creates meanings.

> [...] when I play my game of mobile objects, I'm often tempted to move the photographs of my aunt, uncle, grandparents, and the twins near the knife and the fragment of the box. Then the game flirts with terror. It moves me so close to the edge that I have a sensation of falling, as if I had hurled myself off the edge of a building. I plummet downward, and in the speed of the fall I lose myself in something formless but deafening. It's like entering a scream – being a scream.[22]

This game of mobile objects is a metaphor for the narrative process of the novel as a whole. It marks the text as a posttraumatic narrative, which is driven by its own search for orientation and sense-making, but contains an extreme sense of fragility and brokenness, which keeps threatening the stability of the self and of the text.

The terrorist attacks of 9/11 have probably been the most spectacular event that has shaped the literary response to trauma in the first decade of the twenty-first century. I am not dealing here with this response in any representative way but only look briefly at how this collective national shock and global media event is related to writing about trauma as we have discussed it so far. More than other catastrophes with as many or even more victims, 9/11 was experienced as exceptional, unheard of, and unimaginable, raising the fundamental question of its representability in language and art. In political and media reactions, this initial sense of shock and incomprehensibility however was soon translated into new moral-ideological purpose and aggressive self-assertion, and the crisis of the most deeply-held beliefs about America as a land of invulnerable power and limitless opportunity was repressed in the openly declared crusade against an external enemy, the war on terror. In literary reactions, however, the trauma was confronted – with some temporal delay – in its disturbing psychocultural and ethical complexities, and it seems that this different attitude and response to the traumatic event went along with an explicit or implicit critique of its moral-ideological simplification and political instrumentalization. Art

22   *Ibid.*, 364–5.

Spiegelman's *In the Shadow of No Towers* tries to capture in the genre of comics and from the perspective of one character – basically himself – an event which resists visual and textual appropriation by art – and yet in this self-reflexive, metatextual gesture indicates one way of approaching this trauma; Jonathan Safran Foer's *Extremely Loud and Incredibly Close* decentres the response to trauma into different perspectives, linking 9/11 to earlier forms of collective traumatization, e.g. in World War II; Siri Hustvedt's *The Sorrows of an American* includes 9/11 as one contemporary background for the individual traumas of everyday life as evidenced not only in the semi-autobiographical fate of the narrator-protagonist and his family and friends, but also in various cases of psychiatric patients.

A contemporary trauma narrative which exclusively focuses on 9/11 is Don DeLillo's *Falling Man*, which deals in the retrospect of several years with the traumatizing effects of that catastrophe on survivors, and on the challenge of an appropriate artistic response to it. The narrative follows no clear or coherent plot line, deliberately confuses the identity of the individual characters, and includes disruptive as well as repetitive and circular elements that indicate the loss of personal and narrative control over the material. In the blurring of the relationship between reality and fiction, between identity and otherness, mind and body, inside and outside world, the novel approaches the complexities of trauma without reducing them to any easy aesthetic and ethical solutions. Even the terrorists are included in this shifting of perspectives, and in the sense of a shared common humanity that becomes even more urgent and evident at the moment of its most terrible violation.

DeLillo does allude to the powerful visual and media representations of 9/11 that had flooded the public imagination until he wrote his novel, but he also inscribes their radical insufficiency into his intermedial reflections. When he refers to scenes in his novels as film-like, they are, as it were, films without pictures. After Keith, the central character, has barely escaped from the North Tower before it collapsed, he is talking to himself: 'He said, "I'm standing here," and then louder, "I'm standing here." In the movie version, someone would be in the building, and emotionally damaged woman or a homeless man, and there would be dialogue and close-ups.'[23] But there is

---

23   Don DeLillo, *Falling Man* (London: Picador, 2007), 27.

no one else besides him, and the environment is as blurred and unreal as his own sense of personality and identity. Unlike Foer in *Extremely Loud and Incredibly Close*, DeLillo does not include the famous photograph of a man falling from one of the towers, but only a verbal description of the photograph, translating this globally reproduced image of another's unimaginable pain into words. Whereas Foer in *Extremely Loud and Incredibly Close* uses a computer simulation of the falling man photograph in a medial distancing that indicates his respect for the real falling man, and indeed imaginatively reverses the catastrophe by transforming it into a serial arrangement of pictures in which the falling man appears to be flying upwards instead, DeLillo restricts himself to the medium of language as the sole source of representing the unrepresentable. DeLillo self-reflexively doubles this procedure by including narrative sequences about the artist figure of the Falling Man, who made his appearances throughout New York soon after 9/11 to confront his involuntary spectators with his performances, in which he jumped from buildings, falling and then hanging from a rope in the position of the real falling man on the photograph. Thus the authentic event is reenacted in the performance act of the Falling Man, who memorializes the original tragedy in his artistic reenactment, which is then imaginatively reenacted in DeLillo's narrative. Once again, as we have seen in other trauma narratives as well, language and narration are both necessary and inadequate for this task, representing a radical insufficiency that is reflected in the discontinuities, the repetitions, and gaps of the narrative, which communicate to the reader the absence of a centre that remains, however, uncannily present. DeLillo illustrates this missing centre metafictionally in reference to the female protagonist Lianne, who is trying to remember a haiku poem:

> Lianne used to read haiku, sitting crosslegged on the floor, in the weeks and months after her father died. She thought of a poem by Bashō, or the first and third lines. She didn't remember the second line. *Even in Kyoto – I long for Kyoto.* The second line was missing but she didn't think she needed it.[24]
>
> [...]

---

24 *Ibid.*, 33.

Even in New York, she thought. Of course she was wrong about the second line of
the haiku. She knew this. Whatever the line was, it was surely crucial to the poem.
Even in New York – I long for New York.[25]

The missing links, open gaps, and indeterminacies of the text are the source
for the readers' interpretation of the events, which allow them access to
deeper dynamics and complexities of trauma but at the same time confront
them with the limits and indeed the impossibility of any definitive discursive knowledge and textual appropriation of trauma.

5. Concluding Remarks

As we have seen, literary history from classical times through romanticism into modernity consists to a considerable degree of trauma narratives, providing a repertoire of themes and forms on which modern and
postmodern narratives of trauma can draw. Of course, the unprecedented
mass catastrophes in the twentieth century represented a new scale and
dimension which substantially affected and changed literary responses
to trauma – in the writings during and after the First World War, and
particularly after the Holocaust in the later twentieth century. In spite of
their exceptional status, however, these narratives remain connected, at
least in principle, to a long tradition of literary representations of 'other
people's pain,' whose ethical implications are tied to their fictional status
and to the fact that the other people and their fates whose pain the reader is
witnessing or sharing are the fates of imaginary people in a depragmatized
and metadiscursive space of textuality, which however may paradoxically
enhance its communicational intensity and its signifying power towards
a collectively experienced historical reality.

25   *Ibid.*, 35.

Bibliography

Caruth, Cathy, *Unclaimed Experience: Trauma, Narrative, and History* (Baltimore: Johns Hopkins University Press, 1996).

DeLillo, Don, *Falling Man* (London: Picador, 2007).

Devoine, Françoise, and Jean-Max Gaudilliere, *History Beyond Trauma. Whereof One Cannot Speak, Thereof One Cannot Stay Silent* (New York: Other Press, 2005).

DiPrete, Laura, *'Foreign Bodies': Trauma, Corporeality, and Textuality in Contemporary American Culture* (London and New York: Routledge, 2006).

European Journal of English Studies (Special Issue on Trauma and Literature) 7/3 (2003).

Faulkner, William, *The Sound and The Fury* (New York: Vintage, 1984 [1929]).

Hustvedt, Siri, *What I Loved* (London: Hodder and Stoughton, 2003).

Kaplan, E. Ann, *Trauma Culture: The Politics of Terror and Loss in Media and Literature* (New Jersey: Rutgers University Press, 2005).

LaCapra, Dominick, *Writing History, Writing Trauma* (Baltimore: Johns Hopkins University Press, 2001).

MacCurdy, Marian Mesrobian, *The Mind's Eye: Image and Memory in Writing about Trauma* (Amherst: University of Massachussetts Press, 2007).

Morrison, Toni, *Beloved* (Harmondsworth: Penguin, 1991 [1987]).

Sauter, Michael, 'Ethische Aspekte des kulturökologischen Literaturmodells am Beispiel von Philip Roths *The Human Stain*', in Hubert Zapf, ed., *Kulturökologie und Literatur* (Heidelberg: Winter, 2008), 309–21.

Silko, Leslie Marmon, *Ceremony* (Harmondsworth: Penguin, 1977).

Sontag, Susan, *Regarding the Pain of Others* (New York: Farrar Straus, 2003).

Tal, Kalai, *Worlds of Hurt: Reading the Literatures of Trauma* (Cambridge and New York: Cambridge University Press, 1996).

Turner, Mark, 'The Art of Compression' in Mark Turner, ed., *The Artful Mind. Cognitive Science and the Riddle of Human Creativity* (New York: Oxford University Press, 2006), 93–114.

Vickroy, Laurie, *Trauma and Survival in Contemporary Fiction* (Charlottesville: University of Virginia Press, 2002).

Zapf, Hubert, 'New Directions in American Literary Studies: Ecocriticism and the Function of Literature as Cultural Ecology' in Ansgar Nünning and Jürgen Schlaeger, eds, *English Studies Today. Recent Developments and New Directions* (Trier: WVT, 2007), 139–64.

——, ed. (in collaboration with Christina Caupert, Timo Müller, Erik Redling, and Michael Sauter), *Kulturökologie und Literatur. Beiträge zu einem transdisziplinären Paradigma der Literaturwissenschaft* (Heidelberg: Winter, 2008).

RUDOLF FREIBURG

Trauma as Normalcy:
Pain in Philip Roth's *The Human Stain*

When Julian Barnes translated Alphonse Daudet's autobiographical description of his suffering from the pain of syphilis into English under the title *In the Land of Pain* (2002),[1] he prepared the ground – to some extent – for his following masterpiece *Nothing To Be Frightened Of* (2008),[2] a philosophical and literary discussion of death and total elimination, a description of the gradual degeneration or abrupt collapse of human consciousness into eternal nothingness. Pain and death, he made clear in both books, reveal oxymoronic qualities; nobody who experiences severe pain directly will feel able to write or talk about it; pain may start as an inconspicuous and vague sensation in one's consciousness as described by Tolstoy in his unforgettable short story 'The Death of Ivan Ilyich' (1886),[3] or, for example, in Daudet's life story, but it can also invade the most intimate parts of one's being, excluding everything else; the terror of extreme pain leaves no room for altruism, thoughts about peace or justice, family or history; pain can dominate the whole of human nature or – if the suffering is extreme – what is left of it. Pain and its multifarious phenomena, the agonies and 'unimaginable' forms of distress, in a certain way resemble the self-reflexivity of ecstasy; as reports of torture prove, pain may destroy the

---

1   Alphonse Daudet, *In the Land of Pain*, ed. and trans. Julian Barnes (London: Jonathan Cape, 2002); for the difficult relationship between pain and language, see Barnes's 'Introduction', *ibid.*, v–xv, v: '[...] pain is normally the enemy of descriptive powers. [...] pain, like passion, drives out language.'
2   Julian Barnes, *Nothing To Be Frightened Of* (London: Jonathan Cape, 2008).
3   See Leo Tolstoy, *The Death of Ivan Ilyich and Other Stories*, trans. Anthony Briggs (London: Penguin, 2006).

love between couples, the familiarities between friends, and it may radically
erase a person's confidence in the hitherto familiar world;[4] great physical
agony but also psychological pain may wipe out decades of intense belief
in God.[5] Pain – in this sense – is autonomous and auto-reflexive, selfish to
the extreme, causing ever newer and more intense forms of suffering that
exist beyond the pale, beyond language and – of course – beyond any form
of meaning. The intensity of pain creates idiosyncratic states of consciousness, inexpressible in language, unrepresentable in words or pictures. They
isolate the victim from his surroundings, forcing him to become a stranger
to all others and even to himself. These intense forms of suffering represent an ontological sphere that could be defined as the world of complete
'otherness', ungraspable, unfamiliar and untranslatable. It is small wonder
that any attempt to represent this 'otherness' has to end in vagueness; only
paradoxes, oxymora, elliptic sentences, allusions, aposiopeses, metaphors,
extreme symbols and conceits, synecdoche and of course silence might be
able to articulate to a certain degree what this different world implies. The
more intensely pain is felt, the greater the ensuing silence will be, and as
the mythological *exemplum* of great pain, the figure of Philomela raped by
Tereus, who then – as Ovid describes in his *Metamorphoses*[6] – cut out her
tongue in order to cover up his crime, illustrates, it is that loss of speech
which quite often accompanies suffering. Like pain, death too, shocks by
generating alienation and traumatic absence of words. The realm of death
is the paradigm of extreme 'otherness', *totidem aliter*. It cannot be familiar-
ized. It is there – unavoidable, incontestable, unacceptable – but present
as the most existential trauma *per se*.

4   An impressive example of the destructive power of pain and torture is Jean Améry's,
     'Die Tortur', in Jean Améry, *Jenseits von Schuld und Sühne: Bewältigungsversuch eines
     Überwältigten* (Munich: Szczesny, 1966), 41–70.
5   In this way pain and suffering are closely linked to the problem of theodicy; see
     Rudolf Freiburg, '"Moments that murdered my God and my Soul": Der Theodizee-
     Diskurs im Spiegel ausgewählter Holocaust-Literatur', in Gerd Bayer and Rudolf
     Freiburg, eds, *Literatur und Holocaust* (Würzburg: Königshausen & Neumann,
     2008), 111–40.
6   See Ovid, *Metamorphosen*, trans. and ed. Michael von Albrecht (Stuttgart: Reclam,
     1994), 313–21.

But the victim may recover from pain, the moribund may survive severe illness or the aftermath of an accident and the desire to talk about pain, to describe it, to analyse it, even to heal it by the sheer power of words or the aesthetics of poetic language, which – as Paul Celan's poetry proves better than any other depiction of the Holocaust – may be the most appropriate means of coping with pain and suffering.[7] The immediacy of pain and death leaves no room for narration and description; but once the victim can observe his own history of suffering, or once others as witnesses concentrate on this history, a new process sets in. Without any doubt, other people's pain, caused either by private accidents and tragedies, by regional or even global catastrophes, is fascinating. It reveals the nature of that awe-inspiring notion of the sublime described by Edmund Burke,[8] it lures the spectator into its magic dark spell, which often changes his life as a result.[9] As disturbing as it might be, Susan Sontag's idea is true: 'There is beauty in ruins.'[10] Hans Blumenberg's famous paradigm of 'shipwreck with spectator' has often been employed as an explanation for the survivor's pleasure in enjoying the beauty of ruins,[11] and also to illustrate the behaviour of eyewitnesses of catastrophic events. Other people's pain can be a threat; a great lesson in the existential 'school of affliction' – as Richardson's Clarissa would have

7   See Dennis J. Schmidt, 'Black Milk and Blue: Celan and Heidegger on Pain and Language', in Aris Fioretos, ed., *Word Traces: Readings of Paul Celan* (Baltimore: Johns Hopkins University Press, 1994), 110–29; see also Leith Morton, 'The Paradox of *Pain*: The Poetry of *Paul Celan* and So Sakon', *Literature and Aesthetics: The Journal of the Sydney Society of Literature and Aesthetics* 1/1 (1991), 82–96.
8   See Edmund Burke, *A Philosophical Enquiry into the Origin of Our Ideas of the Sublime and Beautiful* (1757), ed. J. T. Boulton (London: Routledge, 1958).
9   Seen in this way Burke's theory of the sublime harks back to Plato's idea that men as 'rational beings' also 'have an appetite for sights of degradation and pain and mutilation'; see Susan Sontag, *Regarding the Pain of Others* (New York: Farrar, 2003), 97.
10 *Ibid.*, 76; Sontag mainly concentrates on the aesthetics of photography in her essay; see also *ibid.*: 'Photographs tend to transform, whatever their subject; and as an image something may be beautiful – or terrifying, or unbearable, or quite bearable – as it is not in real life.'
11 See Hans Blumenberg, *Schiffbruch mit Zuschauer: Paradigma einer Daseinsmetapher* (Frankfurt am Main: Suhrkamp, 1979).

put it.[12] It may represent an object of empathy and understanding,[13] and a target of reproach. Other people's pain can launch learned discussions of theodicy, as was the case when the great earthquake destroyed Lisbon in 1755 or when 'out of the blue' planes attacked the Twin Towers in New York in September 2001.[14]

But other people's pain can also be exploited. It can be turned into an object of ruthless commodification and it can serve the ends of political propaganda and ideological indoctrination.[15] The history of pain and suffering may also be used to define and redefine one's own nature as an individual; as a 'founding trauma' collective pain may serve a nation to reanimate long forgotten virtues and strengths in order to reshape national identity.[16] Observing the calamities of others is, as Susan Sontag says, 'a quintessential modern experience' transforming the harsh reality of war into 'living room sights and sounds'.[17]

Literature and pain in general have a long history in common; novels and dramas reflect the most appalling tragedies soaked in blood, scenes of violence, torture and also sadomasochistic descriptions of the maltreated bodies of others. The fascination readers and spectators experience in the face of depicted suffering is immense since it allows them the virtual experience of something radically alien, often evil, possibly even sexually arousing, as may best be proved by citing examples from the time-honoured tradition of gothic fiction. But literature has also always displayed a soothing nature

12   See Samuel Richardson, *Clarissa or The History of A Young Lady* (1747–8) (London: Penguin, 1985), 991.

13   See Mitchell Green, 'Empathy, Expression, and what Artworks Have to Teach', in Garry L. Hagberg, ed, *Art and Ethical Criticism* (Oxford: Blackwell, 2008), 95–122.

14   See Rudolf Freiburg and Susanne Gruß, eds, *'But Vindicate the Ways of God to Man': Literature and Theodicy* (Tübingen: Stauffenburg, 2004); see also Kristiaan Versluys, '9/11: The Discursive Responses', in *Out of the Blue: September 11 and the Novel* (New York: Columbia University Press, 2009), 1–17.

15   See the examples Sontag gives in *Regarding the Pain of Others*, 10.

16   See Valentina Adami, *Trauma Studies and Literature: Martin Amis's 'Time's Arrow' as Trauma Fiction* (Frankfurt am Main: Lang, 2008), 18.

17   See Sontag, *Regarding the Pain of Others*, 18.

and like Boethius' famous *Consolatio Philosophiae* (524) it has revealed a healing function,[18] with which the destructive forces of immense suffering could – if not be cured – at least be alleviated. One has only to think of the long tradition of elegiac poetry from the graveyard poets to Alfred Tennyson, Thomas Hardy and Paul Celan in order to understand the therapeutic function of poetical texts and narratives in general.

As a disillusioned connoisseur of death and as a moralistic and Pyrrhonian commentator on the universal theatre of pain where 'Everyman' stars as the tragic figure doomed to perish after an existence of calamities,[19] Philip Roth is surely one of the most significant voices of the contemporary American school of *littérature engagée*.[20] Throughout his career, Roth delved deep down into the enigmas of human nature, analysing problems of individual and national identity and simultaneously interpreting American and international history as the chronology of suffering, as a 'nightmare' from which – just like James Joyce's Stephen Dedalus in the Nestor episode in *Ulysses* (1922)[21] – he would like to awake. As an American Jewish writer, Roth has always been critical and provocative at the same time.[22] Primarily the Holocaust, as an example of the immense extent of other

18   See Boethius, *Consolatio Philosophiae (524): lateinisch-deutsch; Trost der Philosophie*, trans. and ed. Ernst Gegenschatz and Olof Gigon (Düsseldorf: Artemis & Winkler, 2004).

19   See the harsh comment on life in Philip Roth, *Everyman* (London: Jonathan Cape, 2006); the book's dark cover looks like a tombstone.

20   For a brief sketch of Philip Roth's biography see Jens Martin Gurr, 'Philip Roth, *The Human Stain* (2000)', in Susanne Peters, ed., *Teaching Contemporary Literature and Culture, vol. II: Novels; Part II* (Trier: WVT, 2008), 443–62, 443.

21   See James Joyce, *Ulysses* (1922), ed. Jeri Johnson (Oxford: Oxford University Press, 1998), 34.

22   For the complex role that Roth plays as a 'Jewish' writer see Aharon Appelfeld, 'The Artist as a Jewish Writer', in Asher Z. Milbauer and Donald G. Wilson, eds, *Reading Philip Roth* (Houndsmill and London: Macmillan, 1988) 13–16; see also Victoria Aarons, 'American-Jewish Identity in Roth's Short Fiction', in Timothy Parrish, ed., *The Cambridge Companion to Philip Roth* (Cambridge: Cambridge University Press, 2007), 9–21.

people's pain, is omnipresent in his work;[23] but he also critically analyses all forms of false glorification and veneration of suffering that might serve purposes of a more ideological and political kind. From *The Ghost Writer* (1979) on, Roth criticized the commodification of the Holocaust, attacking any kind of hyperbolic sentimentality about American identification with the fate of the European Jews and he did not tire of launching satiric tirades at the exploitation of the Holocaust as a false 'pillar' of Jewish identity politics and the grotesqueness of what is satirically called 'Holocaust pornography'.[24]

The American Trilogy plays a significant role in Philip Roth's *œuvre*:[25] *I Married a Communist* (1998) studies the period of McCarthyism in America, *American Pastoral* (1997) analyses the nature of American identity during the time of the Vietnam War and its ensuing Peace Movement, and *The Human Stain* (2000) describes the disgrace of Athena's former dean and professor of classics, Coleman Silk, against the backdrop of the famous affair that Bill Clinton had with Monica Lewinsky in 1998 which eventually led to the attempt to impeach the President.[26] The plot of the novel is quite simple: Coleman Silk, former Dean of Athena,[27] has successfully turned the college into a highly effective university, but in doing so,

---

23 See Michael Rothberg, 'Roth and the Holocaust', in Parrish, *The Cambridge Companion to Philip Roth*, 52–67.

24 *Ibid.*, 54, 60: '[...] there might be something *pornographic* about making images and ultimately commodities out of the Holocaust. It is as if the fundamental obscenity of the events themselves cannot be represented without a pornographic contamination of the person doing the representing'.

25 Instead of 'American Trilogy' these three novels are also occasionally referred to as the 'Newark Trilogy'; see Michael Kimmage, 'In History's Grip: Philip Roth's "Newark Trilogy"', *PhiN* 32 (2005), 15–31; Newark is chosen as a place of 'ugliness', an 'urban disaster' that displays 'lack of history'; *ibid.*, 16.

26 See also Gurr, 'Philip Roth, *The Human Stain* (2000)', 447.

27 Roth felt inspired by the authentic case of his former neighbour, Anatole Broyards, who had also changed his own identity, when he created his 'protagonist' Coleman; see Elaine B. Safer, 'The Human Stain: Irony and the Lives of Coleman Silk', in *Mocking the Age: The Later Novels of Philip Roth* (New York: State University of New York, 2006), 117–32, 131.

he has bullied many of his colleagues. When commenting on the absence of two coloured students in one of his classes he says 'Does anyone know these people? Do they exist or are they spooks?'[28] This remark is interpreted as a vicious discrimination of African-Americans. Deeply injured by the behaviour of his colleagues, who fail to support him, Coleman takes his leave with intense indignation. When his wife dies several days later, he blames society's absurd 'spirit of pursuit' for her untimely death, asking his neighbour, Roth's well-known *alter ego* or *alter brain* – as the writer prefers to call him – Nathan Zuckerman, to write the story of his abuse. Meanwhile Coleman has started an affair with Faunia Farley who cleans the college and works in a dairy. Faunia is divorced from her husband, Les Farley, since – as a consequence of his Vietnam-trauma – Les used to beat her and kept on blaming her for the death of their two children. Coleman's affair with Faunia irritates his French colleague, Delphine Roux, who obviously also has a crush on the still attractive professor. Delphine sends an anonymous letter to Coleman accusing him of abusing a poor woman half his age; Coleman seeks legal help, determined to fight the wrong accusations. While Les Farley becomes increasingly jealous and aggressive, since he cannot tolerate the notion of his former wife having an affair with a Jew, as he says, Delphine Roux publishes an advertisement in search of a suitable academic partner, blacks excluded. Losing her concentration for just a moment she posts the advertisement by email erroneously sending it to the complete staff of Athena College. The email leaves no doubt that Delphine would be delighted to find a partner who would have to be exactly like Coleman. When she recognizes her mistake she pretends that her office was vandalized and she accuses Coleman of having broken into her computer and of having sent the fatal email. That night Coleman and Faunia die in a car accident, which was obviously caused by Les Farley. That, at least, is what Nathan Zuckerman thinks. At Coleman's funeral, Zuckerman meets Coleman's sister Ernestina, who tells him her brother's life story. It becomes clear that Coleman was not born

---

28 Philip Roth, *The Human Stain* (Boston, New York: Houghton Mifflin, 2000), 6; further references to this text are included in the text in brackets.

a Jew, but an African-American who – to eschew all disadvantages caused
by the 'wrong' race in post-war American society – had determined to
assume a new identity.[29] In order to 'pass' as a 'white Jew' Coleman had even
forbidden his mother to see him or her grandchildren ever again, causing
her tremendous pain.[30] The book ends with a meeting between Zuckerman and Les Farley on a frozen pond where Les is trying to fish, the last
sentence being an elegy with the murderer adopting the role of the lonely
outsider stranded in the immaculate landscape of the lost American pastoral: 'There it was, if not the whole story, the whole picture. Only rarely,
at the end of our century, does life offer up a vision as pure and peaceful as
this one: a solitary man on a bucket, fishing through eighteen inches of ice
in a lake that's constantly turning over its water atop an arcadian mountain
in America' (361). Roth's *The Human Stain* clearly reveals the features of a
campus novel, but it has also been interpreted as a 'Washington novel',[31] an
'American tragedy',[32] as an attack on the notion of 'American innocence',[33]
as a 'satire on political correctness',[34] and also as a 'fable about the moral

29   For a discussion of the role of race in *The Human Stain*, see Dean J. Franco, 'Being
     Black, Being Jewish, and Knowing the Difference: Philip Roth's *The Human Stain*;
     Or, It Depends on What the Meaning of "Clinton" Is', in Daniel Walden, ed., *Philip
     Roth's America: The Later Novels* (Lincoln: University of Nebraska Press, 2004),
     88–103.
30   For a comparative study of the motif of 'passing' in the novel and the film, see Rachel
     Gelder, 'Passing and Failing: Reflections on the Limitations of Showing the Passer
     in *The Human Stain*', *Women & Performance: A Journal of Feminist Theory*, 15/1
     (2005), 293–312.
31   For a discussion of the political significance of 'Washington' in *The Human Stain*, see
     Jeffrey Charis-Carlson, 'Philip Roth's Human Stains and Washington Pilgrimages',
     Studies in American Jewish Literature 23 (2004), 104–21.
32   See Bonnie Lyons, 'Philip Roth's American Tragedies', in Jay L. Halio and Ben
     Siegel, eds, *Turning Up the Flame: Philip Roth's Later Novels* (Newark: University
     of Delaware Press, 2005), 125–30, 125.
33   See Derek Parker Royal, 'Contesting the Historical Pastoral in Philip Roth's American
     Trilogy', in Jay Posser, ed., *American Fiction of the 1990s: Reflections of History and
     Culture* (London and New York: Routledge, 2008), 120–33, 131.
34   Safer, '*The Human Stain*: Irony and the Lives of Coleman Silk', 117.

and intellectual state of America as a whole.'[35] If it is true of the American Trilogy that all three novels can be read as 'American problem' novels and as 'acid dissertations on the heart of American darkness',[36] *The Human Stain* might also be characterized both as the 'Great American Album of Pain' and as a 'condition-of-America-novel'. It is incontestable that Roth mainly negotiates questions of personal and national identity in his novel and that *The Human Stain* could be looked upon as 'moral romance, the *Scarlet Letter* of race, class, and gender',[37] but the extent to which these questions are linked with aspects of pain and especially trauma has not yet been thoroughly discussed.[38]

The novel's affiliation with pain is clearly illustrated by the book's motto, which associates *The Human Stain* with the tragedy of Sophocles' *King Oedipus*, and by the book's title itself, which symbolizes the deep deterioration of human nature.[39] The novel shows a generic kinship with tragic drama and its central aesthetic doctrine of *hamartia, pathos* and *catharsis*, and it leans heavily on the technique of employing pain to create the tragic conflicts of the plot. The stage that Roth presents in *The Human Stain* teems with suffering people: As an adolescent Coleman was discriminated against because of the colour of his skin. Above all he was derided by a white prostitute who had him thrown out of the whorehouse, and made him spend 'the worst evening of his life' in an extremely shabby bar with dirty toilets in a bleak red-light district (180–4). Later, as a renowned university professor and scholar of classical literature, Coleman suffers from the unfair injuries caused by the misunderstanding of his rather harmless remark about

---

35 See Gurr, 'Philip Roth, *The Human Stain* (2000)', 447.
36 See Mark Schechner, 'Roth's American Trilogy', in Parrish, *The Cambridge Companion to Philip Roth*, 142–57, 142.
37 *Ibid.*, 152.
38 For a discussion of the function of trauma in Roth's *American Pastoral*, see Kathleen L. Macarthur, 'Shattering the American Pastoral: Philip Roth's Vision of Trauma and the American Dream', in Walden, *Philip Roth's America: The Later Novels*, 15–26.
39 The reference to tragedy is only one symptom of the highly complex intertextuality of Roth's novel; for further references to Shakespeare, Faulkner, Henry James, Kafka or Kundera, to name but a few, see Derek Parker Royal, 'Roth, Literary Influence, and Postmodernism', in Parrish, *The Cambridge Companion to Philip Roth*, 22–34, 22.

'spooks' and from his ensuing loss of authority,[40] but even more so from the death of his wife. Nathan Zuckerman, the genuine narrative voice of the story, reveals his own autobiography as a series of personal drawbacks, especially his suffering from the consequences of old age in general and from prostate surgery – which caused incontinence and left him impotent – in particular.[41] Delphine Roux, the attractive, elegant and highly gifted French scholar only suffers slightly. She cannot get over the fact that despite her personal achievements and charms, a congenial paramour is hard to find. Coleman's mother could never get over the loss of her brilliant son, who disavowed her and forbade her to see her grandchildren, breaking her heart by doing so. Coleman's own children suffer from the background of an alienated family life. The children Coleman's daughter teaches have to struggle with 'the crippling shortcomings' of illiteracy (164), just like Faunia Farley, Coleman's young lover. She assumes the role of a female Job in *The Human Stain*. As a child she was molested by her stepfather and betrayed by her own mother, who did not believe her when she told her that she was frequently abused. Fleeing from her own family she found herself in a ruthless American society that exploited her as a female worker and also as a sexual object. Her life story reveals itself as the chronology of sexual abuses that humiliated her, leaving her no room for self-esteem and honour. The two canisters with urns containing the ashes of her two dead children serve as the unforgettable emblem of her unbearable affliction. Too poor to be able to afford a decent burial for them, Faunia lives with these sad remnants of her kids that remind her day after day that she may

---

40   See the implied paradox of the sentence 'Thrown out of a Norfolk whorehouse for being black, thrown out of Athena College for being white' (Roth, *The Human Stain*, 16).

41   Age itself is a trauma in Roth's Fiction when one thinks of the definition of 'old age isn't a battle, old age is a massacre' that he presents in *Everyman*, 156. See also Georgiana Banita, 'Philip Roth's Fictions of Intimacy and the Aging of America', in Heike Hartung and Roberta Maierhofer, eds, *Narratives of Life: Mediating Age* (Münster: LIT, 2009), 91–112. For the role of scatology in general and incontinence in particular in Roth's philosophy see David Brauner, 'American Anti-Pastoral: Incontinence and Impurity in American Pastoral and *The Human Stain*', in Walden, *Philip Roth's America: The Later Novels*, 67–76.

be guilty of their death. With her own history of two suicide attempts, she is clearly the most unfortunate human being in the novel. Not faring much better, Les Farley, her ex-husband can be seen as a later American analogue to Septimus Warren Smith, the tragic figure suffering from shell-shock in Virginia Woolf's novel *Mrs Dalloway* (1925).[42] As a victim of the Vietnam War who clearly shows the symptoms of post-traumatic stress disorder, Leslie proves extremely aggressive towards Bill Clinton, whom he despises, towards Jews in general and towards Coleman in particular. Les Farley is deeply disoriented; his disorders range from schizophrenia, amnesia, unmotivated trembling, sudden flashbacks of the experience of atrocities in Vietnam to the ungovernable wish to kill all and sundry, an urge that makes him kill Coleman and Faunia towards the end of the book. But, as the impressive beginning of the novel illustrates, America and President Clinton, too,[43] suffer because the nation is paralyzed by the dominant affair of that year, by 'Monicagate':

> It was the summer in America when the nausea returned, when the joking didn't stop, when the speculation and the theorizing and the hyperbole didn't stop, when the moral obligation to explain to one's children about adult life was abrogated in favour of maintaining in them every illusion about adult life, when the smallness of people was simply crushing, when some kind of demon had been unleashed in the nation and, on both sides, people wondered 'Why are we so crazy?', when men and women alike, upon awakening in the morning, discovered that during the night, in a state of sleep that transported them beyond envy or loathing, they had dreamed of the brazenness of Bill Clinton. I myself dreamed of a mammoth banner, draped dadaistically like a Christo wrapping from one end of the White House to the other and bearing the legend A HUMAN BEING LIVES HERE. It was the summer when – for the billionth time – the jumble, the mayhem, the mess proved itself more subtle than this one's ideology and that one's morality. It was the summer when a president's penis was on everyone's mind, and life, in all its shameless impurity, once again confounded America. (3)

42   See Virginia Woolf, *Mrs Dalloway* (1925) (Harmondsworth: Penguin, 1975), 17–19 and 154–67.

43   Toni Morrison called Bill Clinton 'our nation's first black president'; see Franco, 'Being Black, Being Jewish, and Knowing the Difference', 98.

Roth satirizes what he calls the 'ecstasy of sanctimony' (2). The title of
the book refers to the deep disorders in human nature. *The Human Stain*
reminds one of the theological notion of original sin, and it also symbolizes the stains or pigments of skin thus addressing the main theme of the
novel, the traumatic experience of racism. Finally, the title alludes to the
most notorious stain in that phase of American history, the stain caused by
the President's semen on Monica Lewinsky's famous dress.[44] In the novel it
is Faunia who introduces the idea of the stained human being when – after
fleeing from Coleman and seeking refuge in nature – she remarks:

> The human stain […]: we leave a stain, we leave a trail, we leave our imprint. Impurity,
> cruelty, abuse, error, excrement, semen – there's no other way to be here. Nothing
> to do with disobedience. Nothing to do with grace or salvation or redemption. It's
> in everyone. Indwelling. Inherent. Defining. The stain that is there before its mark.
> Without the sign it is there. The stain so intrinsic it doesn't require a mark. The stain
> that *precedes* disobedience, that *encompasses* disobedience and perplexes all explana-
> tion and understanding. It's why all the cleansing is a joke. A barbaric joke at that.
> The fantasy of purity is appalling. It's insane. What is the quest to purify, if not *more*
> impurity? (242, emphasis in the original)

The human stain causes pain. It is the genetically predetermined habit of
all human beings to create evil, to torment each other and to cause each
other severe bitterness. The dark and disillusioned mentality of this quotation reminds one of the New Anthropology as invented by the English
and French satirists of the seventeenth and eighteenth centuries, Hobbes,
Mandeville, Swift, de Sade and Voltaire. The stain and the pain it causes is
no revelation of a *nemesis divina*, no God-given evil that is meant to serve
the sadistic demands of metaphysical beings who take delight in watching
the agonies of the human race, as Soame Jenyns in an essay ridiculed by

44   For these interpretations of the title see, for instance, Gurr, 'Philip Roth, *The Human
     Stain* (2000)', 452; see also Brett Ashley Kaplan, 'Reading, Race and the Conundrums
     of Reconciliation in Philip Roth's *The Human Stain*', in Halio and Siegel, *Turning
     Up the Flame*, 172–93, 181.

Samuel Johnson once thought.[45] The stain is rather the inevitable result
of typically human weaknesses of character and nature, but also of the
failures caused by the deficiencies of epistemological instruments, like
insight, intuition and – above all – reason that are proved inappropriate
in this process.

As a female version of the biblical Job, Coleman's paramour Faunia,
whose name obviously refers to the Roman God of beasts, thus symbolis-
ing her degeneration into a semi-animalistic state of being as well as her
sympathies with animals, especially with the crow Prince (247),[46] is a good
lesson in studying the function of other people's pain in literature. Her
extremely melancholic personal fate adds a sensational touch to a story
in which nothing much happens. Portrayed as an abused young girl, who
then 'voluntarily' sets out on a sad sexual career, Faunia satisfies the rather
voyeuristic desires of the reading public. The close affinity between sexuality and death represents this alluring world of '*otherness*': Faunia hides the
urns containing the ashes of her dead children under the bed on which
she probably also makes love to her numerous admirers. Her children die
in a fire when she herself is accused of having been engaged in a sexual act
with a stranger; *fellatio*, as rumour has it, was also responsible for Coleman's
lethal accident, since his attention was shifted from the road to Faunia's
sexual advances in the car. Faunia's life story is teeming with scenes of sexuality but is also embedded in a context of death. The slightly pornographic
scenery of her sexual affair with one of Athena's janitors is contrasted with
the sheer horror of the description of Faunia's job of cleaning 'the stains'
in a hut in which a desperate man had committed suicide. For the reader,
the materialistic presentation of the collateral damage this suicide caused
is almost impossible to bear, but despite the nausea, which it creates in his
consciousness, it is, at the same time, fascinating. The erroneous notion that
pain is always that of other people renders it alluring, tempting, fascinating,

45   See Rudolf Freiburg, 'The Pleasures of Pain?: Soame Jenyns *versus* Samuel Johnson',
     in Freiburg and Gruß, *Literature and Theodicy*, 225–43.
46   See Ross Posnock, 'Being Game in *The Human Stain*', in *Philip Roth's Rude Truth: The
     Art of Immaturity* (Princeton: Princeton University Press, 2006), 193–235, 220.

because the reports concerned send a shiver down the spine of the reader who is on the lookout for *nouveaux frissons* in his comparably unadventurous life in the twenty-first century. Like in so many other novels by Philip Roth, *eros* and *thanatos* are closely linked to each other, leading to the question whether such an authorial strategy in depicting life is ethically justifiable. And one must also ask if a white middle-class American writer like Roth has the right to imagine the distress of an African-American young man who is discriminated against, and if he as a male writer has both the sensitivity and the necessary understanding to describe an abused woman like Faunia.

The ethical implications of Roth's novels are highly complex.[47] As an experienced novelist Roth knows how to keep his readers curious, he is a master at shaping introductions that from the very first sentence on guarantee suspense and philosophical insight. But his descriptions of pain and suffering, the detailed account of scenes of gore and nausea are clearly not introduced for voyeuristic purposes alone, although – like Julian Barnes – he is fully aware of the appeal of catastrophes when he makes his *alter brain*, Zuckerman, remark:[48]

> Feeding that great opportunistic maw, a novelist's mind. Whatever catastrophe turns up, he transforms into writing. Catastrophe is cannon fodder for him. But what can *I* transform this into? I am stuck with it. As is. Sans language, shape, structure, meaning – sans the unities, the catharsis, sans everything. More of the untransformed unforeseen. And why would anyone want more? (170, emphasis in the original)

47   For a general discussion of the relationship between literature and ethics, see Paul Guyer, 'Is Ethical Criticism a Problem?', in Hagberg, *Art and Ethical Criticism*, 3–32; see also Christine Lubkoll and Oda Wischmeyer, eds, *'Ethical Turn': Geisteswissenschaften in neuer Verantwortung* (Munich: Fink, 2009).

48   See Julian Barnes, *A History of the World in 10 ½ Chapters* (1989) (London: Picador, 1990), 125: 'How do you turn catastrophe into art? Nowadays the process is automatic. A nuclear plant explodes? We'll have a play on the London stage within a year. A President assassinated? You can have the book or the film or the filmed book or the booked film. War? Send in the novelists. A series of gruesome murders? Listen for the tramp of the poets. We have to understand it, of course, this catastrophe; to understand it, we have to imagine it, so we need the imaginative arts.'

The quotation can be read as a reflection about the formlessness of pain and catastrophe. The absence of language and structure anticipate the most significant problem in the representation of other people's pain, the notion that a traumatic experience cannot be represented appropriately. Any form of representation, any attempt to give a structure to the chaotic material catastrophes and accidents are made of, has to be interpreted as a process of continuous distortion, as the attempt to blur the lines between factual history, tragic as it may be, and its creative reconstruction in one's imagination.[49] Thus the novel is also a study of the affiliations between epistemology and ontology, and it argues that 'meaning and knowledge are not simple and undifferentiated but multiple and elusive'.[50] There is even a slight tendency towards postmodern techniques of representation that could contribute to the endeavour to mirror the incoherence of the ongoing events and the lack of certitude in factual knowledge.[51] The chronology of the story is far from simple: single bits of information are strewn in at various phases during the narration and Roth thus ignores any clear rules of simple linearity.[52]

Nevertheless, Roth sets out to minutely analyse the function of pain in the process of forming identities. As for Zuckerman, Coleman, or even

49 Traumatologists are aware of this difference between 'narrative' and 'historical' truth; see Marianne Leuzinger-Bohleber, Gerhard Roth, and Anna Buchheim, *Psychoanalyse, Neurobiologie, Trauma* (Stuttgart: Schattauer, 2008), 10–12; for the difficulty of finding authentic truth in the reports of victims also see Dori Laub, 'Truth and Testimony: The Process and the Struggle', in Cathy Caruth, ed., *Trauma: Explorations in Memory* (Baltimore and London: Johns Hopkins University Press, 1995), 61–75.

50 See also Isabel Soto, 'Everyone Knows (?): Philip Roth's *The Human Stain*', in Carme Manuel and Paul Scott Derrick, eds, *Nor Shall Diamond Die: American Studies in Honour of Javier Coy* (Valéncia: Biblioteca Javier Coy d'Estudis Nord-Americans, 2003), 499–506, 504.

51 For the relationship between the trauma novel and postmodernism see Ronald Granofsky, *The Trauma Novel: Contemporary Symbolic Depictions of Collective Disaster* (Frankfurt am Main: Lang, 1995), 11–12.

52 See also Adami, *Trauma Studies and Literature*, 7: 'In fact, trauma fiction usually overlaps with postmodern fiction in its refusal of closure and coherence, proposing disruptive forms of narrative that depart from conventional plot structures.'

Les Farley, pain is depicted as a highly important factor which influences the outcome of all processes of identity shaping, especially those that might be ranked under the category of 'self-fashioning'. Roth's notion of identity can be defined as 'performative'; there might be a gist of identity, a kernel of personality that cannot be changed, but Roth prefers to suggest that identity keeps on being constructed throughout life, with pain playing one of the most important roles in this process. His idea of personal identity is that of an 'impersonation',[53] the acting out of various potentialities that are all simultaneously existent. 'Asserting one's identity, as Roth understands it, is always a transgressive act. This means that for Roth no form of identity – ethnic or otherwise – can ever be fixed,'[54] or, to put it differently, '[...] constructing the self is an open ended and always ongoing process.'[55] Like contemporary traumatologists such as Cary Caruth, he interprets history as a sequence of national and international traumata and he looks upon the twentieth and twenty-first centuries as 'catastrophic ages',[56] which shape the

---

53   See Royal, 'Roth, Literary Influence, and Postmodernism', 28.

54   Timothy Parrish, 'Introduction: Roth at Mid-Career', in Parrish, *The Cambridge Companion to Philip Roth*, 1–8, 2.

55   Royal, 'Roth, Literary Influence, and Postmodernism', 30.

56   See Cathy Caruth, 'Introduction', in Caruth, *Trauma: Explorations in Memory*, 3–11; especially 11: 'In a catastrophic age, that is, trauma itself may provide the very link between cultures: not as a simple understanding of the pasts of others but rather, within the traumas of contemporary history, as our ability to listen through the departures we have all taken from ourselves.' There is, however, the danger that such an identification of history with trauma becomes too generalized; see Dominick LaCapra, *Writing History, Writing Trauma* (Baltimore: Johns Hopkins University Press, 2001), 64: 'When absence and loss are conflated, melancholic paralysis or manic agitation may set in, and the significance or force of particular historical losses (for example, those of apartheid or the Shoah) may be obfuscated or rashly generalized. As a consequence one encounters the dubious ideas that everyone (including perpetrators or collaborators) is a victim, that all history is trauma, or that we all share a pathological public sphere or a "wound culture".' For Roth's notion of 'history perceived as trauma' as 'disruption or assault' and as 'the force that destabilizes and destroys' see also Kimmage, 'In History's Grip: Philip Roth's "Newark Trilogy"', 17.

particular identity of individuals just as well as the identity of a nation.[57] This is the main reason why Roth uses the Clinton-Lewinsky affair as a backdrop to Coleman Silk's *liaison* with Faunia Farley. 'In all three novels [of the American Trilogy] he writes the individual subject into the fabric of history, and by doing so he illustrates that identity is not only a product, but also at the mercy of the many social, political, and cultural forces that surround it.'[58]

In his novels, Roth shoulders the responsibility of minutely describing the gradual transformation of human beings into something different and alien to themselves. Faunia becomes a rather detached, completely disillusioned observer of life, whose numbness in accepting pleasures and pain clearly reveal the outlines of a trauma that is lingering on in the depths of her complex personality. Her fate proves the ideas pronounced by traumatologists that 'trauma is a disruptive experience that disarticulates the self and creates holes in existence; it has belated effects that are controlled only with difficulty and perhaps never fully mastered.'[59] Like schizophrenia, nightmares, flashbacks such as those that her husband Les keeps on experiencing, 'numbing' in Faunia's case lays bare the deep wound that hurts her beyond the possibility of articulating it; the death of her children has turned her into a kind of twentieth-century Niobe, paralyzed to the utmost extent, a person that could be looked upon as being dead and alive at the very same moment.[60] Like Philomela, she has lost not only her dignity and self-esteem in life but also the gift of talking about it; thus her words are elliptic and enigmatic, if she talks at all. She has fled into the subterfuge of illiteracy, but the attentive reader soon finds out that this is her particular reaction to the pangs of loss and grief. The immensity of her distress has overcome what traumatologists designate as the *nécessité de la*

---

57 For Caruth trauma is a 'symptom of history'; quoted from Adami, *Trauma Studies and Literature*, 24.
58 Royal, 'Contesting the Historical Pastoral in Philip Roth's American Trilogy', 120.
59 LaCapra, *Writing History, Writing Trauma*, 41.
60 For the long history of the paradox of being dead and alive at the same time see Günther Blaicher, ed., *Death-in-Life: Studien zur historischen Entfaltung der Paradoxie der Entfremdung in der englischen Literatur* (Trier: WVT, 1998).

narration.[61] Roth characterizes Faunia with empathy and understanding and one has to refute the opinion of one of Roth's rather severe critics who comments: 'But he [Roth] hasn't a clue about Les Farley, who is Brand-X Vietnam Vet, all shattered nerves and tripwire rage, or Faunia, who is generic underclass, complete with childhood molestation and goatish appetites: the overscale eroticism that is a Roth trademark.'[62] The same critic also finds fault with Faunia, who – as a simple woman, who has to clean toilets, – cleverly pronounces philosophical insights worthy of King Lear.[63] Roth's endeavour to portray Faunia as a 'savage wise woman', however, can be understood easily; he intends to show the alienation of a human being whose pain has transformed her into a world-weary person that can no longer share the cares and desires of the average American subject. As an existential outsider, whose obvious eroticism does not, as Schechner maintains, guarantee Roth's predilection for salacious scenes, but which can rather be deciphered as the desperate attempt to feel at least a tiny bit alive amid all the numbness and despair that surrounds her, Faunia has learned to see life as a series of faults and blemishes, to consider the creation as a deeply stained artefact that makes its inhabitants suffer without end. Of course, her wisdom is not that of King Lear, at least not if one regards Lear as the representative of nobility, as a former King and intelligent ruler of an Empire; but it is precisely the 'savage wisdom' (40) of a traumatized person,[64] of Lear as a victim, whose whole existence was

61   See Martina Kopf, *Trauma und Literatur: Das Nicht-Erzählbare erzählen – Assia Djebar und Yvonne Vera* (Frankfurt am Main: Brandes & Apsel, 2005), 61.
62   Schechner, 'Roth's American Trilogy', 156.
63   *Ibid.*, 155.
64   In a very personal essay that compares the national tragedy of 9/11 with the murder of her two close friends Susanne and Half Zantopp, Irene Kacandes has described this sudden acceptance of a 'savage wisdom'; see Irene Kacandes, '9/11/01 = 1/27/01: The Changed Posttraumatic Self', in Judith Greenberg, ed., *Trauma at Home: After 9/11* (Lincoln: University of Nebraska Press, 2003), 168–83, 172: 'And yet, I came out of those experiences with views of the nature of the world and my own mortality that seem truer, if less comforting, than the views I had before. When I first saw the images of the planes crashing into the World Trade Center, I was not incredulous. Rather, what I saw were strangers killing strangers out of hate, out of an unwillingness and

shattered by unbearable atrocities and a catastrophic fate with the most horrific of all injuries: it is through the loss of their children that the two figures resemble each other. Here, indeed, beaten Faunia and betrayed King Lear meet in that region of existential storms and vicissitudes where intelligence no longer plays any role,[65] where the instinct to survive and the wish to commit suicide alternate with each other from moment to moment. Like all severely traumatized people, Faunia hesitates between the desire to talk about her suffering and the wish to remain forever silent as Philomela does; she thus shows the typical behaviour of victims that Judith Herman designates as the 'dialectics of trauma'.[66] And it is also the wisdom of the injured person not to get involved any longer in alleged catastrophes that compared to one's own fate disclose themselves as trivial; this is Faunia's comment on the Clinton-Lewinsky-affair:

> Poor Monica might not get a good job in New York City? You know what? I don't care. Do you think Monica cares if my back hurts from milking those fucking cows after my day at the college? Sweeping up people's shit at the posts office because they can't bother to use the fucking garbage can? Do you think Monica cares about that? She keeps calling the White House, and it must have been just terrible not to have her phone calls returned. And it's over for you? That's terrible too? It never *began* for me. Over before it *began*, try having an iron pipe knock you down. [...] It's not that important. It's not important *at all*. I had two kids. They're dead. If I don't have the energy this morning to feel bad about Monica and Bill, chalk it up to my two kids, all right? If that's my shortcoming, so be it. I don't have any more left in me for all the great troubles of the world. (235, emphasis in the original)

To witness other people's pain also means – and this is an old ethical message of literature in general – that the spectator can learn from the examples described.[67] Pain changes a person's capacity for sympathy and empathy,

---

cultivated inability to see the humanity of the other. What I saw were two adolescent boys stabbing my friends to death.'

65   See William Shakespeare, *King Lear*, ed. Kenneth Muir (London: Methuen, 1982 [1964]), III, ii, 99–105.
66   See Kopf, *Trauma und Literatur: Das Nicht-Erzählbare erzählen*, 32.
67   See Angela Kallhoff, ed., *Marta C. Nussbaum: Ethics and Political Philosophy. Lecture and Colloquium in Münster 2000* (Münster: LIT, 2001); see also Noël Carroll,

it may harden the subject concerned as in Faunia's case but it also helps to
compare one's own suffering with other suffering that is far greater. In this
way, Faunia's life story can be looked upon as a therapy for Coleman who
– up to this point, before meeting her – was almost totally absorbed in his
own relatively banal suffering; in regard to Coleman Faunia thinks:

> What does she hate most? That he really thinks his suffering is a big deal. He really
> thinks that what everybody thinks, what everybody says about him at Athena Col-
> lege, is so life-shattering. It's a lot of assholes not liking him – it's not a big deal. And
> for him this is the most horrible thing that ever happened? Well, it's not a big deal.
> Two kids suffocating and dying, that's a big deal. Having your stepfather put his
> fingers up your cunt, that's a big deal. Losing your job as you're about to retire isn't
> a big deal. That's what she hates about him – the privilegedness of his suffering. He
> thinks he never had a chance? There's real pain on this earth, and he thinks *he* didn't
> have a chance? You know when you don't have a chance? When, after the morning
> milking, he takes that iron pipe and hits you in the head with it. I don't even see it
> coming – and *he* didn't have a chance! Life owes *him* something! (234–5, emphasis
> in the original)

But by comparing Coleman's suffering with her own traumata, Faunia, of
course, is no longer just a victim but rather she now adopts the role of the
observer of other people's pain. What, indeed, seems to be a trivial degree
of suffering to her, is a major trauma for Coleman; pain is relative and
Coleman does not pretend to suffer, he suffers genuinely. For a highly-
gifted man like Coleman each form of humiliation is a major injury; his
decision to 'pass' for a white Jew by concealing his true African-American
origins is the desperate act of an extremely intelligent young man, who
is not willing to accept the fate of degradation and indignation that his
father lived through and that killed him in the end. Coleman, the symbolic
name signifying the colour of black, Silk, the name adumbrating Coleman's desire for elegance and social acceptance,[68] cannot stand the oppos-
ing forces he is exposed to when he just moves from one place to another:

'Narrative and the Ethical Life', in Hagberg, ed., *Art and Ethical Criticism*, 35–62,
and Joshua Landy, 'A Nation of Madame Bovarys: On the Possibility and Desirability
of Moral Improvement through Fiction', *ibid.*, 63–94.

68   See Gurr, 'Philip Roth, *The Human Stain* (2000)', 452.

'At East Orange High the class valedictorian, in the segregated South just another nigger. In the segregated South there were no separate identities, not even for him and his roommate. No such subtleties allowed, and the impact was devastating. Nigger – and it meant *him*' (102–3). To counterfeit inferiority, when actually he feels justified in striving for excellence in all fields of knowledge and even at sport, where he triumphs as a highly successful boxer, is simply beyond Coleman's imagination and as a typical 'American Berserk,'[69] he would rather give up all forms of group-adherence than accept a fate of life-long indignity. For no amount of money, 'honour' or sexual gratification would he be willing to lead the life his father had; this is the quintessence of his father's experience:

> 'Any time a white deals with you,' his father would tell the family, 'no matter how well intentioned he may be, there is the presumption of intellectual inferiority. Somehow or other, if not directly by his words then by his facial expression, by his tone of voice, by his impatience, even by the opposite – by his forbearance, by his wonderful display of *humaneness* – he will always talk to you as though you are dumb and then, if you're not, he will be astonished.' (103, emphasis in the original)

For Coleman, the 'tragic mulatto,'[70] it is precisely the pain of being maltreated and abused by words such as 'nigger' that forces him to change his identity. Coleman's pain lies at the root of his metamorphosis and his wish to become a completely *other* man. Put abstractly, this means, that pain, and especially traumatic pain, serves as a catalyst to split the individual from his peer group in particular, and from society in general.[71] This process may be interactive and reversed, but in Coleman's case it causes his alienation from his familiar world and the beginning of a new life. The space of

---

69 See Timothy Parrish, 'Roth and Ethnic Identity', in Parrish, *The Cambridge Companion to Philip Roth*, 127–41, 139: 'The American Berserk of the past fifty years is also the context out of which *The Human Stain*'s Coleman Silk, arguably Roth's most remarkable protagonist, emerges.'

70 Schechner, 'Roth's American Trilogy', 155.

71 For the highly complex relationship between individual suffering and its social implications see Kai Erikson, 'Notes on Trauma and Community', in Caruth, *Trauma: Explorations in Memory*, 183–99, 185: 'Trauma has a social dimension.'

'*otherness*', to which the suffering individual is catapulted, becomes highly interesting as an ethical *terra incognita*. The isolated and alienated 'I' may invade a space in which it can establish new rather idiosyncratic rules of what has to be considered right and wrong; the new 'I' settles in an ethical 'no-man's-land' that to him at least appears as a space of liberty and freedom. Roth describes and destroys this notion of finding a separate space of happiness; he rather suggests that the dialectics of pain and freedom are again followed by pain, as Coleman's life story proves. There is no escape from history in general, nor from American traumatic history in particular.[72] The endeavour to get rid of the 'ethics of we' (108) – however justified the intention may be if one thinks of the experienced series of Coleman's humiliations – is doomed to failure. Coleman's plan to become 'the greatest of the great *pioneers* of the I' and to get radically involved in the process of '*self*-discovery' and the 'passionate struggle for singularity' (108) expires in a personal catastrophe. Just like Delphine Roux's plan for self-revelation, Coleman's prospects are predetermined to come to nothing. Delphine, whose name is reminiscent of the Delphic oracle and the secret wisdom of *gnothi seauton* or *nosce te ipsum*, says: 'I will go to America and be the author of my life [...]; I will construct myself outside the orthodoxy of my family's given, I will fight *against* the given, impassioned subjectivity carried to the limit, individualism at its best' (273). These versions of the American dream are nullified by Roth's cynical fables of the individual's immersion in the tragedy of traumatic history.

No other protagonist of the novel illustrates the close affiliation of individual suffering with national history as clearly as Les Farley does; twelve pages of the novel are dedicated to the study of Farley's traumatic sufferings in detail (213–25). Some critics claim that the figure of Farley is unconvincing and artificial;[73] others suggest that by describing the trauma therapy, which Les, together with other Vietnam veterans, undergoes in a Chinese restaurant, Roth intended to offer a farcical presentation of the presence of war in American society towards the end of the twentieth cen-

72   See also Kimmage, 'In History's Grip: Philip Roth's "Newark Trilogy"', 18.
73   See Schechner, 'Roth's American Trilogy', 156.

tury.[74] But although one may concede that both dark humour and cynicism permeate the depiction of the restaurant scenes, Roth's intention is much more serious. By linking the fates of Coleman, Faunia, Zuckerman and Les, but also by suggesting the closeness of these fates to that of Monica Lewinsky and Bill Clinton, and thus of America as a whole, Roth suggests that trauma works on a universal level, that trauma, as Cary Caruth has maintained in various publications, must be looked upon as a universal symptom of history. In *The Human Stain* Les clearly reveals himself as a severely traumatized person according to Caruth's definition:

> While the precise definition of post-traumatic stress disorder is contested, most descriptions generally agree that there is a response, sometimes delayed, to an overwhelming event or events, which takes the form of repeated, intrusive hallucinations, dreams, thoughts or behaviors stemming from the event, along with numbing that may have begun during or after the experience, and possibly also increased arousal to (and avoidance of) stimuli recalling the event.[75]

Les Farley's behaviour is eccentric and bizarre; as a stalker he keeps on following his ex-wife wherever she goes, and – as it turns out towards the end of the story – he has not only gathered information about Coleman and Faunia but also about Nathan Zuckerman. Les is portrayed as extremely dangerous; he has beaten up his wife, he has obviously caused the accident that killed Coleman and Faunia; and the restaurant scene proves beyond doubt that he would kill for the slightest reason, just when he is taken by surprise or when he feels disturbed. Nothing seems to be normal for Les any more; when he orders a Chinese meal he feels threatened by the mere presence of other guests and especially by the waiter who clearly reminds him of Vietnam. Eating his food is agony for him.[76] He can hardly last through one complete dinner without just wanting to get out or to vomit on the floor (218). Les shows clear symptoms of so called post-traumatic stress disorder (PTSD), which is mentioned many times in the book (353,

---

74 Safer, 'The Human Stain: Irony and the Lives of Coleman Silk', 120.
75 Caruth, 'Introduction', 4.
76 For the significance of 'eating' as a leitmotif of trauma literature, see Granofsky, *The Trauma Novel: Contemporary Symbolic Depictions of Collective Disaster*, 14–16.

355). The therapy group consists of several traumatized Vietnam veterans whose limbs shake, who keep on muttering obscene four-letter-words, or whose 'health had been close to [being] destroyed by every variety of skin and respiratory and neurological ailment' (216). The traumatized veterans seem to be completely isolated from the world that surrounds them. The other guests in the restaurant – again observers of other people's pain – treat them as if they were aliens. They are frightened and disturbed, and indeed this is what traumatologists confirm, that victims are treated as if they were suffering from a contagious disease.[77] For the veterans the world of the war and the world of American normalcy seem to take place on two different planets, and it is interesting to learn that many Holocaust survivors described their own sufferings in the same way.[78] In only forty-eight hours the soldiers were transported from the hellish world of the Vietnam war back to their American home towns (224), without having a chance to realize the extent of their own psychological injuries. It is the element of 'latency',[79] well-known in all traumatological studies, which can be looked upon as the incubation period of the imminent disease. Les has had barbarous experiences in Vietnam as he tells Zuckerman towards the end of the book (352–4). He lost one of his pals in battle, and when he returned home, normalcy appeared as insanity to him (353); he started to drink and to have unexplainable flashbacks, so typical of the traumatic sufferer (354). The 'traumatic memory', unlike the 'narrative memory', is completely inflexible, its contents are literal and not symbolic, and the victim, as Les's case shows, is forced to repeat the same traumatic experience again and again

77   Kopf, *Trauma und Literatur: Das Nicht-Erzählbare erzählen*, 47.
78   For the idea of 'planet Auschwitz', see for example Stephen T. Katz, 'The Crucifixion Of The Jews: Ignaz Maybaum's Theology Of The Holocaust', in Steven T. Katz, Shlomo Biderman and Gershon Greenberg, eds, *Wrestling with God: Jewish Theological Responses During and After the Holocaust* (Oxford: Oxford University Press, 2007), 594–601, 597.
79   For the term latency, which is derived from Freudian psychology, see Jane Kilby, 'The Writing of Trauma: Trauma Theory and the Liberty of Reading', *New Formations: A Journal of Culture/Theory/Politics* 47 (2002), 217–30, 220.

in a process that is called *restitutio ad integrum*:[80] 'One of the hallmarks of Post-Traumatic Stress Disorder is the intrusive reexperiencing of elements of the trauma in nightmares, flashbacks, or somatic reactions. These traumatic memories are triggered by autonomic arousal [...] and are thought to be mediated via hyperpotentiated noradrenergic pathways originating in the locus coeruleus of the brain [...].'[81] Les describes his experiences in the following way:

> Thousands and thousands of guys were going through what I was going through. Thousands and thousands of guys waking up in the middle of the night back in Vietnam. Thousands and thousands of guys people are calling up and they don't call them back. Thousands and thousands of guys having these real bad dreams. [...] The subconscious mind. You can't control it. It's like the government. It *is* the government. It's the government all over again. It gets you to do what you don't want to do. (355, emphasis in the original)

The identification of the human mind with the government leaves no doubt that the traumatic processes have infiltrated the individual brain as well as the collective mind. America, just like its subjects such as Les and Faunia, has to be considered as a nation deeply steeped in the emotions of elegy. It is the loss of values and human lives that characterizes that traumatic twentieth century. Faunia's individual ritual of mourning, keeping the urn with the ashes of her two dead children against all advice, is mirrored by the American national monuments of mourning: The past war waged in Vietnam just as the actual Gulf War are traumata in the American history. As so often in his other novels, Roth severely castigates the notion of an 'innocent America'.[82] America like its subjects represented by Faunia and

---

80 See Bessel A. van der Kolk and Onno van der Hart, 'The Intrusive Past: The Flexibility of Memory and the Engraving of Trauma', in Caruth, *Trauma: Explorations in Memory*, 158–82, 163.

81 *Ibid.*, 173; for further detailed analyses of post-traumatic stress disorder see Lena Jelinek, *Memory Fragmentation in Posttraumatic Stress Disorder: Content Specific or Generalised* (Berlin: Wissenschaftlicher Verlag, 2007).

82 See also Royal, 'Contesting the Historical Pastoral in Philip Roth's American Trilogy', 131.

Les, is numbed, does not really live any more. Trauma kills life and feeling. When – as part of the therapy – Les is supposed to visit the moving wall of the Vietnam memorial in Pittsfield he feels nothing:

> Nothing. Swift had heard the Wall crying – Les doesn't hear anything. Doesn't feel anything, doesn't hear anything, doesn't even remember anything. It's like when he saw his two kids dead. This huge lead-in, and nothing. Here he was so afraid he was going to feel too much and he feels nothing, and that is worse. It shows that despite everything, despite Louie and the trips to the Chinese restaurant and the meds and no drinking, he was right all along to believe he was dead. At the Chinese restaurant he felt something, and that temporarily tricked him. But now he knows for sure he's dead because he can't even call up Kenny's memory. He used to be tortured by it, now he can't be connected to it in any way. (252–3)

As an implication of this traumatic suffering ethical questions have to be put anew. Is a traumatized subject responsible for his deeds any more? If one listens to Les's own opinion the answer has to be *no*. Any attempts made by the doctor of Medical Ethics to understand Les' behaviour are doomed to fail; Les answers with a series of negations that characterize him as a man no longer of this world and its *ratio*. Common sense, as well as value systems, has been erased by the traumatic experience (257).

The scope of pain depicted in Roth's *The Human Stain* is impressive and it ranges from the fairly slight injuries that Delphine Roux's self-confidence as an attractive woman and a talented scholar suffers, over Coleman's indignation, and Zuckerman's impotence to the serious, life-shattering traumata of Faunia and Les Farley. In a certain way the book inverts the definition of trauma, which is normally seen as an exceptional state that follows a deep impact on the protective shield of human consciousness. The victim that suffers from trauma may – like Freud's famous survivor of a railway accident – walk away apparently unhurt; but after a certain period of latency the meanwhile well-known symptoms of post-traumatic stress disorder set in. In Roth's view the fairly peaceful notion of an innocent American pastoral life in the twentieth century clearly reveals the nature of such a Freudian latency; the alleged peace turns out to be a false tranquillity that only covers the features of several individual and national injuries. America may live on as if it still were isolated from world history, its self-appointed apostles of righteousness and justice may feel self-assured by launching initiatives against Clinton and his administration, but the activities of Coleman's and Clinton's opponents disclose the bigotry of 'piety binge' and the savage mentality of the 'spirit of pursuit'.[83] Coleman may be a successful scholar, but he keeps on suffering from the consequences of his fatal decision to pass as a 'white Jew', falling victim to the contagious spirit of over-exaggerated 'political correctness' towards the end of the book.[84] With masterly strokes Roth paints a gruesome picture of the condition of America's normalcy as one that is prone to collapse, to give up its allegedly safe value systems and to fall back into extremely conservative and right-wing politics of self-assuredness which uses the pain of others in order to consolidate its own feeling of moral supremacy. Roth's ingenuous trick consists in showing that in the American 'wound culture' there is no real distinction between victims and perpetrators; suffering is universal, victims become observers as in Faunia's case, and observers may easily fall into the hands of a probable murderer such as Les Farley. In a certain way Roth, like Monica Lewinsky did, according to one of the Athenian young college teachers, sticks 'a thermometer up the *country's* ass' (148).

> It's not as though Marx or Freud or Darwin or Stalin or Hitler or Mao had never happened – it's as though Sinclair Lewis had not happened. It's, he thought, as though *Babbitt* had never been written. It's as though not even that most basic level of imaginative thought had been admitted into consciousness to cause the slightest disturbance. A century of destruction unlike any other in its extremity befalls and blights the human race – scores of ordinary people condemned to suffer deprivation upon deprivation, atrocity upon atrocity, evil upon evil, half the world or more subjected to pathological sadism as social policy, whole societies organized and fettered by the fear of violent persecution, the degradation of individual life engineered on a scale unknown throughout history, nations broken and enslaved by ideological criminals who rob them of everything, entire populations so demoralized as to be unable to get out of bed in the morning with the minutest desire to face the day ... all the terrible touchstones presented by this century, and here they are up in arms about Faunia Farley. Here in America either it's Faunia Farley or it's Monica Lewinsky! The

83 Kaplan, 'Reading, Race and the Conundrums of Reconciliation', 172–93, 187–8.
84 See *ibid.*, 173: 'Indeed, according to the logic of *The Human Stain*, racial reconciliation can only be achieved by eschewing identity politics.'

luxury of these lives disquieted so by the inappropriate comportment of Clinton and Silk! *This*, in 1998, is the wickedness they have to put up with. *This*, in 1998, is their torture, their torment, and their spiritual death. Their source of greatest moral despair, Faunia blowing me and me fucking Faunia. I'm depraved not simply for having once said the word 'spooks' to a class of white students – and said it, mind you, not while standing there reviewing the legacy of slavery, the fulminations of the Black Panthers, the metamorphoses of Malcolm X, the rhetoric of James Baldwin, or the radio popularity of *Amos 'n' Andy*, but while routinely calling the roll. (153–4, emphasis in the original)

Normalcy is disclosed as a fake, an illusion; even more: Roth leaves no doubt that in America, trauma is omnipresent, trauma is normalcy; being hurt and injured, being humiliated and deprived of one's rights, being sexually abused or misused by the administration to wage an anonymous and absurd war that sends one home as a future victim suffering from PTSD – this seems to be the normal state of things. Any reader of Roth's fiction in general, and of *The Human Stain* in particular will have to recognize that there is no 'other people's pain' but that the pain of the others sooner or later will become part and parcel of one's own suffering. Trauma as 'failed experience', as the 'unclaimed experience' characterizes all of Roth's protagonists and it is also the traumatic failed experience with which he keeps on fighting against the wrong versions of the alleged American dream. There is no room left for the idea of an American version of political innocence. Traumatized itself, by the Vietnam War and especially by the attack on the Twin Towers on 9/11/2001, it is sure to contribute to traumatizing other nations; as was proved several years later under the administration of George W. Bush, the Gulf War and the atrocities of Abu Ghraib Prison in Baghdad.[85]

85   For the support I received when writing this article I would like to thank Nina Abassi, Janine Reinhard, Evelin Werner and Rosemary Zahn.

Bibliography

Aarons, Victoria, 'American-Jewish Identity in Roth's Short Fiction', in Timothy Parrish, ed., *The Cambridge Companion to Philip Roth* (Cambridge: Cambridge University Press, 2007), 9–21.

Adami, Valentina, *Trauma Studies and Literature: Martin Amis's 'Time's Arrow' as Trauma Fiction* (Frankfurt am Main: Lang, 2008).

Améry, Jean, *Jenseits von Schuld und Sühne: Bewältigungsversuch eines Überwältigten* (Munich: Szczesny, 1966).

Appelfeld, Aharon, 'The Artist as a Jewish Writer', in Asher Z. Milbauer and Donald G. Wilson, eds, *Reading Philip Roth* (Houndsmill and London: Macmillan, 1988), 13–16.

Banita, Georgiana, 'Philip Roth's Fictions of Intimacy and the Aging of America', in Heike Hartung and Roberta Maierhofer, eds, *Narratives of Life: Mediating Age* (Münster: LIT, 2009), 91–112.

Barnes, Julian, *A History of the World in 10 ½ Chapters* (London: Picador, 1990).

——, *Nothing To Be Frightened Of* (London: Jonathan Cape, 2008).

Bayer, Gerd, and Rudolf Freiburg, eds, *Literatur und Holocaust* (Würzburg: Königshausen & Neumann, 2008).

Blaicher, Günther, ed., *Death-in-Life: Studien zur historischen Entfaltung der Paradoxie der Entfremdung in der englischen Literatur* (Trier: WVT, 1998).

Blumenberg, Hans, *Schiffbruch mit Zuschauer: Paradigma einer Daseinsmetapher* (Frankfurt am Main: Suhrkamp, 1979).

Boethius, *Consolatio Philosophiae: lateinisch-deutsch; Trost der Philosophie*, trans. and ed. Ernst Gegenschatz and Olof Gigon (Düsseldorf: Artemis & Winkler, 2004).

Brauner, David, 'American Anti-Pastoral: Incontinence and Impurity in American Pastoral and *The Human Stain*', in Daniel Walden, ed., *Philip Roth's America: The Later Novels* (Lincoln: University of Nebraska Press, 2004), 67–76.

Burke, Edmund, *A Philosophical Enquiry into the Origin of Our Ideas of the Sublime and Beautiful*, ed. J. T. Boulton (London: Routledge, 1958).

Caruth, Cathy, ed., *Trauma: Explorations in Memory* (Baltimore and London: Johns Hopkins University Press, 1995).

Carroll, Noël 'Narrative and the Ethical Life', in Garry L. Hagberg, ed., *Art and Ethical Criticism* (Oxford: Blackwell, 2008), 35–62.

Charis-Carlson, Jeffrey, 'Philip Roth's Human Stains and Washington Pilgrimages', *Studies in American Jewish Literature* 23 (2004), 104–21.

Daudet, Alphonse, *In the Land of Pain*, ed. and trans. Julian Barnes (London: Jonathan Cape, 2002).

Erikson, Kai, 'Notes on Trauma and Community', in Cathy Caruth, ed., *Trauma: Explorations in Memory* (Baltimore and London: Johns Hopkins University Press, 1995), 183–99.

Franco, Dean J., 'Being Black, Being Jewish, and Knowing the Difference: Philip Roth's *The Human Stain*; Or, It Depends on What the Meaning of "Clinton" Is', in Daniel Walden, ed., *Philip Roth's America: The Later Novels* (Lincoln: University of Nebraska Press, 2004), 88–103.

Freiburg, Rudolf, and Susanne Gruß, eds, *'But Vindicate the Ways of God to Man': Literature and Theodicy* (Tübingen: Stauffenburg, 2004).

——, 'The Pleasures of Pain?: Soame Jenyns *versus* Samuel Johnson', in Rudolf Freiburg and Susanne Gruß, eds, *'But Vindicate the Ways of God to Man': Literature and Theodicy* (Tübingen: Stauffenburg, 2004), 225–43.

Gelder, Rachel, 'Passing and Failing: Reflections on the Limitations of Showing the Passer in *The Human Stain*', *Women & Performance: A Journal of Feminist Theory*, 15/1 (2005), 293–312.

Green, Mitchell, 'Empathy, Expression, and what Artworks Have to Teach', in Garry L. Hagberg, ed., *Art and Ethical Criticism* (Oxford: Blackwell, 2008), 95–122.

Granofsky, Ronald, *The Trauma Novel: Contemporary Symbolic Depictions of Collective Disaster* (Frankfurt am Main: Lang, 1995).

Gurr, Jens Martin, 'Philip Roth, *The Human Stain* (2000)', in Susanne Peters, ed., *Teaching Contemporary Literature and Culture, vol. II: Novels; Part II* (Trier: WVT, 2008), 443–62.

Guyer, Paul, 'Is Ethical Criticism a Problem?', in Garry L. Hagberg, ed., *Art and Ethical Criticism* (Oxford: Blackwell, 2008), 3–32.

Hagberg, Garry L., ed., *Art and Ethical Criticism* (Oxford: Blackwell, 2008).

Halio, Jay L., and Ben Siegel, eds, *Turning Up the Flame: Philip Roth's Later Novels* (Newark: University of Delaware Press, 2005).

Jelinek, Lena, *Memory Fragmentation in Posttraumatic Stress Disorder: Content Specific or Generalised* (Berlin: Wissenschaftlicher Verlag, 2007).

Joyce, James, *Ulysses*, ed. Jeri Johnson (Oxford: Oxford University Press, 1998).

Kacandes, Irene, '9/11/01 = 1/27/01: The Changed Posttraumatic Self', in Judith Greenberg, ed., *Trauma at Home: After 9/11* (Lincoln: University of Nebraska Press, 2003), 168–83.

Kallhoff, Angela, ed., *Marta C. Nussbaum: Ethics and Political Philosophy. Lecture and Colloquium in Münster 2000* (Münster: LIT, 2001).

Kaplan, Brett Ashley, 'Reading, Race and the Conundrums of Reconciliation in Philip Roth's *The Human Stain*', in Jay L. Halio and Ben Siegel, eds, *Turning Up the Flame: Philip Roth's Later Novels* (Newark: University of Delaware Press, 2005), 172–93.

Katz, Stephen T., 'The Crucifixion Of The Jews: Ignaz Maybaum's Theology Of The Holocaust', in Steven T. Katz, Shlomo Biderman and Gershon Greenberg, eds, *Wrestling with God: Jewish Theological Responses During and After the Holocaust* (Oxford: Oxford University Press, 2007), 594–601.

Kilby, Jane, 'The Writing of Trauma: Trauma Theory and the Liberty of Reading', *New Formations: A Journal of Culture/Theory/Politics* 47 (2002), 217–30.

Kimmage, Michael, 'In History's Grip: Philip Roth's "Newark Trilogy"', *PhiN* 32 (2005), 15–31.

Kopf, Martina, *Trauma und Literatur: Das Nicht-Erzählbare erzählen – Assia Djebar und Yvonne Vera* (Frankfurt am Main: Brandes & Apsel, 2005).

LaCapra, Dominick *Writing History, Writing Trauma* (Baltimore: Johns Hopkins University Press, 2001).

Landy, Joshua, 'A Nation of Madame Bovarys: On the Possibility and Desirability of Moral Improvement through Fiction', in Garry L. Hagberg, ed., *Art and Ethical Criticism* (Oxford: Blackwell, 2008), 63–94.

Laub, Dori, 'Truth and Testimony: The Process and the Struggle', in Cathy Caruth, ed., *Trauma: Explorations in Memory* (Baltimore and London: Johns Hopkins University Press, 1995), 61–75.

Leuzinger-Bohleber, Marianne, Gerhard Roth, and Anna Buchheim, *Psychoanalyse, Neurobiologie, Trauma* (Stuttgart: Schattauer, 2008).

Lubkoll, Christine, and Oda Wischmeyer, eds, *'Ethical Turn': Geisteswissenschaften in neuer Verantwortung* (Munich: Fink, 2009).

Lyons, Bonnie, 'Philip Roth's American Tragedies', in Jay L. Halio and Ben Siegel, eds, *Turning Up the Flame: Philip Roth's Later Novels* (Newark: University of Delaware Press, 2005), 125–30.

Macarthur, Kathleen L., 'Shattering the American Pastoral: Philip Roth's Vision of Trauma and the American Dream', in Daniel Walden, ed., *Philip Roth's America: The Later Novels* (Lincoln: University of Nebraska Press, 2004), 15–26.

Morton, Leith, 'The Paradox of *Pain*: The Poetry of *Paul Celan* and So Sakon', *Literature and Aesthetics: The Journal of the Sydney Society of Literature and Aesthetics* 1/1 (1991), 82–96.

Ovid, *Metamorphosen*, trans. and ed. Michael von Albrecht (Stuttgart: Reclam, 1994).

Parrish, Timothy, ed., *The Cambridge Companion to Philip Roth* (Cambridge: Cambridge University Press, 2007).

Posnock, Ross, *Philip Roth's Rude Truth: The Art of Immaturity* (Princeton: Princeton University Press, 2006).

Richardson, Samuel, *Clarissa or The History of A Young Lady* (London: Penguin, 1985).

Roth, Philip, *The Human Stain* (Boston, New York: Houghton Mifflin, 2000).

——, *Everyman* (London: Jonathan Cape, 2006).

Rothberg, Michael, 'Roth and the Holocaust', in Timothy Parrish, ed., *The Cambridge Companion to Philip Roth* (Cambridge: Cambridge University Press, 2007), 52–67.

Royal, Derek Parker, 'Roth, Literary Influence, and Postmodernism', Timothy Parrish, ed., *The Cambridge Companion to Philip Roth* (Cambridge: Cambridge University Press, 2007), 22–34.

Royal, Derek Parker, 'Contesting the Historical Pastoral in Philip Roth's American Trilogy', in Jay Posser, ed., *American Fiction of the 1990s: Reflections of History and Culture* (London and New York: Routledge, 2008), 120–33.

Safer, Elaine B., *Mocking the Age: The Later Novels of Philip Roth* (New York: State University of New York, 2006).

Schechner, Mark, 'Roth's American Trilogy', in Timothy Parrish, ed., *The Cambridge Companion to Philip Roth* (Cambridge: Cambridge University Press, 2007), 142–57.

Schmidt, Dennis J., 'Black Milk and Blue: Celan and Heidegger on Pain and Language', in Aris Fioretos, ed., *Word Traces: Readings of Paul Celan* (Baltimore: Johns Hopkins University Press, 1994), 110–29.

Shakespeare, William, *King Lear*, ed. Kenneth Muir (London: Methuen, 1982).

Sontag, Susan, *Regarding the Pain of Others* (New York: Farrar, 2003).

Soto, Isabel, 'Everyone Knows (?): Philip Roth's *The Human Stain*', in Carme Manuel and Paul Scott Derrick, eds, *Nor Shall Diamond Die: American Studies in Honour of Javier Coy* (Valéncia: Biblioteca Javier Coy d'Estudis Nord-Americans, 2003), 499–506.

Tolstoy, Leo, *The Death of Ivan Ilyich and Other Stories*, trans. Anthony Briggs (London: Penguin, 2006).

van der Kolk, Bessel A., and Onno van der Hart, 'The Intrusive Past: The Flexibility of Memory and the Engraving of Trauma', in Cathy Caruth, ed., *Trauma: Explorations in Memory* (Baltimore and London: Johns Hopkins University Press, 1995), 158–82.

Versluys, Kristiaan, *Out of the Blue: September 11 and the Novel* (New York: Columbia University Press, 2009).

Woolf, Virginia, *Mrs Dalloway* (Harmondsworth: Penguin, 1975).

SUSANA ONEGA

Trauma, Shame and Ethical Responsibility for the Death of the Other in J. M. Coetzee's *Waiting for the Barbarians*[1]

In a book entitled *African Pasts: Memory and History in African Literatures*, Tim Woods rejects the traditional postcolonial critical interpretation of the representation of history in African literatures 'as a jettisoning of the politics of colonialism', on the reflection that, frequently, this is stated without thinking that '[c]olonialism for Africans is a history which is essentially *not over*, a history whose repercussions are not only omnipresent in all cultural activities but whose traumatic consequences are still actively evolving in today's political, historical, cultural and artistic scenes.'[2] From this Woods goes on to state that, for all their differences, African literatures usually 'represent history through the twin matrices of memory and trauma' and that they are 'continually preoccupied with exploring modes of representation to "work-through" [their] different traumatic colonial pasts.'[3] Drawing on Frantz Fanon's reminder that European colonialism forced an existential deviation and traumatic severing from place and past on 'the African',[4] Woods argues that contemporary African writers not only have to find strategies 'to aid in the reconceptualisation of culture, but also of history and memory, and to organize and articulate the trauma and disruption

---

1   The research carried out for the writing of this essay is part of a research project financed by the Spanish Ministry of Science and Innovation (MICINN) and the European Regional Development Fund (ERDF) (code HUM2007–61035).
2   Tim Woods, *African Pasts: Memory and History in African Literatures* (Manchester and New York: Manchester University Press, 2007), 1 (emphasis in the original).
3   *Ibid.*
4   Frantz Fanon, *Toward the African Revolution* (Harmondsworth: Pelican, 1970).

that colonialism brought about to African communities'.[5] As he argues, the traumatic effects of the cultural deviation and severing brought about by colonization can be perceived in 'the literatures' prevailing metaphors of holes, gaps, lacunae, interruptions, cracks and fissures' and in the tendency to 'come back again and again to the problems of how to represent the continent's past',[6] while the difficulty in representing the past is often expressed through the metaphor of the injured body: 'the African body is continually "on show" in colonial and postcolonial discourse: objectified, manacled, incarcerated, whipped, tortured, branded, categorized, starved.'[7] In keeping with this, Woods defines African writing as an 'art of trauma' evincing specific linguistic and aesthetic problems derived from the need to 'tame and ultimately heal its wounds through symbolic transformations, where historical trauma is so often figured as personal amnesia.'[8]

This definition of African literatures brings to the fore the limitations of the standard dedication of trauma studies to the analysis of Holocaust, Vietnam War and African-American literatures, acting as a salutary reminder of the narrowness of the field under Western eyes. Indeed, contemporary African literatures must meet the challenge not only of providing healing narratives for the trauma of colonization but also of its aftermath, since the process of decolonization has been characterized by such dramatic and horrifying episodes of genocide and displacement as the Hutu massacre of Tutsis in Rwanda, the massive killings and exodus in the Congo civil war, or the Saharauis' thirty-year exile in the desert.

Needless to say, the main individual and collective traumas contemporary South African literature must meet stem from the overwhelming and all-encompassing culture of racial hatred and violence institutionalized by the apartheid regime. J. M. Coetzee's South African novels are excellent examples of this ethical demand and of the extraordinary difficulty of putting into words the traumatic effects of apartheid on the victims as well

---

5   Woods, *African Pasts*, 5.
6   *Ibid.*, 6.
7   *Ibid.*, 7.
8   *Ibid.*

as on the perpetrators. In the pages that follow, I will attempt to substantiate this view through the analysis of *Waiting for the Barbarians*, Coetzee's third novel and the first that brought the work of this extraordinary South African novelist to public notice.

Psychic Trauma, the Repression of Affect and the Healing Power of Words

As early as 1893, Freud and Breuer, in their study 'On the Psychic Mechanisms of Hysterical Phenomena', defined psychical trauma as a malfunctioning of the conscious memory triggered off by the subject's incapacity to react adequately to a shocking event. Even if the event is purely physical, as in the case of railway accidents or the attack of a dog, the memory malfunction itself is not caused by 'the trifling physical injury' but rather by '[a]ny experience which calls up distressing affects – such as those of fright, anxiety, shame or physical pain'.[9] In many other cases, the trauma is produced solely by a psychic shock, for example the moral injury inflicted by the ill-treatment of a superior, or the witnessing of the pain of a beloved one.[10] The ensuing memory malfunction takes the form of amnesia.[11] Characteristically, the 'fading of a memory or the losing of its affect' crucially depends on *'whether there has been an energetic reaction to the event that*

---

9   *'[T]hese experiences are completely absent from the patients' memory when they are in a normal psychical state, or are only present in a highly summary form*. Not until they have been questioned under hypnosis do these memories emerge with the undiminished vividness of a recent event'. Sigmund Freud and Josef Breuer, 'On the Psychical Mechanism of Hysterical Phenomena: Preliminary Communication' (1893), in James Strachey, Anna Freud, Alix Strachey and Alan Tyson, eds and trans., *The Standard Edition of the Complete Psychological Works of Sigmund Freud*, vol. II (London: Vintage, 2001), 1–18, 5–6 (emphasis in the original).

10   *Ibid.*, 14.

11   *Ibid.*, 9 (emphasis in the original).

provokes an affect. [...] If there is no such reaction, whether in deeds or words, or in the mildest cases in tears, any recollection of the event retains its affective tone to begin with.' However, 'language serves as a substitute for action; by its help, an affect can be "abreacted" almost as effectively.'[12] In other words, what prevents the assimilation of the traumatic experience by the usual mental processes is not so much the violence of the traumatic experience itself as the lack of adequate reaction to it, the repression of affect. As a consequence, the event is completely forgotten but the memory of the trauma remains in the unconscious, 'like a foreign body which long after its entry must continue to be regarded as an agent that is still at work'.[13] As Freud later pointed out in *Moses and Monotheism*, this foreign body makes its ghostly presence felt, sometimes after a period of 'latency' of many years, when a second shock triggers off a 'partial return of the repressed memory' in the form of fragmentary and incomprehensible 'mnemic residues', that are experienced as the compulsive repeated reenactment of the original traumatic event with all the traumatizing force of its original occurrence.[14] Although Freud saw these compulsive repetitions as positive attempts to gain conscious control over the repressed experience, he also believed that it was virtually impossible to overcome psychic trauma without help. As already pointed out, the cure is achieved only when the traumatized patient is induced through hypnosis to go back to the initial traumatic moment and made to 'abreact' the trauma, that is, to put it into words.[15] The importance Freud and Breuer granted to the cathartic effect of abreaction is significant for our purposes, as it brings to the fore the crucial role of narrative in the healing of trauma. The transformation of the fragmentary and incomprehensible 'mnemic residues' of the traumatic experience into a coherent narrative involves two main tasks: the

12   *Ibid.*, 8 (emphasis in the original).
13   *Ibid.*, 9.
14   Sigmund Freud, *Moses and Monotheism: Three Essays* (1939 [1934–38]), in James Strachey, Anna Freud, Alix Strachey and Alan Tyson eds and trans., *The Standard Edition of the Complete Psychological Works of Sigmund Freud*, vol. XXIII (London: Vintage, 2001), 66–92.
15   Freud and Breuer, 'On the Psychical Mechanism of Hysterical Phenomena', 6.

filling of memory gaps that render the compulsive repetitions of the event incomprehensible, and the establishment of a temporal distance between the subject's present and the past of the traumatic event. Thus, while the compulsive repetition of the traumatic event is experienced by the subject as a reenactment (LaCapra's 'acting out')[16] of the original experience with the 'undiminished vividness of a recent event' over and over again (see above), narrative memory permits the mastering (or 'working through')[17] of the trauma by situating it in the past of its original occurrence. The fact that the traumatic event can only be perceived belatedly and fragmentarily, as the ghostly trace of a forcefully repressed psychic wound, points to the difficulty of putting it into words. However, the task is rewarding, since as Cathy Caruth notes, the voice of trauma always conveys a hidden truth: '[Trauma] is always the story of a wound that cries out, that addresses us in the attempt to tell us of a reality or truth that is not otherwise available This truth, in its delayed appearance and its belated address, cannot be linked only to what is known, but also to what remains unknown in our very actions and our language.'[18]

With Caruth's and Woods's words in mind, it can be stated that the African writers' self-allotted and difficult task of putting into words the trauma of colonization, (or, in the case of South African writers, the trauma of apartheid), is informed by the need to reveal unknown and painful truths as the way to tame and ultimately heal the wounds caused by it. As Woods suggests, quoting Derek Wright, the intrinsic difficulty of this task goes a long way into explaining the general turn to experimentalism observable in the work of African writers in the late 1980s.[19] As Woods further notes,

16 Dominik LaCapra, *Writing History, Writing Trauma* (Baltimore and London: Johns Hopkins University Press, 2001), 21.

17 *Ibid.*, 21–2.

18 Cathy Caruth, *Unclaimed Experience: Trauma, Narrative, and History* (Baltimore: Johns Hopkins University Press, 1999), 4.

19 'In the second half of the 1980s there appeared in African writing a kind of fiction which challenged the customary ontological boundaries of a hitherto broadly realist mainstream tradition [...]. In this writing different and disparate worlds coexist; [...] the relations between history and fiction are problematic; and it is hard to

this assumption of experimental techniques provoked the irate reaction of realism-biased African readers who considered postmodernism as 'a perpetuation of colonialism by other means of representation'. To this, the writers themselves retorted that, far from ideological submission, the 'strategies of interrogation' associated with postmodernist intertextuality and linguistic free play in fact prompted the reader to assume what André Brink has described as 'a new (moral) responsibility for his/her own narrative, as well as for the narrative we habitually call the world'.[20] This controversy may be placed within the wider context of the debate that gave way, in the decade of the 1980s, to an 'ethical turn' in the related fields of critical theory and moral philosophy, as a reaction against the scepticism and relativism propounded by extreme postmodernist thinkers such as Jean-François Lyotard and Jean Baudrillard, and certain uses of deconstruction, especially in the wake of the controversy surrounding the discovery of Paul de Man's pro-Nazi writings in 1987.[21]

In South Africa, one of the writers who first became a target of attack due to his use of (late modernist rather than postmodernist)[22] experimental

          tell in exactly what ways and at what levels human character is constituted.' Derek
          Wright, 'Postmodernism as Realism: Magic History in Recent West African Fiction',
          in *Contemporary African Fiction*. Bayreuth African Studies 42 (Bayreuth: Bayreuth
          University, 1997), 181. Quoted in Woods, *African Pasts*, 241.
20   André Brink, 'Interrogating Silence: New Possibilities Faced by South African
          Literature', in Derek Attridge and Rosemary Jolly, eds, *Writing South Africa:
          Literature, Apartheid and Democracy 1970–1995* (Cambridge: Cambridge University
          Press, 1998), 14–28, 23. Quoted in Woods, *African Pasts*, 242.
21   For an analysis of this debate, see Susana Onega, 'Ethics, Trauma and the Contemporary
          British Novel', in Sibylle Baumbach, Herbert Graves and Ansgar Nünning, eds,
          *Literature and Values: Literature as a Medium for Representing, Disseminating and
          Constructing Norms and Values* (Trier: WVT, 2009), 195–204. See also Jean-Michel
          Ganteau and Susana Onega, 'Introduction', in Susana Onega and Jean-Michel
          Ganteau, eds, *The Ethical Component in Experimental British Fiction since the 1960s*
          (Newcastle: Cambridge Scholars Publishing, 2007), 1–9.
22   I concur with Andrew Gibson's view that, together with Toni Morrison, W. G.
          Sebald and Orhan Pamuk, J. M. Coetzee is a clear exponent of 'vestigial modernism',
          that is, of novelists who attempt 'to write a comparatively representational fiction'
          while simultaneously 'fleshing out what remains an abstract structure in Beckett's

techniques was J. M. Coetzee. With few exceptions, his five South African novels, written between 1974 and 1990,[23] that is, during the period of mounting socio-political unrest that climaxed in the State of Emergency (1986–90), were generally considered by South African critics and creative writers alike as too self-conscious and experimental, lacking the linguistic transparency supposedly required to convey the 'truth' about South African history. Thus, in an often quoted review of *Life and Times of Michael K.*, Nadine Gordimer criticized Coetzee's characterization of the eponymous protagonist on the contention that he did not meet Georg Lukác's requirement that characters should represent both individuality and typicality, so as to bring to the fore 'the integral relation between private and social destiny'.[24] Coetzee responded to this attack by flatly rejecting the adequacy of realism to meet the aesthetic and ethical demands of the age, arguing that the contemporary novel was 'after bigger game than that'.[25] Again, in a 1987 talk entitled 'The Novel Today', Coetzee rejected the normative 'supplementarity' of the novel with respect to history and advocated a dialectical 'rivalry' with the discourse of history based on the novel's own 'discursive procedures'.[26] Coetzee's detachment from the

---

work.' I also share Gibson's outlook on Coetzee as the contemporary writer who best exemplifies the fusion of vestigial modernism with realism. Andrew Gibson, '"Thankless Earth, But Not Entirely": Event and Remainder in Contemporary Fiction', in Bárbara Arizti and Silvia Martínez-Falquina, eds, *'On the Turn': The Ethics of Fiction in Contemporary Narrative in English* (Newcastle: Cambridge Scholars Publishing, 2007), 3–19, 11.

23   *Dusklands* (1974), *In the Heart of the Country* (1976), *Waiting for the Barbarians* (1980), *Life & Times of Michael K.* (1983) and *Age of Iron* (1990).

24   Nadine Gordimer, 'The Idea of Gardening', *New York Review of Books* (2 January 1984), 6.

25   Stephen Watson, 'Speaking: J. M. Coetzee' (Interview with Stephen Watson), *Speak* 1/3 (1978), 23–4, 24. For a more nuanced analysis of the Gordimer-Coetzee controversy on the function of literature, see the chapter on 'Gordimer, Coetzee and the Public Intellectual' in Eva-Marie Herlitzius, *A Comparative Analysis of the South-African and the German Reception of Nadine Gordimer's, André Brink's and J. M. Coetzee's Works* (Münster: LIT, 2005), 214–18.

26   J. M. Coetzee, 'The Novel Today', *Upstream* 6/1 (1988), 2–5, 3.

Marxist-influenced mainstream South African literature of the 1980s and his defense of the independence and aesthetic value of art has often been misinterpreted as confirmation of the writer's lack of political commitment. As Eva-Marie Herlitzius has pointed out, 'only a few critics stress the more complex approach of Coetzee's fiction in trying, not only to circumvent the representational strategies of colonial literature, but also to go a step further by questioning the possibility of ethical and/or political action in general.'[27]

Coetzee's lack of faith in the possibility of ethical and/or political action in apartheid South Africa, like Samuel Beckett's acknowledgement, in the aftermath of the Second World War, that 'there is nothing to express, nothing with which to express, nothing from which to express, no power to express, no desire to express, together with the obligation to express,'[28] may be said to stem from the realization of the extraordinary difficulty of the writer's task and the inadequacy of traditional literary forms to put into words the unspeakable traumas of our contemporary age. Published in 1980, *Waiting for the Barbarians* constitutes a paradigmatic example of Coetzee's struggle to meet this end, as it attempts to give voice to the pain of 'the barbarians', that is, the savage Hottentots, the most feared and unknown representatives of the white minority's absolute other, whose evocation was enough to justify the sustained policy of segregation and violence that ruled racial relations in South Africa from the creation of the state in 1910 until the formal abolition of apartheid in 1994 and the passing of the Promotion of National Unity and Reconciliation Act in 1995. This difficulty is increased by the fact that the narrator, who is the only character with the possibility of putting into words the pain of 'the barbarians', is a white country magistrate, that is, a collaborator of the apartheid state.

27   Herlitzius, *A Comparative Analysis*, 215.
28   Samuel Beckett, *Proust and the Three Dialogues with Georges Duthuit* (London: Calder, 1965), 103.

Collective Hysteria and Covert and Manifest Violence in *Waiting for the Barbarians*

During the apartheid period, South Africa developed a highly institution-alized policy of racial segregation that, in the mid-1980s, reached a peak of violence and unrest, when the wave of popular contestation over the government's 'total strategy' of ideological and repressive control was met by the proclamation of a 'state of emergency from July 1985 to early 1986, followed by a still more vigorous nationwide State of Emergency which extended from June 1986 to 1990.'[29] In keeping with the double individual and collective nature of the traumas caused by this unmitigated policy of racial discrimination and hate, the action of *Waiting for the Barbarians* develops in a timeless present and is situated in a remote fort on the border of 'Empire',[30] far away from the state's capital. This handling of space and time confers on the events narrated a highly symbolic, archetypal character, while the fact that, after the Anglo-Boer War, the South African frontier was pinpointed by numerous similarly fortified farming enclaves works in the contrary direction acting as a realism-enhancing mechanism. At the same time, the fact that the autodiegetic narrator recounts the events while he is experiencing them echoes Freud's description of the neurotic's incapacity to situate the traumatic event in the past and his or her com-pulsion to reenact it with the undiminished vividness of a recent event.[31]

---

29 Dominic Head, *J. M. Coetzee* (Cambridge: Cambridge University Press, 1997), 131.

30 J. M. Coetzee, *Waiting for the Barbarians* (London: Vintage, 2004), 6. References are given in the text.

31 As Matt DelConte argues, simultaneous present tense narration is highly artificial since 'a narrator narrating events as he experiences them' is mimetically impossible. DelConte implicitly adds a metafictional element to this 'four-wall present tense', when he says that it is also mimetically impossible for this type of narration to be addressed to a narratee at the same ontological level, so that 'the narrative transmis-sion seems to transcend the ontology of the fiction: considering that the narrator seems aware that no one within his ontology can access the narration, the narrator

The same paradoxical combination of archetypal, realistic, and neurotic features informs the characterization of the protagonist, an aging country magistrate from an ancient, English-speaking family, whose representative character is enhanced by the facts that he does not have a name and that he has liberal humanist ideas, like most real high-rank civil servants after the Anglo-Boer War. As Ian Evans explains:

> It is significant that the state's 'Native policy' at this time was informed by the ideology of benevolent paternalism and that the upper reaches of the civil service were dominated by liberal administrators. These men were wary of black opposition and were ideologically opposed to the sorts of overtly repressive controls that South Africa's farmers and white workers increasingly favoured. [...] [They] declined to surrender authority to violent white citizens [...] [and] senior administrators even hesitated to utilize the full range of the powers they lawfully possessed to control Africans.[32]

Like his real counterparts, the country magistrate in *Waiting for the Barbarians* follows a policy of benevolent paternalism and *laissez faire*. He also leads an easy-going life of sexual promiscuity and sociability that characterizes him as a *bon-vivant* and a peace-loving *homme moyen sensuel* with the only remaining aspiration of getting early retirement and a full pension. Under his rule, the fort leads a languid and prosperous existence in harmony with nature and with the various tribes that surround it. This situation comes to an abrupt end with the unexpected visit of Colonel of Police Joll, the member of the 'Third Bureau' sent from the remote state capital to the fort 'under the emergency powers' (2, 1). As Joll himself explains, his visit has to do with the spread of alarming stories that had begun to reach the capital about 'unrest among the barbarians'. However,

---

seems to narrate as if somehow conscious that someone outside his/her ontology can hear the story.' Matt DelConte, 'A Further Study of Present Tense Narration: The Absentee Narrator and Four-Wall Present Tense in Coetzee's *Waiting for the Barbarians* and *Disgrace*', *Journal of Narrative Theory* 37/3 (2007), 427–46, 433.

32   Ian Evans, *Cultures of Violence: Lynching and Racial Killing in South Africa and the American South* (Manchester and New York: Manchester University Press, 2009), 89.

experience tells the magistrate that the rumours are unfounded and that, as he confides to the colonel,

> once every generation, without fail, there is an episode of hysteria about the barbarians. There is no woman living along the frontier who has not dreamed of a dark barbarian hand coming from under the bed to grip her ankle, no man who has not frightened himself with visions of the barbarians carousing in the home, breaking the plates, setting fire to the curtains, raping his daughters. These dreams are the consequence of too much ease. Show me a barbarian army and I will believe. (8–9)

The emergency measures that Joll has come to implement are, then, based solely on the collective hysteria of the white minority, trapped in the compulsive acting out of their ancestral fear of 'the barbarians'. The use of the term 'barbarian' to refer to the tribes of nomadic Hottentots, beyond the state's border points to their condition of absolute others, as the word was used in ancient Greece to designate anyone who was not Greek.[33] Furthermore, the fact that the proclamation of emergency measures does not respond to a real threat is immaterial, as the cultivation of the white minority's ancestral fears of attack by an awesome eternal enemy allows the state to deprive its subjects of their civil rights and to strengthen its absolutist power, as the disingenuous Byzantine narrator in Constantine Cavafy's poem, 'Waiting for the Barbarians', does not fail to realize:

> [...] night has fallen and the barbarians have not come.
> And some who have just returned from the border say
> there are no barbarians any longer.
>
> And now, what's going to happen to us without barbarians?
> They were, those people, a kind of solution.[34]

33   Joll uses the term in an indiscriminate sense, as he thinks that 'Prisoner are prisoners', no matter whether they are nomadic Hottentots or fisher people settled by the lake (23).

34   Constantine Cavafy, 'Waiting for the Barbarians' (1904), trans. Edmund Keeley, <http://www9.georgetown.edu/faculty/jod/texts/cavafy.html> accessed 18 September 2010.

The fact that the fear of the 'barbarians' is the product of the collective hysteria of the Whites points to the structural nature of the violence exerted on the black majority. As Ian Evans argues, after the Anglo-Boer War, the pressure for cheap labour by white farmers and mine owners progressively led the centralized state to the deployment of a highly bureaucratized and all-encompassing policy of racial segregation and violence that took for granted the general hardship, poverty, malnutrition and family dislocation of the black population. Drawing on Johan Galtung's distinction between 'structural' (or covert) violence and 'manifest' (or overt) violence, Evans asserts that this violence was structural and therefore largely invisible to the perpetrators, 'who persisted, for example, in portraying the reserves as a bucolic paradise.'[35] As he further explains, 'social orders in which structural violence predominates are distinguished by their ability to "compartmentalize" manifest violence – that is, to confine it to particular spheres'.[36] In keeping with this, in the novel, the sphere of manifest violence is restricted to 'the Third Bureau [...] [the] most important division of the Civil Guards nowadays,' to which Colonel of Police Joll belongs (2), while the magistrate's utopian leanings signal him as a practitioner of structural violence. When the magistrate first hears of Colonel Joll's visit to the fort, he is anxious to collaborate and 'make a good impression on him' (9). However, disagreements soon arise. On their first encounter, Joll boasts about a hunting expedition in which 'thousands of deer, pigs, bears were slain, so many that a mountain of carcasses had to be left to rot'. To this, the nature-loving magistrate retorts by telling him 'about the great flocks of geese and ducks that descend on the lake every year in their migration and about native ways of trapping them' (1). As the magistrate's comment suggests, before the Colonel's arrival, life in the fort was paradisiacal: white farmers and black fishermen and hunters coexisted in harmony with nature, leading a peaceful existence ruled by a cyclical time marked by the migration of birds, the move from the desert to the mountains of the nomadic tribes, and the

35   'Statism encouraged amongst whites the impression that the wide-ranging violence used to institutionalize segregation was no more than "policy" and quotidian "administration."' Thus, structural violence became 'the spine of white prosperity in South Africa – yet it was largely invisible to whites'. Evans, *Cultures of Violence*, 96.
36   *Ibid.*

change of farming activities according to the seasons. At the centre of this harmonious natural world, the fort functioned as hospitable refuge for all, an amiable *hortus conclusus* of 'walnut trees' and 'orchards grown under their burden', where the Magistrate could safely carry his sleeping-mat out on to the ramparts to enjoy the night breeze and contemplate his restful dominion, while the sentry at the gate 'sits cross-legged fast asleep' (2).

The irruption of Colonel Joll into this *locus amoenus* amounts to the magistrate's expulsion from Paradise and the fort's traumatic fall into History. The Colonel's shocking decision to use the most gruesome forms of physical torture to extract the 'truth' from the bodies of two pitiful 'barbarians', a feeble old man and an injured boy caught in a stock raid, teaches the magistrate the difference between the paternalistic and bloodless form of structural violence he himself exerts at the fort and the manifest violence exerted by the envoy of the central state. Joll believes that torture is the only means to get the truth: 'Pain is truth: all else is subject to doubt' (5). His conviction that access to truth depends on the pressure exerted on the body, rather than the soul, brings to mind Michel Foucault's contention, in *Discipline and Punish*, that the main feature that distinguishes the modern penal system from the earlier one is 'a slackening on the hold of the body' and that in 'the metamorphosis of punitive methods on the basis of a political technology of the body [...] might be read a common history of power relations and object relations.'[37] As he further explains, the fact that the crime and punishment were bound up in the form of atrocity was the effect 'of a power that presented rules and obligations as personal bonds, [...] [and] had to demonstrate not why it enforced its laws, but who were its enemies, and what unleashing of force threatened them.'[38] The atrocity of Joll's methods of torture mirrors, then, the atrocity of the totalitarian state he represents. His sadistic treatment of the innocent prisoners is not aimed at extracting a supposed hidden truth but, simply, at establishing 'the barbarians' as the enemy needed by the state to renew and strengthen the Hegelian power/bondage, or master/slave relationship on which its existence depends.

37   Michel Foucault, *Discipline and Punish: The Birth of the Prison*, trans. Alan Sheridan (New York: Random House, 1995), 10, 24.
38   *Ibid.*, 57.

Foucault's contention that, in this regime, disobedience is interpreted as the first sign of rebellion would explain why the magistrate does not dare to oppose Joll's atrocious treatment of the two Hottentot men even though he is thoroughly shocked by it. Prevented by feelings of self-preservation from giving adequate expression to his horror and shame, the magistrate convinces himself that the pain of these alien others is nothing of his business and that he was unaware of its extremity: 'Of the screaming which people afterwards claim to have heard from the granary, I hear nothing' (5). He also accepts without protest the official report about the old man's eventual murder as the result of a 'scuffle [...] during which the prisoner fell heavily against the wall' (6). And although he tries to comfort the stunned boy and alleviate his excruciating pain, he does nothing to redress the injustice or to procure him a safe return to his people, for, as he reflects: 'I did not mean to get embroiled into this' (8). Still, instead of doing 'the wise thing' and return to his hunting and hawking, the magistrate's moral sense eventually prevails: 'for a while I stopped my ears to the noises coming from the hut by the granary where the tools are kept, then in the night I took a lantern and went to see for myself' (9–10). The magistrate's change of attitude and assumption of responsibility is marked by this crucial moment of curiosity. What he sees is so traumatizing that he finds it impossible to put it into words. After opening the door to the granary that Joll has turned into a prison/torture chamber, the only thing the magistrate is able to report is the pitch darkness and the smell of 'the rum-sodden breath' of a young sentry, who stumbled against him and said, snorting with laughter: 'The prisoner called me and I was trying to help him' (13). After this, the narration is interrupted by the incongruous interpolation of an apparently disconnected dream, in which the magistrate sees the fort and surrounding countryside covered in deep snow, and several children at play in the middle of the square building a snowcastle with a red flag on top. Every child melts away at his approach except for one: 'Older than the others, perhaps not even a child, she sits in the snow with her hooded back to [him]'. The magistrate tries 'to imagine the face between the petals of her peaked hood but cannot' (10). The following night, he dreams again, this time, of 'a body lying spread on its back, a wealth of pubic hair glistening liquid black and gold across the belly, up the loins, and down like an arrow into the furrow of the legs. When [he] stretch[es] out a hand to brush the hair it begins to writhe. It is not hair but bees clustered densely atop one another: honey-drenched, sticky, they crawl out of the furrow and fan their wings' (14).

A common metaphor in government and white South African circles in the 1980s was that of the country as a bastion or fortress besieged by communism and radical black nationalists. Yet another current trope in white South African circles, derived from the classical Greek binary oppositions man/woman, mind/body, culture/nature, is that of the country or land as a woman that has to be sexually mastered/conquered. The two dreams are built around these tropes and made complementary by means of a third one: that of looking/being looked at. In the first dream, the metaphor of the country as a besieged fortress is alluded to by the red flag on top of the snowcastle. That of the country as a woman is evoked by the magistrate's impression that the hooded child who is building the door to it is in fact a pubescent girl. In sharp contrast to this young woman, whose body and face are inaccessible to the magistrate's gaze, in the second dream, the pubescent woman/country appears as a spread-eagled naked body that attracts the sexual curiosity of the magistrate and his desire to caress it. This dream, which echoes both the magistrate's womanizing habits and his position as the highest authority of the fort in times of peace, may be said to synthesize in visual form his unconscious participation in the collective white-male fantasy of sexual mastery/imperialist control of the woman/land.

This fantasy of domination is enhanced by the magistrate's archaeological interests, which have led him to pay with his own money for the excavation of 'the ruins of houses that date back to times long before the western provinces were annexed and the fort was built'. His most treasured finding is 'a cache of wooden slips on which are painted characters in a script I have not seen the like of' (15). He spends hours trying to interpret these signs. He counts the slips, arranges and rearranges them in various geometrical combinations and even finds himself trying to read the signs backwards with the help of a mirror (17), but he is incapable of making any sense of them. The unreadability of these signs, like the inscrutability of the face of the hooded girl in the dream, exerts a tremendous fascination on the magistrate, who believes that they hide the key to the understanding/

mastering of the civilization they represent. In keeping with his cyclical conception of time, he fantasizes with the idea of finding evidence of an earlier struggle between colonizers and Hottentots over the possession of the land:

> Perhaps in my digging I have only scratched the surface. Perhaps ten feet below the floor lie the ruins of another fort, razed by the barbarians, peopled with the bones of folk who thought they would find safety behind high walls. Perhaps when I stand on the floor of the courthouse, if that is what it is, I stand over the head of a magistrate like myself, another grey-haired servant of Empire who fell on the arena of his authority, *face to face at last with the barbarians*. (16, emphasis added)

The magistrate's concluding remark enhances the significance of the dream of the hooded girl, pointing to mutual gaze as the foundation of affective relations between self and other, colonizers and colonized.

Mutual Gaze, Shame and Responsibility for the Death of the Other

The post-Freudian theory of affects initiated by Silvan S. Tomkins defines the infant as a socially interactive being from birth. Before the acquisition of language, already from about the three- to five-month period, babies try to relate to other human beings by establishing eye contact with them. As Donald L. Nathanson explains, at this stage, the infant's and mother's 'shared interocular contact is the most intimate of human experiences' and the source of the primary facial responses that Tomkins calls 'innate affects'.[39] Of the negative affects provoked by the failure to establish mutual

---

39   As Nathanson further explains, when human beings establish mutual gaze with a beloved object we feel attached with it and our face reflects the positive affect provoked by this attachment, be it in the form of *interest-excitement, enjoyment-joy*, or *surprise-startle*. By contrast, the failure to establish mutual eye contact makes us 'feel shorn not just from the other but from all possible others.' The negative

eye contact, shame probably is the most multilayered and complex and the most decisive in the construction of the self. As Nathanson explains, shame 'engenders a characteristic action, that of hiding, avoiding being seen, averting gaze. [...] [W]e are embarrassed when, suddenly, we are revealed; and when we are caught looking at someone else.'[40] Although they are often confused, shame differs from guilt: 'In guilt we are punished for an action taken; in shame we are punished for some quality of the self, some unalterable fact. Guilt limits action; shame guards the identity. Shame is the affect associated with narcissism.'[41]

The success or failure to establish mutual gaze determines, then, the adequacy or inadequacy in the construction of the subject's affective relations to other human beings. Starting from a similar relational definition of the subject, the philosopher Emmanuel Levinas goes a step further to contend that, in order to be truly human, we must make an ethical move away from the self and towards the other so as to look at the other in the face.[42] The assumption of ethical responsibility for 'the absolute other', which Levinas compares to the abnegation and hospitality of Rebecca (Genesis 24),[43] produces a crisis of identity, as the subject assumes a position of *kenosis*: 'The feat, for the being, of de-taching itself, of emptying itself of its being, of placing itself "back to front," and, if it can be put thus, the feat of "otherwise than being."'[44]

---

affects provoked by eye-contact failure are *distress-anguish, anger-rage, fear-terror*, or *shame-humiliation*. Donald L. Nathanson, 'A Timetable for Shame', in Donald L. Nathanson, ed., *The Many Faces of Shame* (New York and London: The Guilford Press, 1987), 1–63, 9, 7, 12 (emphasis in the original).

40 *Ibid.*, 249.

41 *Ibid.*, 250.

42 Emmanuel Levinas, *Otherwise than Being: or, Beyond Essence*, trans. Alphonso Lingis (The Hague: Martinus Nijhoff, 1981); *Totality and Infinity: An Essay on Exteriority*, trans. Alphonso Lingis (London: Kluwer Academic Publishers, 1991).

43 Emmanuel Levinas, 'Judaism and the Feminine Element', *Judaism* 18/1 (1969), 33–73.

44 Catherine Chalier, 'Ethics and the Feminine', in Robert Bernasconi and Simon Critchley, eds, *Re-Reading Levinas* (London: Athlone, 1991), 119–46, 121.

As R. Clifton Spargo explains, according to Levinas, this crisis or
'dislocation of the coherence of identity' achieves its most extreme form
in the empathic contemplation of the death of the other: 'By intimating
the capacity to be moved apart from our intentions or preconceptions, our
emotional relation to the death of the other describes a state of receptivity
far surpassing the self's practical capability in the world.'[45] As Spargo further
notes, Levinas, in his analysis of Plato's *Phaedo*, draws the emphasis on the
affective dimension of Socrates' story, which is the story of his unjust death
sentence and execution by the state, and he connects the capacity to weep
for another with the question of ethical responsibility, thereby bolstering
'an ethics that must, by definition, be unsettling.'[46] According to Levinas,
then, the individual who fails to respond affectively to the unjust death of
another person, or tries to divert responsibility onto others is pursued by
'mournful responsibility'. By contrast, the assumption of responsibility and
emotional attachment to the death of the other constitute the definitive
humanizing event: 'I think that *the Human* consists precisely in opening
oneself to the death of the other, in being preoccupied with his or her
death. What I am saying here may seem like a pious thought, but I am
persuaded that around the death of my neighbor what I have been calling
the humanity of man is manifested.'[47]

With these ideas in mind, it is easy to see that the magistrate's hallucinatory dreams are symptomatic of his inadequate emotional response
to the atrocious torture of the two 'barbarians' and the unjust death of

45   R. Clifton Spargo, *Vigilant Memory: Emmanuel Levinas, the Holocaust and the
     Unjust Death* (Baltimore: Johns Hopkins University Press, 2006), 28.
46   'Like grief's excess in the *Phaedro*, which cannot be suppressed even by Socrates'
     wisdom, mournful responsibility pursues the one who fails to perceive it just as
     persistently as it discovers the one who deflects responsibility onto other persons.
     Insofar as the emotive relation to the death of the other corresponds to the factic-
     ity of a signifying excess, humanity might be defined by what exceeds all systems of
     being, according to the excessive fact of the other who already objects to a world too
     well ordered by our conceptual knowledge.' *Ibid.*, 54–5.
47   Emmanuel Levinas, 'The Philosopher and Death' (1982), in *Alterity and Transcendence*,
     trans. Michael B. Smith (New York: Columbia UP, 1999), 157–8. Quoted in Spargo,
     Vigilant Memory, 58–9 (emphasis in the original).

the old man. From this perspective, the fact that, in the magistrate's first dream, the young woman/country is hooded may be said to point both to her radical otherness and to the magistrate's difficulty in making the ethical move that would allow him to establish a face-to-face relation of affective attachment with her. This reading is enhanced by the end of the second dream, where the magistrate's pleasurable feeling of sexual domination/ colonization of the woman/country unexpectedly gives way to revulsion and awe, as what he had taken for desirable pubic hair uncannily meta-morphoses into a swarm of honey-drenched winged insects coming out of the pubic cleavage/furrow of the woman/land. The uncanny revelation of this repulsive and awe-inspiring dimension of the African woman's body/ land, like the anxiety produced by the magistrate's inability to see the face of the hooded girl or to interpret the signs on the wooden slips, confers on the two dreams an element of sublimation in the Freudian sense of the term, pointing to them as the troubled expression of some anxiety-ridden past experience, or in Freud's own words, as 'mnemic residues' carrying the ghostly traces of a forcefully repressed and forgotten trauma, which has surfaced to the magistrate's conscious invoked by the more recent psychic shock of his complicit witnessing of Joll's torturing of the two Hottentot men. As the analysis of the dreams suggests, the magistrate's earlier trauma has a structural or covert, rather than a punctual or manifest character, as it was caused by his decades-long active collaboration in the construction of the Empire, which, as the trope of sexual mastery/imperial domination suggests, requires the rape of the African woman/land. The feeling of shame provoked by his lack of courage to oppose Joll's unjust acts[48] is, then, the catalyst that brings to the fore the magistrate's forcefully repressed struc-tural trauma, which is the trauma of a perpetrator of the covert violence on which the prosperity of Empire depends. The magistrate, then, is prey to two forms of shame: what he calls 'the shame of office' (152), that is, the unacknowledged and repressed shame of his active participation as high-rank civil servant in apartheid state policy; and the more poignant and

---

48   In the magistrate's own words: 'I curse Colonel Joll for all the trouble he has brought
      me, and for the shame too' (21).

acknowledged shame of his complicit witnessing of Joll's atrocious acts
of manifest violence. As he puts it himself: 'It is the knowledge of how
contingent my unease is, how dependent on a baby that wails beneath my
window one day and does not wail the next, that brings the worst shame
to me, the greatest indifference to annihilation. I know somewhat too
much; and from this knowledge, once one has been infected, there seems
to be no recovering' (22–3). The magistrate's recognition of his 'contingent
unease' as the worst form of shame echoes the 'mournful responsibility'
Levinas ascribes to those who fail or refuse to get emotionally involved in
the unjust death of others. It also goes a long way into explaining why it
is the incomprehensible and deeply disturbing dream of the hooded girl,
apparently unrelated to the torture of the 'barbarian' men, which keeps
returning, ghost-like, with slight variations, to trouble the magistrate's sleep.
Also symptomatic of the mournful state provoked by his shame is the fact
that, besides the hallucinatory dreams, the magistrate experiences an ever-
increasing desire to 'sleep like a dead man' (24), that is to say, to perform the
self-denying fantasy of closing the eyes so as not to be seen:[49] 'I feel old and
tired, I want to sleep. I sleep whenever I can nowadays and, when I wake
up, wake reluctantly. Sleep is no longer a healing bath, a recuperation of
vital forces, but an oblivion, a nightly brush with annihilation' (22).

The magistrate's dream of the hooded girl, like his fantasy of an earlier
'grey-haired servant of Empire' like himself being 'face to face at last with
the barbarians' points, then, to mutual gaze as the means of establishing a
humanizing affective relationship between colonizers and colonized capable of dissipating the magistrate's self-annihilating shame. The affective
importance of mutual gaze would also explain his bafflement and unease

49   As Otto Fenichel explains: '"I feel ashamed" means "I do not want to be seen."
Therefore, persons who feel ashamed hide themselves or at least avert their faces.
However, they also close their eyes and refuse to look. This is a kind of magical
gesture, arising from the magical belief that anyone who does not look cannot be
looked at.' Otto Fenichel, *Psychoanalytic Theory of Neurosis* (New York: Norton,
1945), 139. Quoted in Léon Wurmser, 'Shame: The Veiled Companion of Narcissism',
in Nathanson, *The Many Faces of Shame*, 64–92, 67.

about Colonel Joll's sunglasses, which make eye contact impossible.[50] As Matt DelConte cogently argues, the sunglasses 'not only represent the blind eye that Joll turns to his own tortuous treatment of the barbarians; they also become a barrier to prevent the magistrate from seeing into Joll's eyes to understand how one can steel himself enough to torture another, an understanding that might help the magistrate comprehend his own complicity in the Empire.'[51] But the sunglasses not only act as a barrier preventing mutual gaze and empathy, they also establish a disquieting ego/shadow relationship between the colonel and the magistrate, as Douglas Kerr's comment suggests: 'In Joll's eyes with their sinister glasses the magistrate sees only his own doubled image cast back at him.'[52] Thus, the magistrate's incapacity to empathize with the pain and death of the Hottentots and Colonel Joll's refusal to make eye contact with him condemn the magistrate to a position of social and emotional isolation, scornfully described by Joll as that of 'the One Just Man, the man who is prepared to sacrifice his freedom to his principles' (124). As we shall see, this description of the magistrate points to his condition of *pharmacos*.

Soon after the first dreams the magistrate's attention is caught by a young Hottentot woman, caught in a second raid, who had been atrociously tortured by Joll and made to witness her father's murder, and who had been left behind when the surviving 'barbarians' were released due to the severity of her wounds. Her near blindness, which had forced her into prostitution and beggary, fascinates the magistrate, who immediately identifies her vacant eyes with the blurred face of the hooded girl in the dream. Yielding to an irrepressible impulse, he takes her home and submits her to an ever-more intimate ritual of cleansing and caressing of her atrociously

---

50   'I have never seen anything like it: two little discs of glass suspended in front of his eyes in loops of wire. Is he blind? I could understand it if he wanted to hide blind eyes. But he is not blind. The discs are dark, they look opaque from the outside, but he can see through them' (16).

51   DelConte, 'A Further Study of Present Tense Narration', 436.

52   Douglas Kerr, 'Three Ways of Going Wrong: Kipling, Conrad, and Coetzee', *Modern Language Review* 95/1 (2000), 18–27, 26. Quoted in DelConte, 'A Further Study of Present Tense Narration', 437.

tortured body, starting with the washing of her disfigured and swollen feet, thus transforming the nightmarish dreams of the hooded and the naked girls into an apparently pleasurable, pornographic daydream.

In an article fittingly entitled 'Pornography: Daydreams to Cure Humiliation', Robert J. Stoller argues that daydreams are terribly revealing of human behaviour and that one of their basic functions is 'to ward off and then undo the effect of humiliations'. As he argues:

> Daydreams are secrets pieced together from secrets. At their core is humiliation of two sorts. First; to reveal the exact details of the script would be humiliating, too revealing of one's needs. Second; those exact details are invented to hide from their author, and at the same instant reverse, knowledge of humiliations already suffered. Only when these problems are solved [...] can one move on to open pleasure.[53]

From this perspective, the magistrate's daydream, which partially reveals and hides the shameful secrets of his collaboration with the Empire and lack of involvement in the unjust death of the 'barbarians', may be read as the compulsive acting out of the hallucinatory dreams, and so, as part of the process of working through of his trauma. This reading is reinforced by Troy Urquhart's contention that the magistrate's 'compulsion to wash [the Hottentot girl's] hobbled feet, to explore the marks on her body with his hands and thereby understand something about her experience with the Empire parallels his desire to read the wooden slips and understand the experience of their writer.'[54] The comparison, which is made by the magistrate himself,[55] is relevant in that it brings to the fore the compulsive nature of his obsessive desire to extract meaning out of them both as a way of conferring meaning on his own relation to the 'barbarians'. However, he fails not only to interpret the girl's wounds, just as he fails to interpret the wooden slips, he also repeatedly fails to establish eye contact with her,

---

53 Robert J. Stoller, 'Pornography: Daydreams to Cure Humiliation', in Nathanson, *The Many Faces of Shame*, 292–307, 295.

54 Troy Urquhart, 'Truth, Reconciliation, and the Restoration of the State: Coetzee's *Waiting for the Barbarians*', *Twentieth-Century Literature* 52/1 (2006), 1–21, 12.

55 'It has been growing more and more clear to me that until the marks on this girl's body are deciphered and understood I cannot let go of her' (33).

just as he fails to see the face of the hooded girl in the dream. Discomfited by this failure, he parts the Hottentot girl's eyelids 'between thumb and forefinger' and looks into her vacant eyes, while he incredulously ponders: 'Am I to believe that gazing back at me she sees nothing?' (33). And he scrutinizes her blank face once and again in search of 'secrets and answers' (47), while at the same time he is puzzled by his own incapacity to remember her face, or to 'recall her as she was before the doctors of pain began their ministrations': 'Somewhere in the honeycomb of my brain, I am convinced, the memory is lodged; but I am unable to bring it back. [...] I can remember the bony hands of the man who died [her father]; [...]. But beside him, where the girl should be, there is a space, a blankness' (51).

The magistrate's selective amnesia and his inability to understand why he cannot establish eye contact/affective relationship with the Hottentot girl are clear indications of his traumatic state. This trauma is increased by the horrifying message he eventually reads in her blank face, which is 'the image of a face masked by two black glassy insect eyes from which there comes no reciprocal gaze but only my doubled image cast back at me' (47). As the allusion to her 'glassy insect eyes' suggests, in this tantalizing description, the magistrate conflates uncanny mnemic residues of three traumatic images: the hooded girl's inscrutable face in the first dream; the repulsive insects coming out of the pubic cleavage/furrow of the naked body/land in the second dream; and Colonel Joll's mirror-like black sunglasses, all of which convey the same shattering message: that he can expect 'no reciprocal gaze'. The magistrate's horrified comprehension that she sees no difference between him and her torturer makes him wish for the first time to assert his distance from Joll: 'I must assert my distance from Colonel Joll! I will not suffer for his crimes!' (48). Still, at this stage, the elderly civil servant is not yet ready to assume full ethical and affective responsibility for the Hottentot girl/the pain of the other. Echoing Levinas's argument that the assumption of responsibility for the other produces an identity crisis, he wonders whether he was experiencing 'a change in [his] moral being' (46–7), but he rejects the idea on the consideration that his bewildering situation is the result of external factors out of his control:

> I am the same man I always was; but time has broken, something has fallen in upon
> me from the sky, at random, from nowhere: this body in my bed, for which I am
> responsible, or so it seems, otherwise why do I keep it? For the time being, perhaps
> forever, I am simply bewildered. It seems all one whether I lie down beside her and
> fall asleep or fold her in a sheet and bury her in the snow. (47)

The magistrate's melancholic acceptance of his unavoidable fate brings to
mind the typical victim of tragic irony, Aristotle's *pharmacos* or scapegoat.
As Northrop Frye has pointed out, '[t]he *pharmacos* is neither innocent
nor guilty. He is innocent in the sense that what happens to him is far
greater than anything he has done. He is guilty in the sense that he is a
member of a guilty society, or living in a world where such injustices are
an inescapable part of existence.'[56] According to his own perception, the
destitute civil servant finds himself in a similar incongruous and inevitable position, like Adam, Christ, or, more appositely, the immortal titan
Prometheus, who was rejected by the gods for befriending men, just as
the magistrate will be cast off from the society of the white colonizers for
befriending 'the barbarians'.

Incapable of imagining the possibility of change, the magistrate per-
severes in his attempt to explore/master the disfigured body of the Hottentot girl, even though he is unable to feel sexually aroused by her and he
invariably ends up falling asleep: 'I begin to pare and clean her toenails; but
already waves of sleeping are running over me. I catch my head drooping,
my body falling forwards in a stupor. [...] I fold her legs together in my
arms, cradle my head on them, and in an instant am sleep' (32). According
to Urquhart, this ritual allows for two opposed readings: if we associate it
with Jesus Christ's washing of feet in John 13, it may suggest 'that the Magistrate tries to act as the girl's savior, that he tries to purify her after she has
been defiled, first at the hands of Joll and then by living as a prostitute.'[57]

---

56 Northrop Frye, *Anatomy of Criticism: Four Essays* (Princeton, NJ: Princeton
    University Press, 1957), 41.
57 This interpretation would be in keeping with the magistrate's belief in the need of
    purification rituals to cleanse body and soul. For example, in the desert, he puts an
    end to the soldiers' disquiet about the bad luck they associate with the Hottentot
    girl's menstrual bleeding by performing a simple ritual of purification. He also won-
    ders whether Colonel Joll 'has a private ritual of purification carried out behind

But the reading would be ironic, as 'this act of salvation comes only as he makes her, in effect, his whore.'[58] By contrast, if we associate it with Mary Magdalene's washing of Jesus' feet in Luke 7, 'the ritual suggests that it is the Magistrate who has become a prostitute, buying a life of leisure from the Empire by selling himself through silent complicity with a system of torture and oppression, and that he believes at some level that the girl will be his salvation.'[59] Urquhart's either/or interpretation seems excessively categorical, as the magistrate's motives are terribly mixed as befits his incongruous 'neither innocent nor guilty' condition of *pharmacos* and his culturally-biased outlook on the African woman/land as sexually attractive yet monstrous. Once the contradictory nature of the magistrate's feelings and attitudes are taken into consideration it is easy to see that his relationship with the Hottentot girl constitutes a sublime encounter in the romantic sense of the term.

Abjection, Sublimation, Penance and Reparation for the Death of the Other

Various critics have interpreted the magistrate's attempts to read the wooden signs and the Hottentot girl's body/text as evidence of his desire to assert

---

closed doors, to enable him to return and break bread with other men'. And he asks Lieutenant Mandel: 'How do you find it possible to eat afterwards, after you have been ... working with people?' Then he adds: 'But no ordinary washing would be enough, one would require priestly intervention, a ceremonial of cleansing, don't you think? Some kind of purging of one's soul too [...]' (75–6, 13, 138).

58   The irony is increased when it is recalled that Christ's act was meant to denounce the inequality of master/slave relationships and to enforce what may be described as a Levinasian ethics of unconditional love for the other *avant la lettre*: '14 If I then, your Lord and Teacher, have washed your feet, you also ought to wash one another's feet. 15 For I have given you an example, that you should do as I have done to you. 16 Most assuredly, I say to you, a servant is not greater than his master; nor is he who is sent greater than he who sent him.' John 13:14–16.

59   Urquhart, 'Truth, Reconciliation, and the Restoration of the State', 12.

'the moral ideal of a human community';[60] erase the dichotomy colonizer/
colonized, and move forward to a new ethical order founded on Edenic
principles.[61] In this sort of allegorical reading, there is hope of retributive
justice and even, as Susan VanZanten Gallagher suggests, the possibility
that the unspeakable and forcefully erased history of the victims of apartheid be given voice, not by the silenced barbarians themselves, but through
the magistrate's assumption of the role of 'temporary father-interpreter'
of their oppression.[62] However, as Troy Urquart convincingly argues, this
assertion can only be made by ignoring the troubling fact that what the
magistrate is really trying to do is 'to speak for the barbarian by translating
barbarian experience into the language of the Empire.'[63] This crucial point
is made by the magistrate himself when he describes the marks of torture
as a text begging for interpretation,[64] or when he compares his washing/
caressing of the girl's deformed body with Colonel Joll's extraction from
it of 'the sounds of her intimate pain'. As the magistrate wonders, mixing
shame with sexual jealousy:

> Whose was the last face she saw plainly on this earth but the face behind the glowing
> iron? Though I cringe with shame, even here and now, I must ask myself whether, when
> I lay head to foot with her, fondling and kissing those broken ankles, I was not in my
> heart of hearts regretting that I could not engrave myself on her as deeply. (280)

60 David Atwell, *J. M. Coetzee: South Africa and the Politics of Writing* (Berkeley:
    University of California Press, 1993), 78.
61 Michael Valdez Moses, 'The Mark of Empire: Writing, History, and Torture in
    Coetzee's *Waiting for the Barbarians*', *Kenyon Review* 15/1 (1993), 115–27.
62 Susan VanZanten Gallagher, 'Torture and the Novel: J. M. Coetzee's *Waiting for the
    Barbarians*', *Contemporary Literature* 29/2 (1988), 277–85, 280.
63 Urquhart, 'Truth, Reconciliation, and the Restoration of the State', 6.
64 'It has been growing more and more clear to me that until the marks on this girl's
    body are deciphered and understood I cannot let go of her' (33). As Dominic Head
    has noted, this description echoes the brutal scene in Kafka's 'In the Penal Colony',
    in which the word 'ENEMY' is written on the backs of 'a line of barbarian prisoners'
    and 'then thrashed until the word is effaced' (Head, *J. M. Coetzee*, 76). As Martin
    Modlinger suggested to me in a private communication, the Hottentot girl's tortured
    body/text also bring to mind Sethe's 'tree' of scars on her back and her swollen feet, in
    Toni Morrison's later novel *Beloved* (1987). For an analysis of *Beloved* in the context
    of trauma studies see also Hubert Zapf's article in this volume.

Matt DelConte reads these words as testimony of the magistrate's 'envy of the power that Joll exerts over the woman' and he asserts that the novel 'is very much about the sexual colonization of a younger woman by an older man not for physical gratification but to curb the anxiety of impotence. As such, Coetzee is able to conflate the magistrate's sexual colonization with the Empire's more global political colonization of the barbarians.'[65] Although there is no denying that the magistrate's daydreaming of seducing/mastering the African woman/land has a political as well as a sexual component, his repeated failure to have sexual intercourse with the Hottentot girl has nothing to do with old-age impotence, even though this is the explanation he gives himself (49). In fact, at the same time as he is sleeping with her, the magistrate is seeking satisfaction for his sexual needs by frequenting the bird-like prostitute 'whose nickname at the inn is The Star' (45, 49). But his 'guilty feelings spoil the pleasure' and, when he returns home, he 'tiptoe[s] like an erring husband' so as not to awake the Hottentot girl (60). Further, after his return from the desert, the magistrate buys a potion from a herbalist to diminish his sexual appetite. When the herbalist asks him: 'why should a fine healthy man like yourself want to kill off his desires?' he responds: 'It has nothing to do with desire, father. It is simply an irritation, a stiffening. Like rheumatism' (164). As this response suggests, the magistrate's problem is not physical but psychological and responds to his own perception that he is both 'wanting and not wanting her', that is, wanting to have sex with the Hottentot girl and 'shudder[ing] with revulsion' at the thought of her 'blank body [...] without aperture, without entry' (35, 45, 49). In other words, the magistrate's 'sexual langour' (50) and sleeping trances are symptoms of the sublime revulsion he feels for her obdurate and unreadable, monstrous body, as he himself admits: 'What this woman beside me is doing in my life I cannot comprehend. The thought of the strange ecstasies I have approached through the medium of her incomplete body fills me with a dry revulsion, as if I had spent nights copulating with a dummy of straw and leather' (50). Like Susan Barton's refusal of the logic of desire in her relationship with Friday in Coetzee's *Foe*, the magistrate's sexual disinterestedness is indicative, as Mark Mathuray

65   DelConte, 'A Further Study of Present Tense Narration', 438.

explains, of the subject's refusal to possess the object that occasions the sublime moment, according to Kant's characterization of the sublime.[66]

Just as Susan Barton is revolted by Friday's mutilated tongue, and not by his race,[67] so is the magistrate's sublime revulsion provoked by the deformity of the girl: 'is she truly so featureless? With an effort I concentrate my mind on her. I see a figure in a cap and heavy shapeless coat standing unsteadily, bent forward, straddle-legged, supporting itself on sticks. How ugly, I say to myself. My mouth forms the ugly word. I am surprised by it but I do not resist: she is ugly, ugly' (50). The magistrate's words bring to mind the sexual nausea that, according to Sandra Gilbert and Susan Gubar, men feel in the presence of transgressive women, who are consequently made to feel in constant danger and fear of being labelled as mad and/or monstrous.[68] They also echo Julia Kristeva's description of 'the compound of abomination and fascination' generated by the abjection of the object of desire,[69] which Kristeva exemplifies with the child's abjection of the menstrual and excremental body of the mother and Barbara Creed associates with the monstrous-feminine.[70] More concretely, the sexual nausea the magistrate feels in the presence of the deformed body of the Hottentot girl responds to the western commodification of the African woman/country both as a fascinating body that attracts the sexual curiosity of the male gaze and a grotesque and abject object of fun and disgust. As Janell Hobson has pointed out, the most depurate expression of this oxymoronic figure is 'the Hottentot Venus', an early nineteenth-century representation of the

---

66 Mark Mathuray, 'Sublime Abjection', in Elleke Boehmer, Katy Iddiols and Robert Eaglestone, eds, *J. M. Coetzee in Context and Theory* (New York and London: Continuum, 2009), 159–72, 168.

67 *Ibid.*, 160.

68 Sandra Gilbert and Susan Gubar. *The Madwoman in the Attic: The Woman Writer and the Nineteenth-century Literary Imagination* (1979, New Haven and London: Yale University Press, 1984), 34.

69 Julia Kristeva, *Powers of Horror: An Essay on Abjection* (New York: Columbia University Press, 1982), 169.

70 Barbara Creed, 'Horror and the Monstrous-Feminine: An Imaginary Abjection', in Donald James, ed., *Fantasy and the Cinema* (London: BFI, 1989), 63–89; *The Monstrous Feminine* (London and New York: Routledge, 1993).

African woman that combines two pre-existing tropes: the Black Venus and the Savage Hottentot.[71] As Hobson remarks, this grotesque representation of the African woman evinces 'a problem of "seeing" or "mis/seeing" the body beyond the stigmas identified with it'.[72] The magistrate's sexual curiosity for the Hottentot girl is tainted by a similar problem of vision, as he himself acknowledges when he says that his 'gaze [is] pressing in upon her with the weight of a body' and that by seeing her 'as a body maimed, scarred, harmed, she has perhaps by now grown into and become that new deficient body, feeling no more deformed than a cat feels deformed for having claws instead of fingers' (60–1).

Significantly, it is after this guilty reflection that the old civil servant decides to write a letter to the Governor informing him of his decision to 'repair some of the damage wrought by the forays of the Third Bureau [...] and to restore some of the goodwill that previously existed, [by] undertaking a brief visit to the barbarians' (62). The archetypal perilous journey beyond the border and across the desert that he undertakes with the girl and a few accompanying soldiers is really aimed at returning her to her people. The reward for this act of restitution is the materialization of his imagined face-to-face encounter of a magistrate with a Hottentot leader. Although the actual encounter does nothing to patch up 'relations between the men of the future and the men of the past' (62), as he had hoped, the journey helps the magistrate correct his problematic 'miss/seeing' of the girl. Hearing her banter with the soldiers in the pidgin of the frontier he 'is surprised by her fluency, her quickness, her self-possession', and it suddenly dawns on him that 'she is not just the old man's slut: she is a witty, attractive young woman!' (68). Later on, when she speaks with the Hottentot leader in her own language, he is struck by the thought that: 'she could have spent those long empty evenings teaching me her tongue! Too late now' (78). And he comprehends, 'in a moment of astonishment that I could have loved someone from so remote a kingdom' (82). The revelation

71   Janell Hobson, *Venus in the Dark: Blackness and Beauty in Popular Culture* (New York and London: Routledge, 2005), 17.

72   *Ibid.*

that her impenetrability and radical otherness is the result of his own
failure to love signals a fulcrum in the magistrate's assumption of ethical
responsibility for the pain and death of the other, what Alain Badiou would
describe as the moment of adherence to a truth that demands fidelity at
any cost for the self.[73]

When, after his return from the desert, he is accused of '[t]reasonously
consorting' with 'the barbarians', the magistrate celebrates 'the end of his
alliance with the guardians of the Empire' as a liberation (85). Imprisoned
in the same horror chamber were many natives had been tortured, including
the girl and her father, he imagines their 'ghosts trapped between these walls'
(88) and blames himself for having done nothing to protect them. This
thought leads him to conclude that 'there must always be a place for penance and reparation' (88). Thus, although he is terrified by the unimagined
urgency of his basic physical needs and the prospect of pain, he returns to
his cell after a brief escapade on the reflection that he has nowhere else to
go (114). And, although he attempts to pass unnoticed, on the consideration that 'I cannot save the prisoners, therefore let me save myself' (114),
he does interfere when a little girl is given a cane and encouraged to flog
an already viciously tortured 'barbarian' (116). Needless to say, his demonstration of courage and concern both for the pain of the man and for
the moral debasement of the child brings the torturers' rage upon himself:
his hand and nose are broken in a vicious beating, he is forced to denude
himself and put on a woman's calico smock in front of a rowdy crowd,
and made to ascend the ladder of the gallows with a sack on his head and
a rope around the arms and neck. Thus, grotesquely dressed as a woman
and blinded, deprived of dignity and human sympathy, and conscious only
of his atrocious pain, the magistrate finds himself at last 'past shame' in
the abject position of the Hottentot girl (128). The magistrate assumes his
public defilement and torture as part of an unavoidable ritual of penance
and reparation in which he must play the role of scapegoat: 'A scapegoat is
named, a festival is declared, the laws are suspended: who would not flock
to see the entertainment?' (133), but while he assumes that his penance is

73   Alain Baidou, *L'Éthique: Essay sur la conscience du mal* (Caen: Nous, 2003), 60–4.

a form of reparation for the pain and death of 'the barbarians', the torturers and the angry crowd make him pay for their own heavy losses of white
human lives and property in the disastrous war against them.

The ritual climaxes in a terrifying mock hanging that takes the magistrate to a near-death experience. Just as he is on the point of falling from the
ladder, he has a vision of himself standing face-to-face with the Hottentot
leader, 'waiting for him to speak', but he does not say anything (132). Then,
he feels the rope tightening about his neck and wrists and he experiences
a terrible tearing in his shoulders that makes him roar with pain: 'I bellow
again and again, there is nothing I can do to stop it, the noise comes out
of a body that knows itself damaged perhaps beyond repair and roars its
fright' (132–3). While he flies in agony, suspended by the rope, he hears a
sneering comment: 'That is barbarian language you hear' (133). This comment is accurate both literally and symbolically as the magistrate's bellows
is the body language of pain that he had been trying to ignore when 'the
barbarians' uttered it, the language also that Joll inscribed with his torture
tools in the girl's body, and which the magistrate was unable to read. Ironi-
cally, the truth this body language conveys is the only truth Colonel Joll
and Lieutenant Mandel care about:

> They were interested only in demonstrating to me what it meant to live in a body,
> as a body, a body which can entertain notions of justice only as long as it is whole
> and well [...]. They did not come to force the story out of me of what I had said to
> the barbarians and what the barbarians had said to me. So I had no chance to throw
> the high sounding words I had ready in their faces. They came to my cell to show
> me the meaning of humanity, and in the space of an hour they showed me a great
> deal. (127)

Deprived of 'high sounding words' by the inescapability of his embodied self, the magistrate now imagines how much the Hottentot girl must
have suffered at his own hands.[74] And he regrets that she did not tell him
what he ought to have done: 'if you want to love me you will have to turn
your back on him [Joll] and learn elsewhere' (148). Most crucially, he

---

74 '[S]he must have felt a miasma of deceit closing about her: envy, pity, cruelty all
masquerading as desire' (148).

also comprehends now that 'I was not, as I liked to think, the indulgent pleasure-loving opposite of the cold rigid Colonel. I was the lie that Empire tells itself when times are easy, he the truth that Empire tells when harsh wind blows. Two sides of the Imperial rule, no more, no less' (148–9). This admission of guilt signals the end of the stage of compulsive acting out of his perpetrator's trauma, whose symptoms, as we have seen, are the hallucinatory dreams, the pornographic daydream of the Hottentot girl, the sleeping trances, and the memory malfunction. After it, the magistrate dreams once more of the hooded girl, but this time she returns his gaze smiling: 'For an instant I have the vision of her face, the face of a child, glowing, healthy, smiling on me without alarm, before we collide. Her head strikes me in the belly; then, I am gone, carried by the wind. The bump is as faint as the stroke of a moth. I am flooded with relief. "Then I need not have been anxious after all!" I think' (149). The happy completion of the dream dispels its uncanny, traumatizing force, marking the beginning of the phase of working through. This interpretation is reinforced by another episode that takes place soon after. Just as had happened to him when he identified the hooded child with the Hottentot girl, the dream of the smiling child seems to materialize in real life: as he crosses the square covered in snow, the magistrate sees some children playing in the middle. But they are building a snowman instead of a castle, that is, a human being instead of a fort. Watching them, the magistrate thinks that, although it has no arms, '[i]t is not a bad snowman' and he flatly concludes that 'this is not the scene I dreamed of' (169). His refusal to transform this quotidian scene into yet another pornographic daydream provides clear evidence that he has overcome his trauma. Still, we cannot say that he has the key to the establishment of a lasting affective relationship between colonizers and colonized, for he still yearns for the recovery of the white farmers' paradisiacal *hortus conclusus* with the 'barbarian' hordes outside: 'They will graze their sheep and leave us alone, we will plant our fields and leave them alone, and in a few years the frontier will be restored to peace again' (145). And we can neither say that he has achieved the kind of transcendental wisdom that follows the sublime encounter, according to Kant.[75] Rather,

75   As Thomas Weiskel has noted, the structure of the romantic sublime encounter follows three phases. In the first, subject and object stand in a certain relationship; in the

as in other novels by Coetzee, *Waiting for the Barbarians* ends leaving the protagonist in a typical existentialist position: feeling 'stupid', 'lost', and 'press[ing] on along a road that may lead nowhere' (170). The only form of enlightenment and hope for the future the novel offers is the reader's participation in the minimal existential freedom achieved by the magistrate against the oppressive structures of power/the dialectics of history, through the reading of the healing narrative of his difficult and troubled process of ethical awakening and affective involvement in the unjust pain and death of the other.[76]

Bibliography

Atwell, David, *J. M. Coetzee: South Africa and the Politics of Writing* (Berkeley: University of California Press, 1993).

Baidou, Alain, *L'Éthique: Essay sur la conscience du mal* (Caen: Nous, 2003).

Beckett, Samuel, *Proust and the Three Dialogues with Georges Duthuit* (London: Calder, 1965).

Brink, André, 'Interrogating Silence: New Possibilities Faced by South African Literature', in Derek Attridge and Rosemary Jolly, eds, *Writing South Africa: Literature, Apartheid and Democracy 1970–1995* (Cambridge: Cambridge University Press, 1998), 14–28.

Caruth, Cathy, *Unclaimed Experience: Trauma, Narrative, and History* (Baltimore: Johns Hopkins University Press, 1999).

---

second, this relationship breaks down, as the subject is confronted with a situation that exceeds comprehension and leads to an epiphany of absolute limitation; and in the third, the possibility of meaning is rescued, as the subject is allowed to glimpse at and become aware of his/her destiny as a moral being. Thomas Weiskel, *The Romantic Sublime: Studies in the Structure and Psychology of Transcendence* (Baltimore: Johns Hopkins University Press, 1976). Quoted in Mathuray, 'Sublime Abjection', 161–2. Mathuray analyses the absence of this third phase in Susan Barton and Friday's relation as an example of what he calls '*the stalled sublime*'. *Ibid.*, 162 (emphasis in the original).

76   Significantly, the magistrate decides to start writing it after recuperating his job, at the end of the novel (169).

Cavafy, Constantine, 'Waiting for the Barbarians' (1904), trans. Edmund Keeley, <http://www9.georgetown.edu/faculty/jod/texts/cavafy.html> accessed 18 September 2010.

Chalier, Catherine, 'Ethics and the Feminine', in Robert Bernasconi and Simon Critchley, eds, *Re-Reading Levinas* (London: Athlone, 1991), 119–46.

Coetzee, J. M., 'The Novel Today', *Upstream* 6/1 (1988), 2–5.

——, *Waiting for the Barbarians* (London: Vintage, 2004).

Creed, Barbara, 'Horror and the Monstrous-Feminine: An Imaginary Abjection', in Donald James, ed., *Fantasy and the Cinema* (London: BFI, 1989), 63–89.

——, *The Monstrous Feminine* (London and New York: Routledge, 1993).

DelConte, Matt, 'A Further Study of Present Tense Narration: The Absentee Narrator and Four-Wall Present Tense in Coetzee's *Waiting for the Barbarians* and *Disgrace*', *Journal of Narrative Theory* 37/3 (2007), 427–46.

Evans, Ian, *Cultures of Violence: Lynching and Racial Killing in South Africa and the American South* (Manchester and New York: Manchester University Press, 2009).

Fanon, Frantz, *Toward the African Revolution* (Harmondsworth: Pelican, 1970).

Fenichel, Otto, *Psychoanalytic Theory of Neurosis* (New York: Norton, 1945).

Foucault, Michel, *Discipline and Punish: The Birth of the Prison*, trans. Alan Sheridan (New York: Random House, 1995).

Freud, Sigmund, and Josef Breuer, 'On the Psychical Mechanism of Hysterical Phenomena: Preliminary Communication' (1893), in James Strachey, Anna Freud, Alix Strachey and Alan Tyson, eds and trans., *The Standard Edition of the Complete Psychological Works of Sigmund Freud*, vol. II (London: Vintage, 2001), 1–18.

——, *Moses and Monotheism: Three Essays* (1939 [1934–38]), in James Strachey, Anna Freud, Alix Strachey and Alan Tyson, eds and trans., *The Standard Edition of the Complete Psychological Works of Sigmund Freud*, vol. XXIII (London: Vintage, 2001), 66–92.

Frye, Northrop, *Anatomy of Criticism: Four Essays* (Princeton, NJ: Princeton University Press, 1957).

Gallagher, Susan VanZanten, 'Torture and the Novel: J. M. Coetzee's *Waiting for the Barbarians*', *Contemporary Literature* 29/2 (1988), 277–85.

Ganteau, Jean-Michel, and Susana Onega, 'Introduction', in Susana Onega and Jean-Michel Ganteau, eds, *The Ethical Component in Experimental British Fiction since the 1960s* (Newcastle: Cambridge Scholars Publishing, Newcastle, 2007), 1–9.

Gibson, Andrew, '"Thankless Earth, But Not Entirely": Event and Remainder in Contemporary Fiction', in Bárbara Arizti and Silvia Martínez-Falquina, eds, *'On the Turn': The Ethics of Fiction in Contemporary Narrative in English* (Newcastle: Cambridge Scholars Publishing, 2007), 3–19.

Gilbert, Sandra, and Susan Gubar. *The Madwoman in the Attic: The Woman Writer and the Nineteenth-Century Literary Imagination* (1979, New Haven and London: Yale University Press, 1984).

Gordimer, Nadine, 'The Idea of Gardening', *New York Review of Books* (2 January 1984), 6.

Head, Dominic, *J. M. Coetzee*. (Cambridge: Cambridge University Press, 1997).

Herlitzius, Eva-Marie, *A Comparative Analysis of the South-African and the German Reception of Nadine Gordimer's, André Brink's and J. M. Coetzee's Works* (Münster: LIT, 2005).

Hobson, Janell, *Venus in the Dark: Blackness and Beauty in Popular Culture* (New York and London: Routledge, 2005).

Kerr, Douglas, 'Three Ways of Going Wrong: Kipling, Conrad, and Coetzee', *Modern Language Review* 95/1 (2000), 18–27.

Kristeva, Julia, *Powers of Horror: An Essay on Abjection* (New York: Columbia University Press, 1982).

LaCapra, Dominick, *Writing History, Writing Trauma* (Baltimore and London: Johns Hopkins University Press, 2001).

Levinas, Emmanuel, 'Judaism and the Feminine Element', *Judaism* 18/1 (1969), 33–73.

——, *Otherwise than Being: or, Beyond Essence*, trans. Alphonso Lingis (The Hague: Martinus Nijhoff, 1981).

——, *Totality and Infinity: An Essay on Exteriority*, trans. Alphonso Lingis (London: Kluwer Academic Publishers, 1991).

——, *Alterity and Transcendence*, trans. Michael B. Smith (New York: Columbia University Press, 1999).

Mathuray, Mark, 'Sublime Abjection', in Elleke Boehmer, Katy Iddiols and Robert Eaglestone, eds, *J. M. Coetzee in Context and Theory* (New York and London: Continuum, 2009), 159–72.

Moses, Michael Valdez, 'The Mark of Empire: Writing, History, and Torture in Coetzee's *Waiting for the Barbarians*', *Kenyon Review* 15/1 (1993), 115–27.

Nathanson, Donald L., ed., *The Many Faces of Shame* (New York and London: The Guilford Press, 1987).

Onega, Susana, 'Ethics, Trauma and the Contemporary British Novel', in Sibylle Baumbach, Herbert Graves and Ansgar Nünning, eds, *Literature and Values: Literature as a Medium for Representing, Disseminating and Constructing Norms and Values* (Trier: WVT, 2009), 195–204.

Spargo, R. Clifton, *Vigilant Memory: Emmanuel Levinas, the Holocaust and the Unjust Death* (Baltimore: Johns Hopkins University Press, 2006).

Stoller, Robert J., 'Pornography: Daydreams to Cure Humiliation', in Nathanson, *The Many Faces of Shame*, 292–307.

Urquhart, Troy, 'Truth, Reconciliation, and the Restoration of the State: Coetzee's *Waiting for the Barbarians*', *Twentieth-Century Literature* 52/1 (2006), 1–21.

Weiskel, Thomas, *The Romantic Sublime: Studies in the Structure and Psychology of Transcendence* (Baltimore: Johns Hopkins University Press, 1976).

Watson, Stephen, 'Speaking: J. M. Coetzee' (Interview with Stephen Watson), *Speak* 1/3 (1978), 23–4.

Woods, Tim, *African Pasts: Memory and History in African Literatures* (Manchester and New York: Manchester University Press, 2007).

Wright, Derek, 'Postmodernism as Realism: Magic History in Recent West African Fiction', in *Contemporary African Fiction*. Bayreuth African Studies 42 (Bayreuth: Bayreuth University, 1997).

Wurmser, Léon, 'Shame: The Veiled Companion of Narcissism', in Donald L. Nathanson, ed., *The Many Faces of Shame* (New York and London: The Guilford Press, 1987), 64–92.

Notes on Contributors

ALEIDA ASSMANN is Professor of English Literature at the University of Constance (Germany). Her research focuses on history and memory in literary and cultural studies with a special emphasis on cultural memory. She is the author of *Geschichte im Gedächtnis. Von der individuellen Erfahrung zur öffentlichen Inszenierung* (2007), *Der lange Schatten der Vergangenheit. Erinnerungskultur und Geschichtspolitik* (2006) and co-editor (with Sebastian Conrad) of *Memory in a Global Age. Discourses, Practices and Trajectories* (2010).

BETTINA BANNASCH is Professor of Modern German Literature at the University of Augsburg (Germany). Her research interests include Holocaust literature, German-Jewish literature and, most recently, German literature in exile. She is co-editor (with Almuth Hammer) of *Verbot der Bilder – Gebot der Erinnerung. Mediale Repräsentationen der Shoah* (2004) and (with Günter Butzer) *Übung und Affekt. Formen des Körpergedächtnisses* (2007).

COLIN DAVIS is Professor of French at Royal Holloway, University of London. His research is principally in the field of twentieth-century French literature, thought and film. He is particularly interested in ethical criticism and the links between philosophy, literature and film. He is the author of *Ethical Issues in Twentieth-Century French Fiction: Killing the Other* (2000) and *Haunted Subjects: Deconstruction, Psychoanalysis and the Return of the Dead* (2007).

RUDOLF FREIBURG is Professor of English Literature at the University of Erlangen-Nuremberg (Germany). His research interests include eighteenth-century literature, postmodernist literature and the relationship between theodicy, atheism and literature. He has co-edited numerous books, amongst them (with Susanne Gruß) '*But Vindicate the Ways of God to Man': Literature and Theodicy* (2004) and most recently (with Gerd Bayer) *Literatur und Holocaust* (2008).

MARÍA JESÚS MARTÍNEZ-ALFARO is Senior Lecturer of English Literature at the University of Zaragoza (Spain) and a member of the 'Ethics and Trauma in Contemporary Fiction in English' research team at Zaragoza. She is the author of *Text and Intertexts in Charles Palliser's 'The Quincunx'* (1996) and co-editor (with Ramón Plo) of *Beyond Borders: Re-defining Generic and Ontological Boundaries* (2000).

MARTIN MODLINGER is a doctoral candidate in the Department of German and Dutch at the University of Cambridge, where he is writing his thesis on the history and literature of the Terezín Ghetto. He studied English literature and history as well as 'Ethics of Textual Cultures' in Munich, Perth and Erlangen. His interests lie in German and English literature, especially Holocaust literature, and the history of terror and catastrophe. He has co-edited (with A. Bidmon, M. Illi, D. Gruschke, C. Lubkoll and O. Wischmeyer) *'Ethical Turn'? – Geisteswissenschaften in Neuer Verantwortung* (2009) and has published several articles on Holocaust literature and the ethical implications of literature.

SUSANA ONEGA is Professor of English Literature at the University of Zaragoza (Spain) and head of the 'Ethics and Trauma in Contemporary Fiction in English' research team at Zaragoza. Her research interests include experimental modernist and postmodernist literature, trauma studies and ethics in literature. She has edited (with Jean-Michel Ganteau) *The Ethical Component in Experimental British Fiction since the 1960's* (2007) and (with Jean-Michel Ganteau) *Trauma and Ethics in British Fiction* (forthcoming).

SUSANNAH RADSTONE is Professor in the School of Humanities and Social Sciences at the University of East London. Her recent research has focused on the field of memory studies with particular reference to trauma studies and the cinema. She is the author of *The Sexual Politics of Time: Confession, Nostalgia, Memory* (2007) and co-editor (with Bill Schwarz) of *Memory: Histories, Theories, Debates* (2010).

PHILIPP SONNTAG is a doctoral candidate at the Department of English/ American and Romance Studies at the University of Erlangen-Nuremberg (Germany) and a member of the postgraduate programme 'Literature and Culture'. He studied English literature, philosophy and political science as well as 'Ethics of Textual Cultures' in Erlangen. His research interests include contemporary literature, literary theory and the relationship between philosophy and literature, especially ethics and literature. He is currently a lecturer of English Literature at the University of Erlangen-Nuremberg.

HUBERT ZAPF is Professor of American Literature at the University of Augsburg and a faculty member of the honours graduate programme 'Ethics of Textual Cultures' in Augsburg (Germany). His research focuses on literature and cultural ecology, twentieth-century drama, American literary history, and literary and cultural theory. He is the author of *Literatur als kulturelle Ökologie. Zur kulturellen Funktion imaginativer Texte an Beispielen des amerikanischen Romans* (2002) and co-editor (with Sebnem Toplu) of *Redefining Modernism and Postmodernism* (2010).

Index

CULTURAL HISTORY AND LITERARY IMAGINATION

EDITED BY CHRISTIAN J. EMDEN & DAVID MIDGLEY

This series promotes inquiry into the relationship between literary texts and their cultural and intellectual contexts, in theoretical, interpretative and historical perspectives. It has developed out of a research initiative of the German Department at Cambridge University, but its focus of interest is on the European tradition broadly perceived. Its purpose is to encourage comparative and interdisciplinary research into the connections between cultural history and the literary imagination generally.

The editors are especially concerned to encourage the investigation of the role of the literary imagination in cultural history and the interpretation of cultural history through the literary text. Examples of the kind of issues in which they are particularly interested include the following:

- The material conditions of culture and their representation in literature, e.g. responses to the impact of the sciences, technology, and industrialisation, the confrontation of 'high' culture with popular culture, and the impact of new media;

- The construction of cultural meaning through literary texts, e.g. responses to cultural crisis, or paradigm shifts in cultural self-perception, including the establishment of cultural 'foundation myths';

- History and cultural memory as mediated through the metaphors and models deployed in literary writing and other media;

- The intermedial and intercultural practice of authors or literary movements in specific periods;

- The methodology of cultural inquiry and the theoretical discussion of such issues as intermediality, text as a medium of cultural memory, and intercultural relations.

Both theoretical reflection on and empirical investigation of these issues are welcome. The series is intended to include monographs, editions, and collections of papers based on recent research in this area. The main language of publication is English.

Vol. 1   Christian Emden & David Midgley (eds): Cultural Memory and Historical Consciousness in the German-Speaking World Since 1500. Papers from the Conference 'The Fragile Tradition', Cambridge 2002. Vol. 1.
316 pp., 2004. ISBN 3-03910-160-9 / US-ISBN 0-8204-6970-X

Vol. 2   Christian Emden & David Midgley (eds): German Literature, History and the Nation. Papers from the Conference 'The Fragile Tradition', Cambridge 2002. Vol. 2.
393 pp., 2004. ISBN 3-03910-169-2 / US-ISBN 0-8204-6979-3

Vol. 3   Christian Emden & David Midgley (eds): Science, Technology and the German Cultural Imagination. Papers from the Conference 'The Fragile Tradition', Cambridge 2002. Vol. 3.
319 pp., 2005. ISBN 3-03910-170-6 / US-ISBN 0-8204-6980-7

Vol. 4   Anthony Fothergill: Secret Sharers. Joseph Conrad's Cultural Reception in Germany.
274 pp., 2006. ISBN 3-03910-271-0 / US-ISBN 0-8204-7200-X

Vol. 5   Silke Arnold-de Simine (ed.): Memory Traces. 1989 and the Question of German Cultural Identity.
343 pp., 2005. ISBN 3-03910-297-4 / US-ISBN 0-8204-7223-9

Vol. 6   Renata Tyszczuk: In Hope of a Better Age. Stanislas Leszczynski in Lorraine 1737-1766.
410 pp., 2007. ISBN 978-3-03910-324-9

Vol. 7   Christian Emden, Catherine Keen & David Midgley (eds): Imagining the City, Volume 1. The Art of Urban Living.
344 pp., 2006. ISBN 3-03910-532-9 / US-ISBN 0-8204-7536-X

Vol. 8   Christian Emden, Catherine Keen & David Midgley (eds): Imagining the City, Volume 2. The Politics of Urban Space.
383 pp., 2006. ISBN 3-03910-533-7 / US-ISBN 0-8204-7537-8

Vol. 9   Christian J. Emden and Gabriele Rippl (eds): ImageScapes: Studies in Intermediality.
289 pp., 2010. ISBN 978-3-03910-573-1

Vol. 10   Alasdair King: Hans Magnus Enzensberger. Writing, Media, Democracy.
357 pp., 2007. ISBN 978-3-03910-902-9

Vol. 11   Ulrike Zitzlsperger: ZeitGeschichten: Die Berliner Übergangsjahre. Zur Verortung der Stadt nach der Mauer.
241 pp., 2007. ISBN 978-3-03911-087-2

Vol. 12 Alexandra Kolb: Performing Femininity. Dance and Literature in German Modernism.
330pp., 2009. ISBN 978-3-03911-351-4

Vol. 13 Carlo Salzani: Constellations of Reading. Walter Benjamin in Figures of Actuality.
388pp., 2009. ISBN 978-3-03911-860-1

Vol. 14 Monique Rinere: Transformations of the German Novel: *Simplicissimus* in Eighteenth-Century Adaptations.
273pp., 2009. ISBN 978-3-03911-896-0

Vol. 15 Forthcoming.

Vol. 16 Ingo Cornils and Sarah Waters (eds): Memories of 1968: International Perspectives.
396pp., 2010. ISBN 978-3-03911-931-8

Vol. 17 Forthcoming.

Vol. 18 Martin Modlinger and Philipp Sonntag (eds): Other People's Pain: Narratives of Trauma and the Question of Ethics.
252pp., 2011. ISBN 978-3-0343-0260-9